Copulae and Multivariate Probability Distributions in Finance

Portfolio theory and much of asset pricing, as well as many empirical applications, depend on the use of multivariate probability distributions to describe asset returns. Traditionally, this has meant the multivariate normal (or Gaussian) distribution. More recently, theoretical and empirical work in financial economics has employed the multivariate Student (and other) distributions which are members of the elliptically symmetric class. There is also a growing body of work which is based on skew-elliptical distributions. These probability models all exhibit the property that the marginal distributions differ only by location and scale parameters or are restrictive in other respects. Very often, such models are not supported by the empirical evidence that the marginal distributions of asset returns can differ markedly. Copula theory is a branch of statistics which provides powerful methods to overcome these shortcomings. This book provides a synthesis of the latest research in the area of copulae as applied to finance and related subjects such as insurance. Multivariate non-Gaussian dependence is a fact of life for many problems in financial econometrics. This book describes the state of the art in tools required to deal with these observed features of financial data.

This book was originally published as a special issue of *The European Journal of Finance*.

Alexandra Dias is Lecturer in Finance at the University of Leicester, UK.

Mark Salmon is Senior Scientist at BHDG Systematic Trading, UK, Visiting Professor in the Economics Faculty at the University of Cambridge, UK, and Advisor to Old Mutual Asset Managers, UK.

Chris Adcock is Professor of Financial Econometrics at the University of Sheffield, UK, and Visiting Professor of Quantitative Finance at the University of Southampton, UK. He is the founding Editor of *The European Journal of Finance*.

Copulae and Multivariate Probability Distributions in Finance

Edited by
Alexandra Dias, Mark Salmon and Chris Adcock

Routledge
Taylor & Francis Group

LONDON AND NEW YORK

First published 2013
by Routledge
2 Park Square, Milton Park, Abingdon, Oxon, OX14 4RN

Simultaneously published in the USA and Canada
by Routledge
711 Third Avenue, New York, NY 10017

Routledge is an imprint of the Taylor & Francis Group, an informa business

This book is a reproduction of *The European Journal of Finance*, volume 15, issues 7-8. The Publisher requests to those authors who may be citing this book to state, also, the bibliographical details of the special issue on which the book was based.

Trademark notice: Product or corporate names may be trademarks or registered trademarks, and are used only for identification and explanation without intent to infringe.

British Library Cataloguing in Publication Data
A catalogue record for this book is available from the British Library

ISBN 13: 978-0-415-81485-0

Typeset in Times New Roman
by Taylor & Francis Books

Publisher's Note
The publisher would like to make readers aware that the chapters in this book may be referred to as articles as they are identical to the articles published in the special issue. The publisher accepts responsibility for any inconsistencies that may have arisen in the course of preparing this volume for print.

Contents

Citation Information

The chapters in this book were originally published in *The European Journal of Finance*, volume 15, issues 7–8 (October–December 2009). When citing this material, please use the original page numbering for each article, as follows :

About the Editors

Alexandra Dias is Lecturer in Finance at the University of Leicester, UK. She has previously been Lecturer at Warwick Business School, UK, a Credit Analyst at Credit Suisse (Zurich) and a Research Associate at RiskLab, ETH-Zurich. She holds a PhD in Mathematics, an MSc in Actuarial Science and Financial Risk Management and a 'Licenciatura' in Mathematics. Her research interests include financial risk management, portfolio selection, extreme events in finance, and dependence modelling with copulas.

Mark Salmon is Senior Scientist at BHDG Systematic Trading, UK, Visiting Professor in the Economics Faculty at Cambridge University, UK, and Advisor to Old Mutual Asset Managers, UK. He was, until September 2011, Professor of Finance at Warwick Business School where he also directed the Financial Econometric Research Centre, (FERC). He has served as a consultant to a number of city institutions and was an Advisor to the Bank of England for 6 years. He was also a member of a 'Task Force' set up by the European Commission to consider exchange rate policy for the EURO. Mark has been a member of the European Financial Markets Advisory Panel and has worked with the National Bank of Hungary on transition policies towards membership of the European Union. His research interests lie in Financial Econometrics, Behavioural Finance and the design and analysis of systematic investment strategies.

Chris Adcock is Professor of Financial Econometrics at the University of Sheffield, UK, and Visiting Professor of Quantitative Finance at the University of Southampton, UK. He is the founding Editor of *The European Journal of Finance* and is one of the founding Associate Editors of the *Journal of Mathematical Finance*. Chris has acted as an Advisor to a number of international investment managers, and algorithms he has designed have been used by Citibank and DSI International Investment Management (now part of UBS), as well as several other asset management groups. His current research interests are centred around the development of portfolio selection and asset pricing theory.

Preface

In 2007, Alexandra Dias and Mark Salmon organised a two-day workshop at Warwick Business School with the title Copulae and Multivariate Probability Distributions in Finance. The meeting took place in September 2007 and was a great success. Subsequently, *The European Journal of Finance* published a special issue with a selection of papers from the workshop. In addition, the special issue included a *tour d'horizon* of the subject area by Christian Genest, Michel Gendron and Michaël Bourdeau-Brien. Their paper served as an excellent introduction to the special issue.

After the special issue appeared, we were approached by Taylor & Francis to turn the special issue into this edited volume. The aim of the publication of this book is to further disseminate the material in the special issue. The three of us hope that this will both reach a wider audience than just those who read *The European Journal of Finance* and serve as a reminder of the intrinsic interest to be found in the subject matter and of its importance, not only to modern finance but also to other application areas.

As noted by the editor of another volume in this series, books are not created in a vacuum. We are grateful to Emily Ross of Taylor & Francis for the opportunity to publish this book and particularly grateful too for her editorial work. It is also another opportunity to thank Christian and his two colleagues, the other authors and the many referees for their hard work. All concerned have contributed greatly to this publication.

Chris Adcock
University of Sheffield, UK

Alexandra Dias
University of Leicester, UK

Mark Salmon
*BHDG Systematic Trading
and Visiting Professor,
University of Cambridge, UK*

The Advent of Copulas in Finance

Christian Genest[a], Michel Gendron[b] and Michaël Bourdeau-Brien[b]

[a] Département de mathématiques et de statistique, Université Laval, Québec, Canada; [b] Département de finance et assurance, Université Laval, Québec, Canada

The authors provide bibliometric evidence to illustrate the development of copula theory in mathematics, statistics, actuarial science and finance. They identify the main contributors to the field, and the most important areas of application in finance. They also describe some of the remaining methodological challenges.

1. Introduction

This paper is the lead article in a special issue of *The European Journal of Finance* that gives an account of the September 2007 Warwick conference on 'Copulas and multivariate probability distributions in finance'. Its contents illustrate the potential of copula modeling techniques in financial contexts.

Copula theory and applications have developed considerably in recent years. In an article that criticizes its overuse, Mikosch (2006) mentions that between 2003 and 2005 the number of Google hits for the word 'copula' jumped from 10,000 to 650,000. As these lines are being written, the count is well over 750,000. Although it is clear that the most common use of the term 'copula' on the web has nothing to do with science, signs that copula methodology is developing are numerous and beyond dispute. For example, in 1999, MathSciNet listed 60 articles with the word 'copula' in the title; the count had risen to 187 by 2005, and to 295 by August 2008.

What about the field of finance? This question prompted us to survey the academic literature on copulas in June 2006. This was done using 26 bibliographic databases such as Google Scholar, Web of Science, Synergy, Proquest, MathSciNet, Elsevier Science Direct, etc. We identified over 4200 papers that mentioned the word 'copula'. After detailed examination, we eliminated duplicate entries and papers where the word 'copula' either did not refer to the mathematical concept or appeared only in the bibliography. At the end of the process, we were left with 871 documents that we then classified according to various criteria: journal, author, author's institution, area of research, field of application, etc.

This database contains a great deal of information about the advent of copulas in finance which we would like to share with you. The growth of the copula literature is quantified in Section 2 and a breakdown by field of study is provided in Section 3. The means through which copula theory is spreading in finance are described in Section 4. The most active contributors, both outside and within the financial/actuarial/econometric sector, are identified in Sections 5 and 6, respectively.

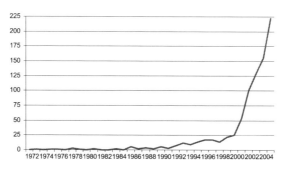

Figure 1. Number of documents on copula theory, 1971–2005.

The main areas of application in finance are listed in Section 7, and some of the current challenges are outlined in Section 8. Concluding comments are given in Section 9.

2. Changes over time

Our database contains 871 documents contributing to copula theory and its applications in different contexts. This literature encompasses 893 authors from 49 different countries and 418 institutions around the world. Overall, 77% of these authors are affiliated to universities; most of the others work in banks, insurance companies and financial institutions. Their writings appeared in some 165 journals and conference proceedings.

The most striking feature of the data set is the rapid growth in the annual number of contributions to the subject. This is illustrated in Figure 1. A more detailed examination reveals that the growth falls into three periods.

(1) Before 1986, the literature was sparse and mostly mathematical. The concept of copula can be traced back at least to the work of Wassily Hoeffding and Maurice Fréchet, though the term itself was coined by Sklar (1959). Many contributions were related to the study of probabilistic metric spaces, as described in the book by Schweizer and Sklar (1983).
(2) Beginning in 1986, one can see a slow, systematic rise in the number of publications. Growth was largely due to the emergence of the concept of copula in statistics and to three conferences devoted to the subject: Rome (1990), Seattle (1993) and Prague (1996).
(3) From 1999 on, the number of contributions grew considerably. The books by Joe (1997) and Nelsen (1999) were influential in disseminating copula theory; the book by Drouet-Mari and Kotz (2001), which focusses on correlation and dependence, is also noteworthy. Actuarial and financial applications were fuelled by Frees and Valdez (1998) and Embrechts, McNeil, and Straumann (1999), who illustrated the potential for copula modeling in these fields.

3. Breakdown by field of study

What is the part of finance to the spectacular growth of copula methodology in the past few years? To investigate this issue, we subjectively grouped the 871 documents in our database into nine mutually exclusive categories: mathematics; statistics; biostatistics; operations research; natural sciences; engineering; actuarial science; economics and finance. We achieved this classification by carefully examining the contents of each document. About 1% did not match any of the categories and were left unclassified.

Figure 2 shows the results of the grouping. Even though people in finance have been interested in copulas only since 2000, they produced the largest proportion of documents, *i.e.* 41%. Next come

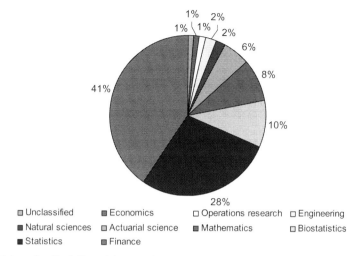

Figure 2. Breakdown by discipline of the 871 documents in the database.

Table 1. List of journals that published the largest number of copula-related articles.

Rank	Journal	Papers published
1	*Journal of Multivariate Analysis*	29
2	*Statistics & Probability Letters*	26
3	*Insurance: Mathematics and Economics*	23
4	*Communications in Statistics: Theory and Methods*	19
5	*Biometrika*	14
6	*Risk Magazine*	14
7	*The Canadian Journal of Statistics*	12
8	*Biometrics*	12
9	*Quantitative Finance*	11
10	*Journal of Nonparametric Statistics*	10

statistics (28%), biostatistics (10%), mathematics (8%) and actuarial science (6%). Interestingly, in June 2006, finance and actuarial science together contributed 47% of the literature, whereas mathematics, statistics and biostatistics together accounted for 46%. No doubt finance-related documents now account for over half of the literature on the subject. We will later discuss the nature of these contributions.

The level of activity in each discipline is also reflected by Table 1, which lists the peer-review journals that carried the largest number of articles concerned with copulas. As of June 2006, statistics continued to lead the rooster. This is not surprising, given that copulas have a long history in this area. Remarkably, *Risk Magazine* and *Quantitative Finance* make the list, even though the earliest papers on the topic appeared there in 2001. A fair proportion of copula-related articles in *Insurance: Mathematics and Economics* also pertain to finance.

4. Types of contribution in finance

We identified 353 finance-related documents in the database. As illustrated by Figure 3, these contributions to copula theory are varied in nature. They include lecture notes, books, theses,

3

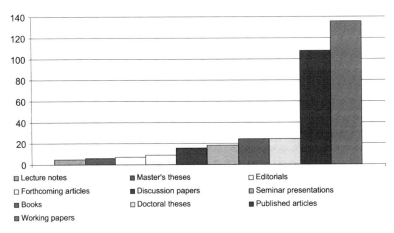

Figure 3. Breakdown by type of the 353 finance-related documents in the database.

editorials, seminar presentations and so on, but the bulk of the contributions consists of working papers or articles that are either published or forthcoming in peer-review journals.

Looking at Figure 3, one can see that working papers account for approximately one-third of the total. This is a larger proportion than published manuscripts, even when forthcoming articles are included. This is the result of a combination of factors.

(1) Many working papers seem to be intended for publication but had not reached that state yet as of June 2006.
(2) Several of them are fairly old and either may have failed to meet the publication standards or encountered resistance from the main-stream financial community.
(3) Many reports are authored by financial analysts working for banks, insurance companies and regulatory agencies faced, *e.g.* with the requirements of the Basel II Accords. These people typically have little time to devote to the lengthy academic publishing process.
(4) Clearly, some working papers were never intended for publication but were rather designed as surveys of a widely scattered literature and aimed at practitioners.

The work of the 'Groupe de recherche du Crédit Lyonnais' is a prime example of web-based dissemination of copula methodology in a financial context. The pedagogical documents written between 2002 and 2004 by Thierry Roncalli and his associates (Éric Bouyé, Valdo Durrleman, Jean-Frédéric Jouanin, Ashkan Nikeghbali, Gaël Riboulet, etc.) have contributed much to the popularity of copulas in finance. To this date, these reports remain freely available at http:// gro.creditlyonnais.fr/content/rd/home_copulas.htm.

Some of the accumulated wisdom transpires in the book by Roncalli (2004).

5. Main contributors outside finance

The 871 documents in our database make it possible to identify the most prolific contributors to copula theory and its applications in different disciplines. In this section, we describe the main research groups in the fields of mathematics, statistics and biostatistics. Some of their work has influenced subsequent contributions in actuarial science, finance and econometrics. The latter developments are reviewed in Section 6.

According to our database, Roger Nelsen is the most prolific author among mathematicians. His book (Nelsen, 1999; re-edited in 2006) is very frequently cited. His American colleagues (Jerry Frank, Greg Fredricks, Berthold Schweizer, etc.) and his collaborators in Spain (Juan Quesada-Molina, José Antonio Rodríguez-Lallena, Manuel Úbeda-Flores, etc.) and in Italy (Carlo Sempi, Fabrizio Durante, etc.) have played a major role, notably in the construction of copula families and in the derivation of bounds that have found applications in finance.

In statistics, the number of contributors is much larger. The 'Québec group' (the first author and his colleagues, viz. Bruno Rémillard, Louis-Paul Rivest, Philippe Capéraà, Belkacem Abdous, etc.) has been by far the most prolific, not only in terms of publications, but also in training graduate students and postdoctoral fellows (Anne-Laure Fougères, Kilani Ghoudi, Mhamed Mesfioui, Jean-François Quessy, Lajmi Lakhal Chaieb, David Beaudoin, etc.) who continue to generate copula-related research. Rank-based methods have been central in the group's contributions to inference for copula models. This nonparametric approach, rooted in the work of Rüschendorf (1976) and Deheuvels (1979), is summarized by Genest and Favre (2007).

Further to the copula conferences held in Barcelona (2000), Québec (2004) and Tartu (2007), research papers have proliferated on statistics-related aspects of copulas and their applications in extreme-value theory, hydrology and so on. Arthur Charpentier, Anne-Catherine Favre, Jean-David Fermanian, Johanna Nešlehová, Olivier Scaillet, Rafael Schmidt and Johan Segers are prominent figures in this new wave of researchers with an interest in the subject.

In biostatistics, the forerunner is clearly David Oakes. As early as the late 1980s, his papers were instrumental in applying copula methodology to Cox's proportional hazards models; see, *e.g.* Oakes (1989) and the book by Hougaard (2001) for the connection between frailty models and the pervasive Archimedean copulas. Truncation and censoring, which are common issues in survival analysis, have been central concerns of biostatisticians interested in copulas, such as Jason Fine, Philippe Lambert or Joanna Shih.

6.   Main contributors in actuarial science, finance and econometrics

In actuarial science, the popularity of copulas owes much to the review article by Frees and Valdez (1998), published in the *North American Actuarial Journal*. Few people know, however, that Carrière and Chan (1986) had already used copulas to compute the bounds of an annuity's value to the last survivor. Although he did not couch problems in terms of copulas, Floriaan De Vylder was also an early contributor to optimization problems on Fréchet spaces in an actuarial context; in particular, see Part II of De Vylder (1996) or Denuit and Charpentier (2004).

Insurance: Mathematics and Economics has published the overwhelming majority of copula-related actuarial papers. It has featured many contributions to the field by Michel Denuit, Jan Dhaene, Étienne Marceau, Mhamed Mesfioui, Shaun Wang, Mario Wüthrich, etc. Their concerns focus mainly on quantifying dependence between claims in a portfolio and its impact on pricing. In addition, Marco Scarsini and Alfred Müller have played a key role in studying copula-based dependence concepts and stochastic orderings used, *e.g.* in the analysis of worst-case scenarios (see, *e.g.* the book by Müller and Stoyan, 2002). This literature is surveyed in the book by Denuit et al. (2005).

In the field of finance, the first and oldest research group is that of Paul Embrechts (ETH Zürich). As early as 1999, Embrechts, McNeil and Straumann were using the concept of copula to alert readers of *Risk Magazine* to the pitfalls of correlation. The papers by Embrechts and his collaborators on the use of copulas in managing financial risks are by far the most numerous and oft cited. They culminated in 2005 with the publication of the book by McNeil, Frey, and

Embrechts (2005). This text is unique in applying both copula theory and extreme value theory to an eclectic mix of subjects: credit risk, market risk, operational risk and insurance. Members of this group include Wolfgang Breymann, Valérie Chavez-Demoulin, Alexandra Dias, Rüdiger Frey, Filip Lindskog, Alexander J. McNeil, Johanna Nešlehová, Philipp Schönbucher, Giovanni Puccetti. Although not direct collaborators, Claudia Czado, Claudia Klüppelberg and Werner Hürlimann can be associated to this group.

In 2000, an independent research group on copulas in finance emerged in Italy, around Umberto Cherubini and Elisa Luciano. They co-authored over 10 papers on option pricing and hedging of credit derivatives. Their work has led them to write, with Walter Vecchiato, a book on copula methods in finance (Cherubini, Luciano, and Vecchiato, 2004). Also worth mentioning is the book on extreme financial risks by Malevergne and Sornette (2006), which places strong emphasis on the theory of copulas and their empirical testing and calibration.

In econometrics, papers in which copula methodology is used explicitly are still relatively rare. Noteworthy contributions have been made, *e.g.* by Xiaohong Chen, Yanqin Fan, Andrew Patton, Mark Salmon, Murray Smith and Bas Werker. Additional applications of copulas in econometrics are mentioned in the review paper by Trivedi and Zimmer (2005). Although it is clear that the flexibility provided by copulas is welcome in problems involving dependence between variables and over time, the jury is still out on how best this can be accomplished, particularly when the underlyings are measured in continuous time.

7.   Major areas of application in finance

Two major phenomena account for the rise of copula modeling in finance: the lack of normality in (log) returns and the dependence between extreme values of various assets. Our database shows that these themes are recurrent in financial applications of copulas. Broadly speaking, contributions to the latter can be grouped into the following four categories.

(1) *Risk management*: Topics included here are those covered in the book by McNeil, Frey, and Embrechts (2005), *i.e.* credit, market, operational risk and risk aggregation. Developments in this area were stimulated by the Basel II Accords and the influential contributions of Embrechts, McNeil, and Straumann (1999) and Li (2000).
(2) *Portfolio management*: Included here are papers dealing with dependence between international financial markets, different classes of assets and currencies. For example, the paper by Patton (2004) on bivariate equity portfolio management falls in this category.
(3) *Pricing of derivatives*: This broad category comprises work on the pricing of exotic options, collateralized debt obligations and credit default swaps. Beginning with their 2002 paper, Cherubini and Luciano have been among the main contributors to this area, which is discussed in detail in the book by Cherubini, Luciano, and Vecchiato (2004).
(4) *Risk measurement*: We have merged in this category the papers discussing value-at-risk, expected shortfall and financial contagion. The paper of Embrechts, Höing, and Juri (2003) provides an early example of VaR studies using copulas.

The 353 documents related to finance were classified according to these four categories. For presentation purposes, 13 documents from the first half of 2006 were excluded. In addition, 23 documents were left unclassified, either because they were general introductions to copulas or because they pertained to other topics such as market microstructure or monetary flows.

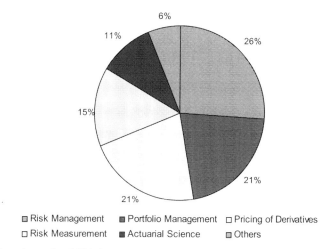

Figure 4. Breakdown by topic of 381 documents related to finance or actuarial science from 1999 to 2005.

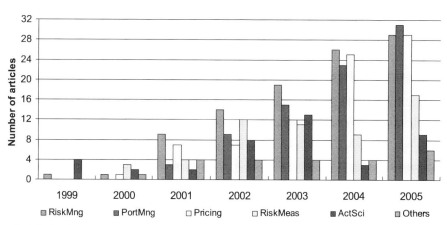

Figure 5. Distribution over time of 381 documents related to finance or actuarial science from 1999 to 2005.

Figure 4 shows the level of activity in each of these areas. Because many actuarial contributions have a close connection to finance, 41 documents relating to that field were included as well. The distribution in time of the same 381 documents is displayed in Figure 5.

Three observations can be made from the graphs.

(1) Copula modeling seems to be spreading more or less evenly in various areas of finance.
(2) The growth rate is roughly linear and similar in portfolio management, risk management and the pricing of derivatives; the use of copulas in risk measurement is roughly constant.
(3) Applications of copulas are more numerous in finance than in actuarial science, despite a late start. This being said, finance is a broader field of research than actuarial science, and the boundary between the two areas is somewhat arbitrary.

8. What does the future hold?

The data we collected make it obvious that the interest of the financial community for copula modeling is blooming and will continue to grow in the foreseeable future. If this approach is to be adopted widely, however, the methodology will need to be expanded to face the challenges of abundant, time-dependent and highly multidimensional financial data.

First, there is a need to develop graphical tools for the selection and validation of copula models. At present, the detection and visualization of dependence is based on chi-plots, K-plots and rank-rank plots for small sample sizes or on kernel- and wavelet-based estimates of the copula density when data are sufficiently abundant (cf. Genest and Favre 2007; Genest, Masiello, and Tribouley 2009). These techniques should be further studied and refined. In the spirit of residual plots for linear regression, graphical diagnostic tools and formal tests also need to be built to check whether data can be represented by specific dependence structures such as Archimedean, meta-elliptical or extreme-value copulas.

Second, further research is needed to assess the added value of copulas in time-series modeling. In recent years, they have been used to capture serial dependence in a univariate context. They have also been employed to characterize the dependence between multivariate residuals from time series that have been modeled either jointly or marginally. See Patton (2009) and references therein for some of the pros and cons of these various approaches. Many technical challenges will need to be met to adapt rank-based inference tools to the treatment of model residuals, and more generally to multivariate data that are not independent.

Third, great opportunities for financial applications lie in the development of high-dimensional multivariate copula models and associated inference techniques. Hierarchical models based on pair-copula vine decompositions seem particularly promising. This approach is described, for example, in the book by Kurowicka and Cooke (2006). See Aas et al. (2009) for a nice introduction and an application involving Norwegian stocks and bonds.

Further methodological challenges bearing on finance – but not limited to it – concern the construction of goodness-of-fit tests for copula models, the adaptation of copula modeling techniques to count data and the development of inference tools for extreme-value structures. For reviews of these topics, see Genest, Rémillard, and Beaudoin (2009), Genest and Nešlehová (2007) and McNeil, Frey, and Embrechts (2005), respectively.

Beyond technical issues, the most pressing challenge for the copula community is the inclusion of their modeling techniques in commercial software packages. Of all factors, the availability of a user-friendly copula toolkit is probably most likely to stimulate the widespread adoption and use of this methodology, particularly among financial analysts and engineers.

9. Conclusion

The bibliometric study presented here documents the advent and spectacular growth of copula theory. As we saw, this explosion of interest is stronger in finance than in any other field but to this date, relatively few contributions have found their way in finance peer-review journals. The initiative of *The European Journal of Finance* thus seems timely, particularly in the wake of the subprime crisis that led analysts, banks and regulators to question the old, Gaussian paradigm.

While our study identifies the main actors and a few key writings in the early development of copula theory, we avoided crowding the paper with references to the literature. We thought it would be more useful to provide the beginner with a list of books that cover the material from various perspectives: actuarial, financial, mathematical, statistical, etc. The bibliography also features a few surveys, viz. Frees and Valdez (1998), Owzar and Sen (2004), Trivedi and Zimmer (2005), Kolev, dos Anjos, and Mendes (2006) and Genest and Favre (2007).

We encourage people to sieve through this material before they start using copulas or contribute to the field. In the footsteps of Mikosch (2006), who used a tale of Hans Christian Andersen to qualify the copula fashion, we suggest that the reader acts as the hero of Charles Perrault's *Le petit poucet* (Hop o' my Thumb) and drops little white pebbles through his or her readings to avoid getting lost in the densest, darkest part of the forest.

Acknowledgements

The authors are grateful to Paul Embrechts, Johanna Nešlehová and Mark Salmon for comments on an earlier version of this paper. Funding in support of this work was provided by the Natural Sciences and Engineering Research Council of Canada, by the Fonds québécois de la recherche sur la nature et les technologies and by the Institut de finance mathématique de Montréal.

References

Aas, K., C. Czado, A. Frigessi, and H. Bakken. 2009. Pair-copula constructions of multiple dependence. *Insurance: Mathematics and Economics* 44, no. 2.

Carrière, J.F. and L.K. Chan. 1986. The bounds of bivariate distributions that limit the value of last-survivor annuities. *Transactions of the Society of Actuaries* 38, no. 1: 51–74.

Cherubini, U. and E. Luciano. 2002. Bivariate option pricing with copulas. *Applied Mathematical Finance* 9, no. 2: 69–85.

Cherubini, U., E. Luciano, and W. Vecchiato. 2004. *Copula methods in finance.* New York: Wiley.

Deheuvels, P. 1979. La fonction de dépendance empirique et ses propriétés: Un test non paramétrique d'indépendance. *Bulletin de la Classe des Sciences, Série V, Académie Royale de Belgique* 65: 274–292.

Denuit, M. and A. Charpentier. 2004. *Mathématiques de l'assurance non-vie: Principes fondamentaux de théorie du risque.* Paris: Economica.

Denuit, M., J. Dhaene, M. Goovaerts, and R. Kaas. 2005. *Actuarial theory for dependent risks: Measures, orders and models.* New York: Wiley.

De Vylder, F. 1996. *Advanced risk theory: A self-contained introduction.* Brussels: Éditions de l'Université libre de Bruxelles.

Drouet-Mari, D. and S. Kotz. 2001. *Correlation and dependence.* London: Imperial College Press.

Embrechts, P., A. Höing, and A. Juri. 2003. Using copulae to bound the value-at-risk for functions of dependent risks. *Finance and Stochastics* 7, no. 2: 145–167.

Embrechts, P., A.J. McNeil, and D. Straumann. 1999. Correlation: Pitfalls and alternatives. *Risk Magazine,* 12, no. 5: 69–71.

Frees, E.W. and E.A. Valdez. 1998. Understanding relationships using copulas. *North American Actuarial Journal* 2, no. 1: 1–25.

Genest, C. and A.-C. Favre. 2007. Everything you always wanted to know about copula modeling but were afraid to ask. *Journal of Hydrologic Engineering* 12, no. 4: 347–368.

Genest, C., E. Masiello, and K. Tribouley. 2009. Estimating copula densities through wavelets. *Insurance: Mathematics and Economics* 44, no. 2.

Genest, C. and J. Nešlehová. 2007. A primer on copulas for count data. *Astin Bulletin* 37, no. 2: 475–515.

Genest, C., B. Rémillard, and D. Beaudoin. 2009. Goodness-of-fit tests for copulas: A review and a power study. *Insurance: Mathematics and Economics* 44, no. 2.

Hougaard, P. 2001. *Analysis of multivariate survival data.* Berlin: Springer.

Joe, H. 1997. *Multivariate models and dependence concepts.* London: Chapman and Hall.

Kolev, N., U. dos Anjos, and B.V. de M. Mendes. 2006. Copulas: A review and recent developments. *Stochastic Models* 22, no. 4: 617–660.

Kurowicka, D. and R.M. Cooke. 2006. *Uncertainty analysis with high dimensional dependence modelling.* New York: Wiley.

Li, D.X. 2000. On default correlation: A copula function approach. *Journal of Fixed Income* 9, no. 4: 43–54.

Malevergne, Y. and D. Sornette. 2006. *Extreme financial risks: From dependence to risk management.* Berlin: Springer.

McNeil, A.J., R. Frey, and P. Embrechts, 2005. *Quantitative risk management: Concepts, techniques, tools.* Princeton University Press.

Mikosch, T. 2006. Copulas: Tales and facts (with discussion). *Extremes* 9, no. 1: 1–86.

Müller, A. and Stoyan, D. 2002. *Comparison methods for stochastic models and risks.* New York: Wiley.

Nelsen, R.B. 1999. *An introduction to copulas.* Berlin: Springer.

Nelsen, R.B. 2006. *An introduction to copulas.* 2nd ed. Berlin: Springer.

Oakes, D. 1989. Bivariate survival models induced by frailties. *Journal of the American Statistical Association* 84, no. 406: 487–493.

Owzar, K. and P.K. Sen. 2004. Copulas: Concepts and novel applications. *Metron* 61, no. 3: 323–353.

Patton, A.J. 2004. On the out-of-sample importance of skewness and asymmetric dependence for asset allocation. *Journal of Financial Econometrics* 2, no. 1: 130–168.

Patton, A.J. 2009. Copula-based models for financial time series. *Handbook of financial time series*, eds. T.G. Andersen, R.A. Davis, J.-P. Kreiss and T. Mikosch, in press. Berlin: Springer.

Roncalli, T. 2004. *La gestion des risques financiers.* Paris: Economica.

Rüschendorf, L. 1976. Asymptotic distributions of multivariate rank order statistics. *The Annals of Statistics* 4, no. 5: 912–923.

Schweizer, B. and A. Sklar. 1983. *Probabilistic metric spaces.* Amsterdam: North-Holland.

Sklar, A. 1959. Fonctions de répartition à *n* dimensions et leurs marges. *Publications de l'Institut de statistique de l'Université de Paris* 8: 229–231.

Trivedi, P.K. and D.M. Zimmer. 2005. Copula modeling: An introduction for practitioners. *Foundations and Trends in Econometrics* 1: 1–111.

Testing for structural changes in exchange rates' dependence beyond linear correlation

Alexandra Dias[a] and Paul Embrechts[b]

[a] *Warwick Business School, Finance Group, University of Warwick, Conventry UK;* [b] *Department of Mathematics, ETH Zurich, Switzerland*

In this paper, we test for structural changes in the conditional dependence of two-dimensional foreign exchange data. We show that by modeling the conditional dependence structure using copulae, we can detect changes in the dependence beyond linear correlation, such as changes in the tail of the joint distribution. This methodology is relevant for estimating risk-management measures, such as portfolio value-at-risk, pricing multi-name financial instruments, and portfolio asset allocation. Our results include evidence of the existence of changes in the correlation as well as in the fatness of the tail of the dependence between Deutsche mark and Japanese yen.

1. Introduction

In financial markets, the price movements of different assets are invariably related. In addition, financial crises, market deregulations, policy shifts, and central bank interventions may cause changes in the way financial asset prices relate to each other. The dynamics of asset dependence is of importance in risk management, asset pricing, portfolio allocation, and forecasting. Not surprisingly, there is considerable interest in the dynamic behavior of correlation between different risks as a function of time. Financial theory and models often assume that (conditional) correlation between assets are possibly time-varying; see, for instance, the dynamic conditional correlation (DCC)-generalized autoregressive conditional heteroskedasticity (GARCH) model from Engle (2002). Loretan and Phillips (1994) studied tests for covariance stationarity, Boyer, Gibson, and Loretan (1999) investigated pitfalls in tests for changes in correlation, Longin and Solnik (2001) related the dynamics of conditional correlation with market trend, and Andreou and Ghysels (2003) analyzed procedures for testing for changes in conditional correlation. There is an enormous amount of econometric literature on the use of regime changes for describing non-stationary economic data. In the context of time series analysis, see, for instance, Hamilton (1990). In the field of monetary policy, regime switches may come about as a consequence of new policy implementation; see Francis and Owyang (2005). In the latter context, tools have been developed to measure the influence of both regime changes as well as policy shocks. A further series of publications concentrates on the relationship between long-memory and the existence of structural changes, so-called 'spurious long-memory process'; see Mikosch and Stărică (2000), Diebold and Inoue (2001), Mikosch and Stărică (2004), and Choi and Zivot (2007).

As with other financial processes, the dependence between exchange rates is exposed to changes due to general economic events. In addition, central bank interventions are likely to have a definitive impact. For the case studied here of the Deutsche mark (DEM) and the Japanese yen (JPY) prior to the introduction of the EURO, an economic event that has a strong impact on the Japanese economy, but not on the German economy, can cause instability in the yen and trigger a move of investment preferences toward the DEM as compared with the JPY. This should weaken the dependence between the two exchange rates. On the other hand, an intervention of the Bank of Japan to ensure a depreciation of the yen once the DEM depreciates against the dollar, to keep Japanese export competitive, might cause an increase in the dependence between the two exchange rates.

We present a methodology for testing for structural changes, the so-called change-points, in the conditional dependence using copulae. Through many examples, we now know that "there is more to dependence as can be measured through (linear) correlation" (Embrechts, McNeil, and Straumann 2002). It turns out that the notion of copula yields an excellent tool for the modeling of nonlinear dependencies. These techniques have now achieved textbook level; see, for example, Joe (1997), Cherubini, Luciano, and Vecchiato (2004), McNeil, Frey and, Embrechts (2005), and Nelsen (2006). Dynamic dependence structures modeled with copulae are, for instance, to be found in Fortin and Kuzmics (2002), Giacomini et al. (2006), Patton (2006a, 2006b) and Rockinger and Jondeau (2006).

In this paper, we extend existing methods in a number of ways. We assume that the multivariate asset-return process is dynamic heteroskedastic, and the asset returns are to be standardized by conditional volatility estimates. We take a two-stage estimation approach. We standardize each univariate return series using GARCH volatility models (see Andersen, Bollerslev, and Diebold (2005)), and then test for changes in the conditional dependence with parametric (copula) models. The two-stage model estimation can be found in the literature on semi-parametric modeling, as in Andreou and Ghysels (2003), or in a full-parametric modeling context as in Engle and Sheppard (2001) and Patton (2006b). The methodology presented here is new in two aspects. First, our procedure allows for testing for changes not only in the conditional covariance or correlation but also for changes in the complete conditional dependence. Second, we assume that both the number of changes and when they happen are unknown. The goal is to uncover structural changes that might not impact on the covariance, such as changes in the tails of the conditional distribution. A change in the conditional tail distribution is not detected when testing for changes in the correlation and has obvious consequences in any computation involving the joint distribution like tail-risk measures, such as value-at-risk or expected shortfall.

We analyze daily US dollar (USD)–DEM and USD–JPY exchange rates from April 1986 till October 1998. For this period, we test for changes in the conditional dependence modeled by a parametric copula. The reason we illustrated the change-point techniques introduced in this paper with a rather old exchange rate data is that it covers a period containing several interesting economic/political events that could lead to non-stationarity in the dependence and that therefore a priori one might expect change-points. We would also like to stress that the methodology introduced has much wider applicability beyond this (old) foreign exchange (FX) data set. The results show clear evidence of changes in the correlation and changes in the tail dependence between the two exchange rates. One of the most relevant results is a significant change in the dependence when the Berlin wall fell, on 9 November 1989: the conditional correlation drops substantially and the tail dependence weakens. The explanation might be that such an event increased the uncertainty in the German economy without having a similar impact in Japan. The burst of the Japanese asset-price bubble seems to have had the opposite effect by strengthening the dependence as we find a change in that direction in the correlation in October 1990, although the tail dependence did not change. We find a further drop in the conditional correlation in June 1997, now possibly due to a bigger impact of the Asian crisis on JPY. The last change that we remark here was detected in October 1995, where the tail dependence weakens so considerably that we can statistically assume asymptotic tail independence until the end of the period covered by the data sample, October 1998.

We detect more changes in the data that are reported later in the paper but for which we did not find immediate related economic events. One possible explanation is that changes in the dependence may also occur smoothly through time instead of suddenly. We are not modeling these smooth changes. Hence, the test statistic will point to a certain date as a change-point when, in reality, it is a smoothly changing process. This is not necessarily a disadvantage. Assuming a constant dependence with changes at certain points will lead to more stable portfolio value-at-risk and (dynamic) asset allocation than if we use dynamic models where the dependence is allowed to change at every point in time. Modeling the conditional dependence as being constant in time, yet allowing for the possibility of breaks to occur, is a compromise between the oversimplifying assumption of constant dependence and the highly parameterized time-varying dependence models. If constant models are too simple for the evidence found in the data, the time-varying models are statistically much more difficult to estimate. By way of an economically relevant example, in this paper, we present a new tool to financial experts, which have potential for a more careful, yet parsimonious analysis of financial data.

This paper proceeds as follows. In Section 2, we present the theory of change-points for copulae. In Section 3, we test for changes in the conditional dependence between USD–DEM and USD–JPY. In the same section, we perform several statistical specification and goodness-of-fit tests. Section 4 contains a summary of the results and concludes the paper.

2. Tests for Structural Changes in the Conditional Dependence

In this section, we concentrate on the theoretic methods we use for the detection of structural changes in the conditional dependence of a multivariate time series. The first step is the standardization of the one-period logarithmic univariate returns, $r_t = p_t - p_{t-1}$, where p_t stands for the logarithmic price of a financial asset at time $t \geq 1$. We decompose the return series as $r_t = \mu_t + \sigma_t \varepsilon_t$, where ε_t are independent and identically distributed (iid) with zero mean and unit variance, and σ_t is the conditional standard deviation at time t. As a consequence, the σ-standardized returns are given by

$$\varepsilon_t = \frac{r_t - \mu_t}{\sigma_t}, \quad t \geq 1.$$

The process σ_t is not observable, and its most widely used (univariate or multivariate) estimators involve autoregressive conditional heteroskedasticity (ARCH) type models, stochastic volatility models, realized volatility measures, and continuous-time models; see Andersen, Bollerslev, and Diebold (2005) for a systematic review of volatility measures and specific references. The test statistics reported in Section 3 confirm the existence of conditional heteroskedasticity in the data set we use. Hence, we filter the returns with ARCH-type volatility models. As these are parametric models, we prevent a possible erroneous inference by performing tests for model specification and structural breaks in the univariate margins in our data analysis.

The stability of the dependence structure of the d-dimensional vector process of filtered returns ε_{it}, for $i = 1, 2, \ldots, d$, is then to be tested for structural breaks. Loretan and Phillips (1994), Longin and Solnik (2001), Andreou and Ghysels (2003), among others, consider the detection of breaks in the conditional covariance. The univariate filtered returns are assumed to be iid, and this is supported for our data by statistical tests reported in Section 3. Hence, the only possible source of instability is the dependence structure that is completely characterized by the copula, as shown by Sklar (1959). We consider a parametric copula-based model for the multivariate conditional filtered returns

$$F(\varepsilon_{1t}, \ldots, \varepsilon_{dt}; \boldsymbol{\theta}_t) = C(F_1(\varepsilon_{1t}), \ldots, F_d(\varepsilon_{dt}); \boldsymbol{\theta}_t)$$

$$= C(\mathbf{u}; \boldsymbol{\theta}_t),$$

where F is the conditional distribution function of the filtered returns, F_i $(i = 1, 2, \ldots, d)$ are the univariate continuous distribution functions of the margins, and C is a copula function with vector parameter $\boldsymbol{\theta}_t$. For ease of exposition, we concentrate on the bivariate case, $d = 2$. The methodologies used here can be extended to higher dimensions by considering an appropriate copula-based model.

2.1 Detecting Change-Points in Copula Parameters

Testing for breaks in the multivariate conditional distribution of the filtered returns is equivalent to testing for breaks in the copula. We analyze this issue through a change-point detection technique for parametric copula models. There are several well-known tests on structural breaks in econometric time-series analysis; see, for instance, Bai (1997), Bai and Perron (1998), Hansen (2001), and Polzehl and Spokoiny (2006). Here, we test for changes in the copula parameters and estimate the size of those changes and the corresponding time of occurrence. For related work, see, for instance, Gombay and Horvàth (1999). For a detailed treatment of the change-point theory underlying our approach, see Csörgő and Horvàth (1997) and references therein, and Dias and Embrechts (2002).

Let $\mathbf{U}_1, \mathbf{U}_2, \ldots, \mathbf{U}_n$ be a sequence of independent random vectors in $[0, 1]^d$ with univariate uniformly distributed margins and copulae $C(\mathbf{u}; \boldsymbol{\theta}_1, \boldsymbol{\eta}_1), C(\mathbf{u}; \boldsymbol{\theta}_2, \boldsymbol{\eta}_2), \ldots, C(\mathbf{u}; \boldsymbol{\theta}_n, \boldsymbol{\eta}_n)$, respectively, where $\boldsymbol{\theta}_i$ and $\boldsymbol{\eta}_i$ are the copula parameters such that $\boldsymbol{\theta}_i \in \Theta^{(1)} \subseteq \mathbb{R}^p$ and $\boldsymbol{\eta}_i \in \Theta^{(2)} \subseteq \mathbb{R}^q$. We consider $\boldsymbol{\eta}_i$ as constant parameters and look for one single change-point in $\boldsymbol{\theta}_i$. Formally, we test the null hypothesis

$$H_0 : \boldsymbol{\theta}_1 = \boldsymbol{\theta}_2 = \cdots = \boldsymbol{\theta}_n \quad \text{and} \quad \boldsymbol{\eta}_1 = \boldsymbol{\eta}_2 = \cdots = \boldsymbol{\eta}_n$$

versus the alternative

$$H_A : \boldsymbol{\theta}_1 = \cdots = \boldsymbol{\theta}_{k^*} \neq \boldsymbol{\theta}_{k^*+1} = \cdots = \boldsymbol{\theta}_n \quad \text{and} \quad \boldsymbol{\eta}_1 = \boldsymbol{\eta}_2 = \cdots = \boldsymbol{\eta}_n.$$

If we reject the null hypothesis, k^* is the time of the change. All the parameters of the model are supposed to be unknown under both hypotheses. If $k^* = k$ were known, the null hypothesis would be rejected for small values of the likelihood-ratio (LR) statistic

$$\Lambda_k = \frac{\sup_{(\boldsymbol{\theta}, \boldsymbol{\eta}) \in \Theta^{(1)} \times \Theta^{(2)}} \prod_{1 \leq i \leq n} c(\mathbf{u}_i; \boldsymbol{\theta}, \boldsymbol{\eta})}{\sup_{(\boldsymbol{\theta}, \boldsymbol{\theta}', \boldsymbol{\eta}) \in \Theta^{(1)} \times \Theta^{(1)} \times \Theta^{(2)}} \prod_{1 \leq i \leq k} c(\mathbf{u}_i; \boldsymbol{\theta}, \boldsymbol{\eta}) \prod_{k < i \leq n} c(\mathbf{u}_i; \boldsymbol{\theta}', \boldsymbol{\eta})}, \quad (1)$$

where we assume that C has a density c. The estimation of Λ_k is carried out through maximum likelihood. Denote

$$L_k(\boldsymbol{\theta}, \boldsymbol{\eta}) = \sum_{1 \leq i \leq k} \log c(\mathbf{u}_i; \boldsymbol{\theta}, \boldsymbol{\eta})$$

and

$$L_k^*(\boldsymbol{\theta}, \boldsymbol{\eta}) = \sum_{k < i \leq n} \log c(\mathbf{u}_i; \boldsymbol{\theta}, \boldsymbol{\eta}).$$

Then, the LR equation can be written as

$$-2 \log(\Lambda_k) = 2 \left(L_k(\hat{\boldsymbol{\theta}}_k, \hat{\boldsymbol{\eta}}_k) + L_k^*(\boldsymbol{\theta}_k^*, \hat{\boldsymbol{\eta}}_k) - L_n(\hat{\boldsymbol{\theta}}_n, \hat{\boldsymbol{\eta}}_n) \right).$$

As k is unknown, H_0 will be rejected for large values of

$$Z_n = \max_{1 \leq k < n} (-2 \log(\Lambda_k)). \tag{2}$$

2.1.1 Asymptotic critical values

The asymptotic distribution of $Z_n^{1/2}$ is known but has a very slow rate of convergence; see Csörgő and Horvàth (1997, 22). In the same reference, we can also find an approximation for the distribution of $Z_n^{1/2}$ derived to give better small-sample rejection regions. Indeed, for $0 < h(n) \leq l(n) < 1$, the following approximation holds

$$P\left(Z_n^{1/2} \geq x\right) \approx \frac{x^p \exp(-x^2/2)}{2^{p/2}\Gamma(p/2)} \left(\log \frac{(1-h)(1-l)}{hl} - \frac{p}{x^2} \log \frac{(1-h)(1-l)}{hl} \right.$$

$$\left. + \frac{4}{x^2} + O\left(\frac{1}{x^4}\right) \right), \tag{3}$$

as $x \to \infty$ and where h and l can be taken as $h(n) = l(n) = (\log n)^{3/2}/n$. Note that in (3), p is the number of parameters that may change under the alternative. This result turns out to be very accurate as shown in a simulation study in Dias and Embrechts (2002), where it is applied to the Gumbel copula.

2.1.2 The time of the change

If we assume that there is exactly one change-point, then the maximum likelihood estimator for the time of the change is given by

$$\hat{k}_n = \min\{1 \leq k < n : Z_n = -2\log(\Lambda_k)\}. \tag{4}$$

In the case that there is no change, $\hat{k}_n$ will take a value near the boundaries of the sample. This holds because under the null hypothesis, and given that all the necessary regularity conditions hold, for $n \to \infty$, $\hat{k}_n/n \overset{d}{\to} \xi$, where $P(\xi = 0) = P(\xi = 1) = 1/2$; see Csörgő and Horvàth (1997, 51). This behavior was verified in a simulation study for the Gumbel copula under the no-change hypothesis in Dias and Embrechts (2002).

2.1.3 Multiple changes

In the case that more than one change-point exists, we use a sequential procedure coupled with the hypothesis testing proposed by Vostrikova (1981) in the context of multidimensional processes with unknown parameters. This method is studied for detecting multiple breaks (one at a time) in the mean of a process in Bai (1997). It is introduced as a computationally advantageous alternative to the simultaneous estimation in Bai and Perron (1998) and detects simultaneously the number and location of the change-points. The sequential method consists of first applying the LR test for one change. If H_0 is rejected, then we have the estimate of the time of the change $\hat{k}_n$. Next, we divide the sample in to two subsamples $\{\mathbf{u}_t : 1 \leq t \leq \hat{k}_n\}$ and $\{\mathbf{u}_t : \hat{k}_n < t \leq n\}$ and test H_0 for each one of them. If we find a change-point in any of the sets, we continue this segmentation procedure until H_0 is not rejected in any of the subsamples. Given the existence of multiple change-points and different change sizes, the method might over- or underestimate the location of a change-point; see Bai (1997). To overcome this question, Bai (1997) proposed a fine-tuning repartition procedure after estimating the m change-points $\hat{k}_1 < \hat{k}_2 < \cdots < \hat{k}_m$ that we use here. Accordingly, each change-point $\hat{k}_i$ is reestimated by applying the test to the subsample $\{\mathbf{u}_t : \hat{k}_{i-1} + 1 \leq t \leq \hat{k}_{i+1}\}$, where $\hat{k}_0 = 0$ and $\hat{k}_{m+1} = n$.

3. Conditional Dependence of USD–DEM and USD–JPY

We analyze here the bivariate daily logarithmic returns[1] USD–DEM and USD–JPY exchange rates. The observations cover the period from 27 April 1986 until 25 October 1998. The data set was kindly provided by Wolfgang Breymann and Olsen Data and previously treated and cleaned as explained in Breymann, Dias, and Embrechts (2003). After the data cleaning, the returns data set consists of 3259 daily observations. Table 1 contains some summary statistics. From these statistics, we observe that both series show a non-significant trend and have negative skewness and excess kurtosis.[2] The unconditional linear-correlation estimate yields a significant correlation between the two series. In order to test for conditional heteroscedasticity, we consider the ARCH effects test proposed by Engle (1982). For the two series, the hypothesis of no-ARCH effects has to be rejected. Our goal in this section is to model the conditional dependence underlying the bivariate USD–DEM and USD–JPY exchange rate returns. By now, a standard approach is based on the notion of conditional copula, as discussed in Patton (2006b). In this two-stage procedure, one first models the marginal dynamics and then the dependence structure.

Table 1. Summary statistics.

	USD–DEM	USD–JPY
Mean	−0.0112	−0.0128
Standard deviation	1.0182	1.0026
Skewness	−0.1234	−0.3171
Kurtosis	4.6838	5.7735
Linear correlation	0.6243	
No-ARCH effects: Lagrange Multiplier (LM) test		
Test statistic	35.25	75.99
p-value	0.000	0.000

Summary statistics for the USD–DEM and USD–JPY returns and test of the null hypothesis of no-ARCH effects from Engle (1982).

3.1 Modeling the Univariate Margins

The marginal tests presented in Table 1 reveal the presence of time-varying variance and heavy tailedness. In our discrete-time setting, we model stochastic volatility effects by GARCH-type models. In particular, we fit univariate autoregressive moving average (ARMA)-GARCH models to each marginal series.

Formally, consider the sequence of iid random variables with zero mean and unit variance $(\varepsilon_t)_{t \in \mathbb{Z}}$. The process $(r_t)_{t \in \mathbb{Z}}$ is an ARMA(p_1, q_1)-GARCH(p_2, q_2) if it satisfies the equations

$$r_t = \mu_t + \epsilon_t,$$

$$\mu_t = \mu + \sum_{i=1}^{p_1} \phi_i (r_{t-i} - \mu) + \sum_{j=1}^{q_1} \theta_j \epsilon_{t-j},$$

$$\epsilon_t = \sigma_t \varepsilon_t,$$

$$\sigma_t^2 = \alpha_0 + \sum_{i=1}^{p_2} \alpha_i (|\epsilon_{t-i}| + \gamma_i \epsilon_{t-i})^2 + \sum_{j=1}^{q_2} \beta_j \sigma_{t-j}^2,$$

(5)

where $\alpha_0 > 0$, $\alpha_i \geq 0$ for $i = 1, 2, \ldots, p_2$, $\beta_j \geq 0$ for $j = 1, 2, \ldots, q_2$, and ε_t is independent of $(r_s)_{s \leq t}$. The parameter γ takes into account that innovations of different signs may have asymmetric impacts on the future variance; see, for example, Bollerslev, Chou, and Kroner (1992) and references therein. We fit the univariate ARMA-GARCH models by maximum likelihood to each marginal series, assuming that the innovations ε_t come from a Student-t distribution with ν degrees of freedom. Table 2 presents the estimates of the parameters of the models with the respective asymptotic standard errors (SEs) in parenthesis. The moving average component could be removed for either series. The USD–DEM data require an autoregressive lag of order 1 and the USD–JPY of order 10. The necessary lags for the ARCH and GARCH components are both of order 1 for the two exchange rates. For the USD–DEM returns, we cannot reject the null hypothesis of $\gamma_i = 0$ for the estimated asymmetry parameter, and in the case of USD–JPY, we reject the same null hypothesis. The rejection of $\gamma_i = 0$ for the USD–JPY, given that the estimate value $\hat{\gamma}$ is negative, indicates that negative shocks on the USD–JPY rate have a larger impact on future volatility than positive shocks.

Table 2. Univariate modeling of the USD–DEM and USD–JPY returns.

	USD–DEM estimate(SE)	USD–JPY estimate(SE)
Constant, $\hat{\mu}$	−0.0046 (0.0161)	0.0226 (0.0153)
AR(1), $\hat{\phi}_1$	−0.0343 (0.0165)	–
AR(10), $\hat{\phi}_{10}$	–	0.0597 (0.0163)
GARCH constant, $\hat{\alpha}_0$	0.0423 (0.0185)	0.1267 (0.0481)
Lagged ϵ^2, $\hat{\alpha}_1$	0.0348 (0.0088)	0.0726 (0.0213)
Lagged variance, $\hat{\beta}_1$	0.9160 (0.0215)	0.7927 (0.0623)
Asymmetry, $\hat{\gamma}_1$	–	−0.1557 (0.0801)
Degrees of freedom, $\hat{\nu}$	5.7967 (0.5557)	4.8894 (0.4119)

This table shows the maximum likelihood estimates and the corresponding asymptotic SEs obtained from fitting ARMA-GARCH models to each of the return series USD–DEM and USD–JPY.

From the fitted ARMA-GARCH model parameters, we recover the residuals or filtered returns, $\hat{\varepsilon}_t$, for each univariate time series $(r_1, r_2, \ldots, r_n)$:

$$\hat{\varepsilon}_t = \frac{r_t - \hat{\mu}_t}{\hat{\sigma}_t}, \quad t = 1, 2, \ldots, n. \tag{6}$$

Once the univariate models are selected and fitted, the dynamics as well as the goodness-of-fit of the t-density must be checked. We use the Ljung–Box (L–B) and the multivariate Portmanteau test, from Hosking (1980), for testing for serial correlation on the filtered returns up to the fourth moment and on the absolute values of the residuals. We assess the goodness-of-fit of the t-density with the Anderson–Darling (A–D) test and the normality of the filtered returns Jarque–Bera (J–B) test. We also test for heteroscedasticity or ARCH effects and for the existence of structural breaks on the univariate filtered returns. In Table 3, we report the p-values obtained for these tests.

The L–B and the Portmanteau tests give indication of no serial or cross-correlation. There is no evidence of remaining ARCH effects. The goodness-of-fit tests for the marginal distributions reject normality, according to the J–B test, and do not reject the Student-t distribution, according to the A–D test. This confirms our choice of a Student-t for the innovations of the models. We also tried to include crossed lagged returns in these models but without success. We also tested the existence of change-points in the parameters of the distribution of the univariate filtered returns. If the marginal models are appropriate, then the filtered returns should come from a Student-t distribution with constant parameters (location, scale, and degrees of freedom). Given the results for non-serial correlation reported in Table 3, we assume each univariate filtered returns series to be independent. We test the null hypothesis of no change-points in any of the three parameters of the univariate Student-t applying (2) and (3). For the USD–DEM, we obtain a test statistic value of $z_{n\,\mathrm{obs}}^{1/2} = 3.195$, which corresponds to a p-value of 0.5829 according to (3). In the case of the USD–JPY filtered returns, we have that $z_{n\,\mathrm{obs}}^{1/2} = 3.880$, which implies a p-value of 0.1025. In both cases, we do not reject the no change-points hypothesis. On the other hand, there is a significant contemporaneous linear correlation between the two filtered time series. The estimated linear correlation is $\hat{\rho} = 0.6180$, which turns out to be of the same order as the one obtained for the (non-filtered) returns. It is this dependence that we want to model using copulae. In the next section, we perform a copula analysis of the bivariate filtered returns.

Table 3. Specification tests on the filtered returns (p-values).

Null hypothesis	USD–DEM	USD–JPY	Multivariate test
No serial correlation of first moment	0.1204	0.5328	0.0614
No serial correl of absol values	0.8456	0.6803	0.8525
No serial correlation of second moment	0.9702	0.9154	0.9690
No serial correlation of third moment	0.1225	0.2474	0.5524
No serial correlation of fourth moment	0.3969	0.2942	0.9481
No ARCH effects	0.9663	0.9183	–
Normally distributed	0.0000	0.0000	–
Student-t distributed	0.6452	0.3105	–
No structural breaks	0.5829	0.1025	–

These are the p-values obtained when testing for serial correlation, cross-correlation, ARCH effects, and structural breaks in the filtered returns of USD–DEM and USD–JPY. The p-values of the normality J–B and Student-t A–D goodness-of-fit tests are also given.

3.2 *Modeling the Conditional Dependence Structure: Copula*

In this section, we model the dependence structure or copula between the two exchange rates USD–DEM and USD–JPY filtered returns. There are many parametric families of copulae; see Joe (1997), McNeil, Frey, and Embrechts (2005), and Nelsen (2006). As we do not know at this stage whether there are or not changes in the conditional dependence, we first perform a static copula analysis in order to restrict the class of parametric copula families that we want to concentrate on. Later in the analysis, once the change-points are detected, we check the appropriateness of the copula model again (see Section 3.4).

Assuming at first stationarity, suppose that the USD–DEM filtered returns are represented by ε_1 and the USD–JPY by ε_2. Assume that $(\varepsilon_1, \varepsilon_2)$ has a multivariate distribution function, F, and continuous univariate marginal distribution functions, F_1 and F_2. In order to investigate the dependence, we fit copula-based models of the type

$$F(\varepsilon_1, \varepsilon_2; \boldsymbol{\theta}) = C(F_1(\varepsilon_1), F_2(\varepsilon_2); \boldsymbol{\theta}), \tag{7}$$

where C is a copula function, which we know to exist uniquely by Sklar's Theorem (Sklar 1959), parameterized by the vector $\boldsymbol{\theta} \in \mathbb{R}^q$ with $q \in \mathbb{N}$. The corresponding model density is the product of the copula density, c, and the marginal densities, f_1 and f_2:

$$f(\varepsilon_1, \varepsilon_2; \boldsymbol{\theta}) = c(F_1(\varepsilon_1), F_2(\varepsilon_2); \boldsymbol{\theta}) f_1(\varepsilon_1) f_2(\varepsilon_2),$$

where c is the copula density of model (7), which is given by

$$c(u_1, u_2; \boldsymbol{\theta}) = \frac{\partial^2 C(u_1, u_2; \boldsymbol{\theta})}{\partial u_1 \, \partial u_2}, \quad (u_1, u_2) \in [0, 1]^2.$$

Denote by $\{(\varepsilon_{1i}, \varepsilon_{2i}) : i = 1, 2, \ldots, n\}$ a general random sample of n bivariate observations. The marginal distribution functions, F_i, $i = 1, 2$, are estimated by the rescaled empirical distribution functions, $F_{in}(z) = 1/(n+1) \sum_{j=1}^{n} \mathbb{I}_{\{y \in \mathbb{R} : y \leq z\}}(\varepsilon_{ij})$. As usual, $\mathbb{I}_A$ denotes the indicator function of the set A. After the marginal transformations to the so-called pseudo-observations $(F_{1n}(\varepsilon_{1i}), F_{2n}(\varepsilon_{2i}))$ for $i = 1, 2, \ldots, n$, the copula family C is fitted. Suppose that its density exists, we then maximize the pseudo-log-likelihood function

$$L(\boldsymbol{\theta}; \boldsymbol{\varepsilon}) = \sum_{i=1}^{n} \log c(F_{1n}(\varepsilon_{1i}), F_{2n}(\varepsilon_{2i}); \boldsymbol{\theta}). \tag{8}$$

The dependence parameter $\hat{\boldsymbol{\theta}}$ that maximizes (8) is the pseudo-log-likelihood estimate introduced by Genest, Ghoudi, and Rivest (1995) in the iid case and further studied by Chen and Fan (2005) in the non-iid case. Note however that the preliminary ARMA-GARCH filtering may increase the variance of the estimates of $\boldsymbol{\theta}$.

The copula families considered are: t, Frank, Plackett, Gaussian, Gumbel, Clayton, symmetrized Joe-Clayton, and the mixtures Gumbel with survival Gumbel, Clayton, with survival Clayton, Gumbel with Clayton, and survival Gumbel with survival Clayton; for details on these classes see Joe (1997), Embrechts, McNeil, and Straumann (2002), McNeil, Frey, and Embrechts (2005), Nelsen (2006), and Patton (2006b). Denoting the copula family A with parameter θ by $C^A(\cdot, \cdot; \theta)$, the fitted mixtures have distribution functions of the form

$$C(u_1, u_2; \theta) = \theta_3 \, C^A(u_1, u_2; \theta_1) + (1 - \theta_3) \, C^B(u_1, u_2; \theta_2). \qquad (9)$$

The above choice of copula models is partly based on previous analyses, on tractability and flexibility, on methodological results and also to allow for a fairly broad class with respect to extremal clustering and possible asymmetry. The Gaussian copula is included mainly for comparison. The models were ranked using the Akaike information criterion:

$$\text{AIC} = -2L(\hat{\theta}; \varepsilon) + 2k,$$

and the Bayesian information criterion:

$$\text{BIC} = -2 \ln \left(L(\hat{\theta}; \varepsilon) \right) + k \ln(n),$$

where n is the number of observations and k the number of parameters of the family fitted. Parameter estimates and asymptotic SEs for all fitted models are listed in Table 4. For the four mixture models, the parameters θ_1, θ_2, and θ_3 are as in (9). For the symmetrized Joe–Clayton copula, θ_1 and θ_2 are the lower and upper tail parameters, respectively. For the t-copula, θ_1 represents the degrees of freedom and θ_2 the correlation. The mixture of Gumbel and survival Gumbel and the t-copula are the best ranked models. While the Gumbel mixture model allows for asymmetry, the t-copula is symmetric. We test for asymmetry of the Gumbel mixture. As the AIC of these two models is close and the BIC favors the t-copula, if the Gumbel mixture is revealed to be symmetric, then we prefer to use the t-model because of the economic interpretation of its parameters and because it is very well known in the econometric literature. We perform a LR test

Table 4. Conditional dependence: copula modeling.

	$\hat{\theta}_1$ (SE)	$\hat{\theta}_2$ (SE)	$\hat{\theta}_3$ (SE)	AIC	BIC
Clayton	1.034 (0.035)	–	–	−1252.289	−1246.200
Frank	4.599 (0.124)	–	–	−1446.464	−1440.375
Gumbel	1.679 (0.023)	–	–	−1500.065	−1493.976
Plackett	7.772 (0.350)	–	–	−1526.993	−1520.904
Gaussian	0.617 (0.009)	–	–	−1552.695	−1546.606
Clayton and survival Clayton	1.548 (0.120)	1.280 (0.099)	0.494 (0.032)	−1599.798	−1581.530
Symmetrized Joe–Clayton	0.417 (0.018)	0.430 (0.017)	–	−1603.307	−1591.129
Clayton and Gumbel	1.665 (0.045)	1.844 (0.249)	0.671 (0.037)	−1629.394	−1611.126
Survival Clayton and survival Gumbel	1.816 (0.071)	1.234 (0.195)	0.656 (0.039)	−1632.435	−1614.167
Gumbel and survival Gumbel	1.588 (0.072)	1.952 (0.117)	0.501 (0.048)	−1642.460	−1624.192
t-copula	6.012 (0.786)	0.620 (0.010)	–	−1640.061	−1627.883

Results from fitting copula models to the filtered returns of USD–DEM and USD–JPY. The table shows the model parameter estimates and the asymptotic SEs. In the case of mixture copulae, θ_1 and θ_2 are the dependence parameters, respectively, for the first and second terms of the mixture. θ_3 is the mixture parameter that gives the proportion of the first term. For the t-copula, θ_1 stands for the degrees of freedom and θ_2 for the correlation. The last two columns display the information criteria, AIC and BIC, obtained for each model.

for possible asymmetry in the Gumbel mixture model (9); we tested for the null hypothesis

$$H_0 : \theta_1 = \theta_2 \quad \text{and} \quad \theta_3 = 0.5$$

versus the alternative

$$H_A : \theta_1 \neq \theta_2 \quad \text{or} \quad \theta_3 \neq 0.5,$$

where $\theta_1, \theta_2,$ and θ_3 are the scalar parameters of the model. A low p-value indicates that a three-parameter asymmetric Gumbel mixture model is significantly better than the one-parameter symmetric model. This turns out not to be the case. We obtain a p-value of 0.1842 favoring the symmetric model. This may seem in contrast to Patton (2006b), where for DEM–USD and JPY–USD daily data, the symmetrized Joe–Clayton copula model indicates asymmetry. We also test for asymmetry in the symmetrized Joe–Clayton copula model for our data set. We obtain a p-value of 0.641, rejecting the hypothesis of asymmetry. A comparison of these results may not be straightforward because the two data sets cover different periods. Based on the above, results we continue the analysis of our data with a t-copula model. Further support for the t-based models can be found from Breymann, Dias, and Embrechts (2003), Daul et al. (2003), Pesaran, Schuermann, and Weiner (2004), Demarta and McNeil (2005), McNeil, Frey, and Embrechts (2005), and Rosenberg and Schuermann (2006).

3.3 *Testing for Structural Changes in the Conditional Dependence Between DEM and JPY*

In this section, we test for the occurrence of change-points in the dependence structure of the conditional distribution of USD–DEM and USD–JPY, modeled by a t-copula. Specifically, we test for change-points in the copula parameters of the filtered returns of USD–DEM and USD–JPY exchange rates data. Concretely, we use the procedures from Section 2 to estimate the change-points in the correlation and degrees of freedom parameters of a t-copula fitted to the filtered returns. For the change-points found, we estimate the size of those changes and the corresponding time of occurrence. We also look for economic events that may have triggered these changes. After filtering the univariate returns using the GARCH type models reported in Table 2 of Section 3.1, given the results in Table 3, we can assume the filtered returns to be a sequence of independent bivariate vectors with no breaks in the univariate margins. Hence, we satisfy the conditions for testing for the existence of change-points in the copula parameters. We use the methods specified in Section 2.1 for detecting the possible change-points in the parameters of the multivariate contemporaneous conditional distribution.

In the first step, we test for change-points assuming that one or two parameters may change: degrees of freedom and/or correlation. This corresponds to $p = 2$ in expression (3). We evaluate Λ_k for $k = 1, 2, \ldots, n$, where $n = 3, 259$; see (1). The test statistic (2) takes the value $z_{n \text{ obs}}^{1/2} = 13.49$ and by (3) we have that $P(Z_n^{1/2} > 13.49) \approx 0$. The null hypothesis of no change-point is to be rejected and the estimated time of the change is $\hat{k}_n = 8$ November 1989; coinciding with the fall of the Berlin wall. See Table 5 row corresponding to I in the first column. The values obtained in this and subsequent tests are displayed in Table 5. Next, the sample is divided into two subsamples, one up to 8 November 1989 and another from the estimated time of change onwards. For each subsample, Λ_k is computed as well as $Z_n^{1/2}$. The rows corresponding to II in the first column of Table 5 have those values. As the obtained p-values are close to zero, we reject the null hypothesis of no change for each subsample and estimate two more change-points, 29 December 1986 and 9 June 1997. The later date corresponds to the beginning of the Asian crisis starting with the devaluation of the Thai Baht. Each subsample is again divided into two, and the procedure is repeated yielding the estimates in the rows corresponding to III. For these results, only for the maximum attained at 23 October 1990, the null hypothesis is rejected at a 5% level. This change-point might be related with the burst in the Japanese asset-price bubble. Next we have to split the subsample 8 November 1989 till 9 June 1997 into two at the date 23 October 1990. From these two tests we estimate a change-point in 18 October 1995. So we still have to split this subsample further. The first from 23 October 1990 until 18 October 1995 and the second from this date up to 9 June 1997. The last change-point is estimated at 26 September 1994. Testing in further subsamples does not lead to a rejection of the no change-point hypothesis. These values are in the rows corresponding to VI of Table 5. In summary, we found six change-points: 29 December 1986, 8 November 1989, 23 October 1990, 26 September 1994, 18 October 1995, and 9 June 1997.

Three questions have to be raised now. The detected change-points were obtained in a sequence of tests where the boundaries of the subsamples depend on the change-points detected in the previous tests, except for the first test performed on the full sample. Also multiple change-points and different change sizes may induce the tests to under- or overestimate the location of the change-point. We solve this question by applying the fine-tuning repartition procedure from Bai (1997), as explained in Section 2.1.3. Hence, each change-point is reestimated by testing on the subsample that has only that particular change-point according to the first sequence of tests. The second question has to do with the subsample sizes. As the boundaries of the subsamples are defined by the estimated change-points, each subsample has a different size. That is not a problem because the approximation for the distribution of the test statistic (3) takes the sample size into account. Yet, some subsamples might have a small size, which raises the question of the power of the test. The smallest subsample tested has a size $n = 176$, and we obtained good results for the power of the test in the case of smaller samples with $n = 100$ in our previous work Dias and Embrechts (2002). For this reason, although this question would deserve a full study by itself, we are confident about the results obtained here. The third question is a reminder that in the

Table 5. Tests for change-points in the conditional dependence.

	$z_{n\,\mathrm{obs}}^{1/2}$	n	$P\left(Z_n^{1/2} > z_{n\,\mathrm{obs}}^{1/2}\right)$	$H_0(0.95)$	Time of change
I	13.49	3259	0.0000000	Reject	8 November 1989
II	6.21	922	0.0000006	Reject	29 December 1986
	5.51	2337	0.0000330	Reject	9 June 1997
III	3.28	176	0.1133105	Not Reject	–
	3.02	746	0.3006019	Not Rejected	–
	5.87	1979	0.0000047	Reject	23 October 1990
	2.35	358	0.9999999	Not Rejected	–
IV	2.71	249	0.4409689	Not Rejected	–
	4.25	1730	0.0087136	Reject	18 October 1995
V	5.99	1302	0.0000022	Reject	26 September 1994
	2.87	428	0.3620263	Not Rejected	–
VI	3.06	1023	0.2917965	Not Rejected	–
	2.21	279	0.9216038	Not Rejected	–

Change-point analysis for USD–DEM and USD–JPY conditional dependence. In the "Time of change" column the dates are the change-points estimated in at least one of the dependence parameters.

sequence of tests performed, the null hypothesis considers that the two parameters may change. The implication is that the fine-tuning repartition procedure has to be applied twice: first, where we test for a change-point in the correlation and constant degrees of freedom; and second, where we test for a change-point in the degrees of freedom and constant correlation. Using this procedure, besides checking the location of the change-point, we identify whether the change occurred, in the correlation, in the degrees of freedom, or in both parameters of the t-copula model.

Table 6 reports the results from the fine-tuning procedure. The change-point estimated in 29 December 1986 is identified to have occurred in the correlation only. On the other hand, the second estimated change-point turns out to be a change-point in the correlation and the degrees of freedom. This change seems to be related with the fall of the Berlin wall in 9 November 1989. The 23 October 1990 is found to have been a change-point in the correlation. It is interesting to note that the former date (23 October 1990) corresponds to the burst in the Japanese asset-price bubble. On 18 October 1990, USD–JPY ended a fall from about 158 to 125. The change-points estimated in September/October 1994 and October 1995 are change-points in the degrees of freedom and in the correlation. Finally, in July 1997, we estimated a change-point in the correlation only. This date corresponds to the beginning of the Asian crisis starting with the devaluation of the Thai Baht. We did not find particular economic events possibly associated with some of the change-points detected. A reason for this could be that smooth rather than sudden changes can occur in the dependence structure. In these cases, we do not expect to find an event justifying a sudden change in the dependence. Hence, in the case of smooth changes, we are modeling the dependence dynamics with jumps at a certain points in time but otherwise constant. This approach can have advantages in terms of its applications when compared with a time-varying modeling where changes occur at every point in time; this is the case, for instance, of the DCC-GARCH or Baba, Engle, Kraft, Kroner (BEKK) model from Engle and Kroner (1995). The change-point approach will give more stable portfolio value-at-risk estimates with changes at a certain points

Table 6. Tests for change-points in the conditional dependence parameters.

$z_{n \, \text{obs}}^{1/2}$	n	$P\left(Z_n^{1/2} > z_{n \, \text{obs}}^{1/2}\right)$	Time of change
Breaks in the t-copula correlation, ρ			
3.70	922	0.0000003	29 December 1986
11.93	997	0.0000000	8 November 1989
5.01	1273	0.0000573	23 October 1990
5.85	1302	0.0000006	26 September 1994
6.51	707	0.0000000	24 October 1995
3.94	787	0.0047889	1 July 1997
Breaks in the t-copula degrees of freedom, ν			
3.72	997	0.0111743	30 October 1989
3.83	1302	0.0078626	17 October 1994
4.50	707	0.0005187	16 October 1995

Results from the fine-tuning procedure, reestimating the change-points on the conditional dependence between USD–DEM and USD–JPY. At the same time, we test for each change-point which of the two t-copula model parameters changed. In the top panel are displayed the change-points in the correlation and in the bottom panel the change-points in the degrees of freedom. Note the closeness of the change-point in the correlation in 8 November 1989 and the change-point in the tail parameter in 30 October 1989. These two breaks might be related with the fall of the Berlin wall in 9 November 1989.

when compared with a time-varying correlation model. Dynamic portfolio asset allocation and pricing are other examples where the same reasoning applies.

The test for change-points, besides detecting the time of the change, also allows to compute the size of the change. Let us consider now that aspect of our empirical study. For the periods between the times of changes, we estimated the parameters of the t-copula model. Although the change-points estimated for the degrees of freedom are close to that estimated for the correlation, they do not coincide precisely. For this reason we exclude the small periods between those from the fitting procedure. Specifically, we do not consider the observations in the periods: 10 October 1989 till 11 November 1989; 26 September 1994 till 17 October 1994; and 16 October 1995 till 24 October 1995. Table 7 has the estimates for the correlation and degrees of freedom obtained for each subsample. We look for an interpretation for the raises and falls estimated in the correlation and in the degrees of freedom (or fatness of the tail distribution). A change in the dependence structure must be the result of an event, economic variable, or policy change, which impacts more in DEM than in JPY or vice versa. For instance, if the DEM falls against the USD, the Japanese central bank might impose a fall in the yen in order to keep the competitiveness of its exportations. This would induce a strengthening of the dependence between the two exchange rates. A raise in the yen against the DEM might be stopped also by the central bank with the same consequences for the dependence. The change in the correlation from 0.315 to 0.585 estimated in October 1990 around the burst of the Japanese asset prices seems to be an example. On the other hand, an event or developments that might anticipate instability in the German economy say, but not in the Japanese economy, should originate a weakening in the dependence between mark and yen. In fact, by the time of the fall of the Berlin wall, we estimate a reduction in the correlation from 0.832 to 0.315. The Asian crisis seems to have had a similar effect, as the correlation decreased from 0.556 to 0.348 in July of 1997.

Table 7. Conditional dependence parameters and coefficient of tail dependence, λ, estimated between change-points.

Period	$\hat{\rho}$ (SE)	$\lambda(\hat{\rho}, \hat{\nu})$
t-copula correlation ρ and coefficient of tail dependence λ		
27 April 1986 till 29 December 1986	0.634 (0.042)	0.288
29 December 1986 till 30 October 1989	0.832 (0.010)	0.482
8 November 1989 till 23 October 1990	0.315 (0.059)	0.053
23 October 1990 till 26 September 1994	0.585 (0.019)	0.149
17 Oct 1994 till 24 October 1995	0.784 (0.024)	0.384
24 October 1995 till 1 July 1997	0.556 (0.029)	0.000
1 July 1997 till 25 October 1998	0.348 (0.046)	0.000
Period	$\hat{\nu}$ (SE)	
t-copula degrees of freedom, ν		
27 April 1986 till 30 October 1989	5.220 (1.075)	
8 November 1989 till 26 September 1994	8.570 (2.408)	
17 October 1994 till 16 October 1995	6.215 (3.049)	
24 October 1995 till 25 October 1998	$+\infty$	

Estimated correlation and degrees of freedom between the change-points detected, using the t-copula model for the dependence between USD–DEM and USD–JPY. The third column of the upper panel of the table has the coefficient of tail dependence values obtained from the estimated model parameters.

As a function of the correlation and degrees of freedom, the coefficient of asymptotic tail dependence for the t-copula model (Embrechts, McNeil, and Straumann 2002) takes the form

$$\lambda(\rho, \nu) = 2\bar{t}_{\nu+1}\left(\sqrt{\nu + 1}\frac{\sqrt{1 - \rho}}{\sqrt{1 + \rho}}\right),$$

where $\bar{t}_{\nu+1}$ denotes the tail, or survival function, of a univariate Student-t distribution with $\nu + 1$ degrees of freedom. The estimated values for the coefficient of asymptotic tail dependence are in the last column of Table 7. We can observe that there is a real impact on the tail dependence when there are changes in the correlation and degrees of freedom. The most notable impact is when the degrees of freedom estimate changes to infinity in October 1995. From there onwards, we can assume asymptotic tail independence between the two exchange rates. In terms of value-at-risk, this means a reduction in the quantile from a heavy- to thin-tailed distribution.

3.4 *Specification Tests and Comparison with a Benchmark Model*

After having estimated the number and location of change-points for the correlation and degrees of freedom in the t-model, we have to check if the model for the dependence structure is well specified. In order to check this, we have to repeat the procedure of choosing the best copula model applied in Section 3.2 for the full sample, but now for each subsample between the change-points. Again, as the change-points estimated for the degrees of freedom are close to that estimated for the correlation, we exclude the small periods between those, as in Section 3.3. The best BIC-ranked model after fitting the 11 models listed in Table 4 to each subsample are reported in Table 8. The results confirm that the t-copula model is the best choice among the proposed models. For the observations after October 1995, the best model is the Gaussian copula. This confirms the infinitely large degrees-of-freedom estimate for the period after October 1995 reported in Table 7. We recall here that the Gaussian copula is the limit of the t-copula when the degrees of freedom of the later go to infinity.

We compare our results obtained by modeling the dependence structure allowing for breaks with a benchmark model where the dependence can also be time-varying. A model that allows for this flexibility is the BEKK model from Engle and Kroner (1995). The dependence structure in the BEKK is modeled by a dynamic variance–covariance matrix, for which the components

Table 8. Best ranked copula model between the change-points.

Period	Model
27 April 1986 till 29 December 1986	t-model
29 December 1986 till 30 October 1989	t-model
8 November 1989 till 23 October 1990	t-model
23 October 1990 till 26 September 1994	t-model
17 October 1994 till 16 October 1995	t-model
24 October 1995 till 1 July 1997	Gaussian model
1 July 1997 till 25 October 1998	Gaussian model

Results from fitting copula models to the filtered returns of USD–DEM and USD–JPY between the estimated change-points. For each subperiod between the change-points, the table has the best ranked model (using the BIC criterion) among the 11 copula models fitted before to the full sample in Section 3.2.

Table 9. Specification tests on the Student-t BEKK filtered returns (p-values).

Null hypothesis	USD–DEM	USD–JPY	Multivariate test
No serial correlation of first moment	0.8940	0.3240	0.8555
No serial correl of absol values	0.7477	0.4034	0.6010
No serial correlation of second moment	0.8963	0.4838	0.8868
No ARCH effects	0.8724	0.4864	–
Normally distributed	0.0000	0.0000	–
Student-t distributed	0.7260	0.1310	–

These are the p-values obtained from L–B tests for serial correlation and cross-correlation for the first moments and absolute values of the returns filtered by the Student-t BEKK model. The table also contains the p-values from the ARCH effects LM test, the normality Jarque–Bera, and Student-t A–D goodness-of-fit tests for the same filtered returns of USD–DEM and USD–JPY.

change on time. This model can be used with Student-t bivariate innovations that are needed for these data. Although the BEKK model does not allow for time-varying degrees of freedom, we can compute the modeled correlation path and compare it with the change-points' results. In the case of the BEKK model, the degrees of freedom of the multivariate Student-t innovations are constant and the same for all the margins and for the dependence structure. These are two relevant constraints because on the one hand the change-point tests revealed the existence of breaks in this parameter and, on the other, for our data the degrees of freedom of each margin and of the copula

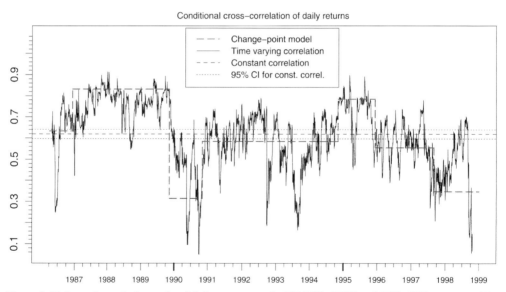

Figure 1. Estimated correlation paths of daily returns on the FX USD–DEM and USD–JPY spot rates. The long-dashed line is the estimated correlation by the change-point tests. This is superimposed on the estimated correlation using the time-varying Student-t BEKK model from Engle and Kroner (1995). The short-dotted line is the time-invariant correlation estimate after the univariate GARCH filtering. The change-points model reacts quicker to important economic events as the fall of the Berlin wall in November 1989 than the time-varying model and ignores smaller possible changes given by the BEKK model.

are different, as we can see in Tables 2 and 8, respectively. A BEKK model has a large number of parameters that have to be simultaneously estimated. The estimation of this model is difficult especially when the innovations are assumed to be Student-t distributed and becomes unwieldy in larger dimensions. The change-points detection is a far more parsimonious approach. In order to use the BEKK, we model the conditional mean of each spot rate USD–DEM and USD–JPY returns using the model in Equations (5) and then estimate a bivariate Student-t BEKK model on the residuals. A Gaussian BEKK model was first fitted but did not pass in the goodness-of-fit tests for the residuals. The specification tests for the Student-t BEKK model are reported in Table 9. The residuals passed all the L–B tests for serial correlation and cross-correlation up to the second moment, the test for ARCH effects, and the A–D goodness-of-fit Student-t test. As expected, they failed the normality test.

To visualize the results, we show in Figure 1 the time-varying correlation path estimated from the BEKK model, superimposed with the estimated change-point cross-correlation for the seven periods between the times of change. The BEKK correlation path is extremely jagged. We pose the question how much of this dynamics in the correlation are actually noise. On the other hand, by construction, the path for the correlation given by the change-points is constant between those. The change-point analysis seems to detect the main features of the changes in the dynamic correlation curve and to ignore smaller changes.

4. Conclusion

The aim of the paper is essentially two-fold. First of all, we want to contribute to the ongoing discussion between practitioners and academics in order to advance the methodological basis for risk-measurement technology. The nonlinear copula-based model presented in this paper contributes to this goal. Second, through the example of the two-dimensional FX data, we have demonstrated a parsimonious conditional dependence model that takes changes in the dependence structure into account. Evidence for the existence of changes in the conditional correlation between FX spot rates has been reported in the literature; see for instance Andreou and Ghysels (2003). Economic events, changes in the economic variables, or central bank measures are liable to produce changes in the co-movements of prices in financial markets and, in particular, in FX rates. We have presented a methodology that combines the use of change-point tests and the decomposition of the multivariate distribution of asset prices in its marginal distributions and dependence structure. We are therefore able to detect structural changes without having to assume a priori a possible date for its occurrence. Further we can detect changes beyond linear correlation, which nevertheless have an important impact in relevant risk measures, pricing, or asset allocation. This is the case for changes found in the heaviness of the tail of the multivariate distribution. The procedure consists on modeling the univariate marginal dynamics with ARMA-GARCH models and testing for changes in the conditional dependence modeled with parametric copula models. The result is a two-stage parsimonious procedure easier to estimate, although able to model dynamics beyond what can be captured by benchmark models as the DCC-GARCH or the BEKK from Engle (2002) and Engle and Kroner (1995), respectively. Applying the methodology presented, we find changes in the correlation and in the heaviness of the tail of the dependence between DEM and JPY modeled by a t-copula. The change points found relate to specific economic events. The most relevant ones are a drop in the correlation and in the heaviness of the tail related with the fall of the Berlin wall in 1989. Another is a strengthening in the correlation around the burst in the Japanese asset-price bubble in the fall of 1990.

Acknowledgements

We acknowledge useful discussions with Alexander McNeil, and anonymous referees and the journal editor for several detailed comments on an earlier version of this paper.

Notes

1. In the remaining of the paper, we refer to the daily logarithmic returns simply as the returns.
2. The values for the kurtosis given are to be compared with a value of 3 for the standard normal distribution.

References

Andersen, T.G., T. Bollerslev, and F.X. Diebold. 2005. Parametric and nonparametric volatility measurement. In *Handbook of financial econometrics*, ed. L.P. Hansen and Y. Ait-Sahalia. Amsterdam: North-Holland.

Andreou, E., and E. Ghysels. 2003. Tests for breaks in the conditional co-movements of assets returns. *Statistica Sinica* 13: 1045–73.

Bai, J. 1997. Estimating multiple breaks one at a time. *Econometric Theory* 13: 551–63.

Bai, J., and P. Perron. 1998. Estimating and testing linear models with multiple structural changes. *Econometrica* 66: 47–78.

Bollerslev, T., R.Y. Chou, and K. Kroner. 1992. ARCH modeling in finance. *Journal of Econometrics* 52: 5–59.

Boyer, B.H., M.S. Gibson, and M. Loretan. 1999. Pitfalls in tests for changes in correlations. International Finance Discussion Paper 597. Board of Governors of the Federal Reserve System. http://www.federalreserve.gov/Pubs/Ifdp/1997/597/ifdp597.pdf.

Breymann, W., A. Dias, and P. Embrechts. 2003. Dependence structures for multivariate high-frequency data in finance. *Quantitative Finance* 3: 1–14.

Chen, X., and Y. Fan. 2005. Estimation of copula-based semiparametric time series models. *Journal of Econometrics* 130, no. 2: 307–35.

Cherubini, U., E. Luciano, and W. Vecchiato. 2004. *Copula methods in finance*. Chichester: Wiley.

Choi, K., and E. Zivot. 2007. Long memory and structural changes in the forward discount: An empirical investigation. *Journal of International Money and Finance* 26, no. 3: 342–63.

Csörgõ, M., and L. Horváth. 1997. *Limit theorems in change-point analysis*. Chichester: Wiley.

Daul, S., E.D. Giorgi, F. Lindskog, and A. McNeil. 2003. Using the grouped *t*-copula. *RISK Magazine* 16, no. 11: 73–6.

Demarta, S., and A.J. McNeil. 2005. The *t*-copula and related copulas. *International Statistical Review* 73, no. 1: 111–29.

Dias, A., and P. Embrechts. 2002. Change-point analysis for dependence structures in finance and insurance. In *Novos Rumos em Estatística*, ed. C. Carvalho, F. Brilhante, and F. Rosado, 9–86. Lisbon: Sociedade Portuguesa de Estatística.; also in *Risk measures for the 21st century*. Chap. 16, ed. G. Szegö, 321–35. New York: JohnWiley and Sons

Diebold, F.X., and A. Inoue. 2001. Long memory and regime switching. *Journal of Econometrics* 105, no. 1: 131–59.

Embrechts, P., A.J. McNeil, and D. Straumann. 2002. Correlation and dependence in risk management: Properties and pitfalls. In *Risk management: Value at risk and beyond*, ed. M. Dempster, 176–223. Cambridge: Cambridge Univ. Press.

Engle, R.F. 1982. Autoregressive conditional heteroscedasticity with estimates of the variance of United Kingdom inflation. *Econometrica* 50, no. 4: 987–1007.

Engle, R.F. 2002. Dynamic conditional correlation: A simple class of multivariate generalized autoregressive conditional heteroscedasticity models. *Journal of Business and Economic Statistics* 20, no. 3: 339–50.

Engle, R.F., and K.F. Kroner. 1995. Multivariate simultaneous generalized ARCH. *Econometric Theory* 11, no. 1: 122–50.

Engle, R.F., and K. Sheppard. 2001. Theoretical and empirical properties of dynamic conditional correlation MVGARCH. Working Paper No. 2001-15, University of California, San Diego.

Fortin, I., and C. Kuzmics. 2002. Tail-dependence in stock return-pairs. *International Journal of Intelligent Systems in Accounting, Finance & Management* 11, no. 2: 89–107.

Francis, N., and M.T. Owyang. 2005. Monetary policy in a markov-switching VECM: Implications for the cost of disinflation and the price puzzle. *Journal of Business and Economic Statistics* 23, no. 3: 305–13.

Genest, C., K. Ghoudi, and L.-P. Rivest. 1995. A semiparametric estimation procedure of dependence parameters in multivariate families of distributions. *Biometrika* 82, no. 3: 543–52.

Giacomini, E., W.K. Härdle, E. Ignatieva, and V. Spokoiny. 2006. Inhomogeneous dependency modelling with time varying copulae. SFB 649 Discussion Paper 2006-075, Weierstrass Institute for Applied Analysis and Stochastics. http://sfb649.wiwi.hu-berlin.de/papers/pdf/SFB649DP2006-075.pdf.

Gombay, E., and L. Horváth. 1999. Change-points and bootstrap. *Environmetrics* 10: 725–36.

Hamilton, J.D. 1990. Analysis of time series subject to changes in regime. *Journal of Econometrics* 45, no. 1–2: 39–70.

Hansen, B.E. 2001. The new econometrics of structural change: Dating breaks in US Labor Productivity. *Journal of Economic Perspectives* 15: 117–28.

Hosking, J.R.M. 1980. The multivariate portmanteau statistic. *Journal of the American Statistical Association* 75, no. 371: 602–8.

Joe, H. 1997. *Multivariate models and dependence concepts.* London: Chapman & Hall.

Longin, F., and B. Solnik. 2001. Extreme correlation of international equity markets. *Journal of Finance* LVI, no. 2: 649–76.

Loretan, M., and P.C.B. Phillips. 1994. Testing the covariance stationarity of heavy-tailed time series: An overview of the theory with applications to several financial data sets. *Journal of Empirical Finance* 1, no. 2: 211–28.

McNeil, A.J., R. Frey, and P. Embrechts. 2005. *Quantitative risk management: Concepts, techniques and tools.* Princeton, NJ: Princeton Univ. Press.

Mikosch, T., and C. Stărică. 2000. Is it really long memory we see in financial returns? In *Extremes and integrated risk management*, ed. P. Embrechts, 149–68. London: Risk Books, Waters Group.

Mikosch, T., and C. Stărică. 2004. Non-stationarities in financial time series, the long range dependence and the IGARCH effects. *Review of Economics and Statistics* 86, no. 1: 378–90.

Nelsen, R.B. 2006. *An introduction to copulas.* 2nd ed. Springer Series in Statistics. New York: Springer.

Patton, A.J. 2006a. Estimation of multivariate models for time series of possibly different lengths. *Journal of Applied Econometrics* 21: 147–73.

Patton, A.J. 2006b. Modelling asymmetric exchange rate dependence. *International Economic Review* 47, no. 2: 527–56.

Pesaran, M.H., T. Schuermann, and S.M. Weiner. 2004. Modeling regional interdependencies using a global errorcorrecting macroeconometric model. *Journal of Business Economics and Statistics* 22, no. 2: 129–62.

Polzehl, J., and V. Spokoiny. 2006. Varying coefficient GARCH versus local constant volatility modeling: Comparison of the predictive power. SFB 649 Discussion Paper 2006-033, Weierstrass Institute for Applied Analysis and Stochastics. http://edoc.hu-berlin.de/series/sfb-649-papers/2006-33/PDF/33.pdf.

Rockinger, M., and E. Jondeau. 2006. The copula-GARCH model of conditional dependencies: An international stockmarket application. *Journal of International Money and Finance* 25, no. 5: 827–53.

Rosenberg, J.V., and T. Schuermann. 2006. A general approach to integrated risk management with skewed, fat-tailed risks. *Journal of Financial Economics* 79, no. 3: 569–614.

Sklar, A. 1959. Fonctions de répartition à *n* dimensions et leurs marges. *Publications de l'Institut de Statistique de L'Université de Paris* 8: 229–31.

Vostrikova, L.J. 1981. Detecting "disorder" in multidimensional random processes. *Soviet Mathematics Doklady* 24, no. 1: pp. 55–9.

Models for construction of multivariate dependence – a comparison study

Kjersti Aas[a] and Daniel Berg[b]

[a]*The Norwegian Computing Center, Blindern, Oslo, Norway;* [b]*University of Oslo and Norwegian Computing Center, Oslo, Norway*

A multivariate data set, which exhibit complex patterns of dependence, particularly in the tails, can be modelled using a cascade of lower-dimensional copulae. In this paper, we compare two such models that differ in their representation of the dependency structure, namely the nested Archimedean construction (NAC) and the pair-copula construction (PCC). The NAC is much more restrictive than the PCC in two respects. There are strong limitations on the degree of dependence in each level of the NAC, and all the bivariate copulas in this construction has to be Archimedean. Based on an empirical study with two different four-dimensional data sets; precipitation values and equity returns, we show that the PCC provides a better fit than the NAC and that it is computationally more efficient. Hence, we claim that the PCC is more suitable than the NAC for hich-dimensional modelling.

1. Introduction

A copula is a multivariate distribution function with standard uniform marginal distributions. While the literature on copulae is substantial, most of the research is still limited to the bivariate case. Building higher-dimensional copulae is a natural next step, however, this is not an easy task. Apart from the multivariate Gaussian and Student copulae, the set of higher-dimensional copulae proposed in the literature is rather limited.

Tail dependence properties are particularly important in applications that rely on non-normal multivariate families (Joe 1996). This is especially the case for financial applications. Tail dependence in a bivariate distribution can be represented by the probability that the first variable exceeds its q-quantile, given that the other variable exceeds its own q-quantile. The limiting probability, as q goes to infinity, is called the upper tail dependence coefficient (Sibuya 1960), and a copula is said to be upper tail dependent if this limit is not zero. The Gaussian copula has no tail dependence. Hence, it is generally regarded not to be appropriate for modelling financial data. The d-dimensional Student copula, however, has been used repeatedly for modelling multivariate financial return data. A number of papers, e.g. Mashal and Zeevi (2002), have shown that the fit of this copula is generally superior to that of other d-dimensional copulae for such data. However, the Student copula has only one parameter for modelling tail dependence, regardless of dimension. Hence, if the tail dependence of different pairs of risk factors in a portfolio are very different, it is shown in Aas et al. (2007) that an even better description of the dependence structure can be achieved with a pair-copula construction.

PCC was originally proposed by Joe (1996), and later discussed in detail by Bedford and Cooke (2001, 2002), Kurowicka and Cooke (2006) (simulation) and Aas et al. (2007) (inference). The PCC is hierarchical in nature. The modelling scheme is based on a decomposition of a multivariate density into a cascade of bivariate copula densities. For a d-dimensional problem, the PCC allows for the free specification of $d(d-1)/2$ copulae. The bivariate copulae may be from any family and several families may well be mixed in one PCC.

The use of the PCC is still in its infancy. A different structure for building higher-dimensional copulae, the nested Archimedean construction (NAC), is more commonly used. Even this structure was originally proposed by Joe (1997), and it is also discussed in Nelsen (1999), Embrechts, Lindskog, and McNeil (2003), Whelan (2004), Savu and Trede (2006), McNeil (2008) and Hofert (2008) Similar to the PCC, the NAC is hierarchical in nature and based on pair-copulae. However, it only allows for the modelling of up to $d-1$ bivariate copulae. Moreover, all copulae must be Archimedean, and there are strong restrictions on the parameters.

The purpose of this paper is to compare the PCC and the NAC in terms of structure, computational efficiency and goodness-of-fit (GOF) for two real data sets. In Section 2 we give a short review of the two constructions. Moreover, we examine properties and estimation- and simulation techniques, focusing on the relative strengths and weaknesses. In Section 3 we apply the NAC and the PCC to two data sets. We examine the GOF and validate the PCC out-of-sample with respect to one day value at risk (VaR) for the equity portfolio. Finally, Section 4 provides some summarizing comments and conclusions.

2. Constructions of higher-dimensional dependence

2.1 *The NAC*

The Archimedean copula family (see e.g. Joe (2997) for a review) is a class that has attracted particular interest due to numerous properties which make them simple to analyse. The most common multivariate Archimedean copula, the exchangeable Archimedean copula (EAC), is extremely restrictive, allowing the specification of only one generator, regardless of dimension. Hence, all k-dimensional marginal distributions ($k < d$) are identical. For several applications, one would like to have multivariate copulae which allow for more flexibility. There have been some attempts at constructing more flexible multivariate Archimedean copula extensions, see e.g. Joe (1997), Nelsen (1999), Embrechts, Lindskog, and McNeil (2003), Whelan (2004), Morillas (2005), Savu and Trade (2006), Hofert (2008). In this paper, we discuss one class of such extensions, the NAC. We first review two simple special cases, the fully nested Archimedian construction (FNAC) and the partially nested Archimedian construction (PNAC), in Sections 2.1.2 and 2.1.3, and then we turn to the general case in Section 2.1.4. However, before reviewing the NAC, we give a short description of the EAC in Section 2.1.1, since this construction serves as a baseline.

2.1.1 *The multivariate EAC*
The most common way of defining a multivariate Archimedean copula is the EAC, defined as

$$C(u_1, u_2, \ldots, u_d) = \varphi^{-1}\{\varphi(u_1) + \cdots + \varphi(u_d)\}, \tag{1}$$

where the function φ is a decreasing function known as the generator of the copula and φ^{-1} denotes its inverse (see e.g. Nelsen (1999)). Note that some authors define φ and φ^{-1} oppositely to what we have done here, while we have chosen to follow the convention in the financial literature.

For $C(u_1, u_2, \ldots, u_d)$ to be a valid d-dimensional Archimedean copula, φ^{-1} should be defined in the range zero to one, be monotonically decreasing and $\varphi(1) = 0$. Furthermore, if $\varphi(0) = \infty$ the generator is said to be strict. Archimedean copulas arise naturally in the context of Laplace transforms of distribution functions (Joe 1997). If φ in addition equals the inverse of the Laplace transform of a distribution function G on $\mathcal{R}^+$ satisfying $G(0) = 0,$[1] the copula in (1) is guaranteed to be a proper distribution, meaning that its density function as well as all marginal density functions are positive.

There are exchangeable multivariate Archimedean copulas with more than one parameter, see e.g. Joe (1997), but the most common EACs, like the Gumbel, Frank and Clayton have only one.

2.1.2 The fully nested Archimedean construction

A simple generalization of (1) can be found in Joe (1997) and is also discussed in Embrechts, Lindskog, McNeil (2003), Whelan (2004), Savu and Trade (2006), McNeil (2008) and Hofert (2008). The construction, which is shown in Figure 1 for the four-dimensional case, is quite simple, but notationally cumbersome. As seen from the figure, one simply adds a dimension step-by-step. The nodes u_1 and u_2 are coupled through copula C_{11}, node u_3 is coupled with $C_{11}(u_1, u_2)$ through copula C_{21}, and finally node u_4 is coupled with $C_{21}(u_3, C_{11}(u_1, u_2))$ through copula C_{31}. Hence, the copula for the four-dimensional case requires three bivariate copulae C_{11}, C_{21} and C_{31}, with corresponding generators $\varphi_{11}, \varphi_{21}$ and φ_{31}:

$$C(u_1, u_2, u_3, u_4) = C_{31}(u_4, C_{21}(u_3, C_{11}(u_1, u_2)))$$
$$= \varphi_{31}^{-1}\{\varphi_{31}(u_4) + \varphi_{31}(\varphi_{21}^{-1}\{\varphi_{21}(u_3) + \varphi_{21}(\varphi_{11}^{-1}\{\varphi_{11}(u_1) + \varphi_{11}(u_2)\})\})\}.$$

For the d-dimensional case, the corresponding expression becomes

$$C(u_1, \ldots, u_d) = \varphi_{d-1,1}^{-1}\{\varphi_{d-1,1}(u_d) + \varphi_{d-1,1} \circ \varphi_{d-2,1}^{-1}\{\varphi_{d-2,1}(u_{d-1}) + \varphi_{d-2,1}$$
$$\circ \ldots \circ \varphi_{11}^{-1}\{\varphi_{11}(u_1) + \varphi_{11}(u_2)\}\}\}. \tag{2}$$

In this construction, which Whelan (2004) refers to as fully nested, all bivariate margins are themselves Archimedean copulae. The FNAC allows for the free specification of $d - 1$ copulae and corresponding distributional parameters, while the remaining $(d - 1)(d - 2)/2$ copulae and parameters are implicitly given through the construction. More specifically, in Figure 1, the two

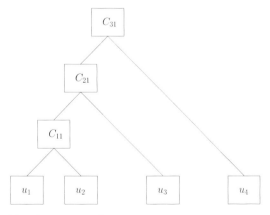

Figure 1. Fully nested Archimedean construction.

pairs (u_1, u_3) and (u_2, u_3) both have copula C_{21} with dependence parameter θ_{21}. Moreover, the three pairs (u_1, u_4), (u_2, u_4) and (u_3, u_4) all have copula C_{31} with dependence parameter θ_{31}. Hence, when adding variable k to the construction, we specify the relationships between k pairs of variables.

The FNAC is a construction of partial exchangeability and there are some technical conditions that need to be satisfied for (2) to be a proper d-dimensional copula. First, all the generators have to be strict with completely monotone inverses. Second, $\varphi_{i+1,1} \circ \varphi_{i,1}^{-1}$ must have completely monotone derivatives for all levels i of the nesting, see e.g McNeil (2008) and Hofert (2008). These conditions put restrictions on the parameters of the copulae involved. For instance, if all the generators are of the same type, e.g. Clayton, Ali–Mikhail–Haq, Gumbel, Frank or Joe type, the degree of dependence, as expressed by the copula parameter, must decrease with the level of nesting, i.e. $\theta_{11} \geq \theta_{21} \geq \cdots \geq \theta_{d-1,1}$, in order for the resulting d-dimensional distribution to be a proper copula. If generators belonging to different families are involved in an NAC, the parameter restrictions are even stronger. For example if $\varphi_{i+1,1}$ and $\varphi_{i,1}$ are the generators for the Clayton and Gumbel copulae, respectively, $\varphi_{i+1,1} \circ \varphi_{i,1}^{-1}$ does not have a completely monotonic derivative for any parameter choice (Hofert 2008). Other families may although be combined. It is for instance possible to choose $\varphi_{i+1,1}$ and $\varphi_{i,1}$ as generators for the Ali–Mikhail–Haq and Clayton copula given that the dependence parameter of the Clayton copula is larger than, or equal to 1. The list of which generators that can be combined is, however, unfortunately not very long. For more information on this, see McNeil (20068) and Hofert (2008).

2.1.3 The partially nested Archimedean construction

An alternative multivariate extension is the PNAC. This construction was originally proposed by Joe (1997) and is also discussed in Whelan (2004), McNeil, Frey, and Embrechts (2006) (where it is denoted partially exchangeable), McNeil (2008) and Hofert (2008).

The lowest dimension for which there is a distinct construction of this class is four, when we have the following copula:

$$C(u_1, u_2, u_3, u_4) = C_{21}(C_{11}(u_1, u_2), C_{21}(u_3, u_4))$$
$$= \varphi_{21}^{-1}\{\varphi_{21}(\varphi_{11}^{-1}\{\varphi_{11}(u_1) + \varphi_{11}(u_2)\}) + \varphi_{21}(\varphi_{12}^{-1}\{\varphi_{12}(u_3) + \varphi_{12}(u_4)\})\}. \quad (3)$$

Figure 2 illustrates this construction graphically. Again the construction is notationally cumbersome although the logic is straightforward. We first couple the two pairs (u_1, u_2) and (u_3, u_4) with copulae C_{11} and C_{12}, having generator functions φ_{11} and φ_{12}, respectively. We then couple these two copulae using a third copula C_{21}. The resulting copula is exchangeable between u_1 and

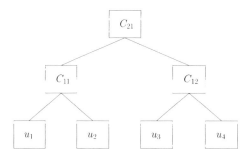

Figure 2. Partially nested Archimedean construction.

u_2 and also between u_3 and u_4. Hence, it can be understood as a composite of the EAC and the FNAC.

For the PNAC, as for the FNAC, $d - 1$ copulae and corresponding distributional parameters are freely specified, while the remaining copulae and parameters are implicitly given through the construction. More specifically, in Figure 2, the four pairs (u_1, u_3), (u_1, u_4) (u_2, u_3) and (u_2, u_4) will all have copula C_{21}, with dependence parameter θ_{21}. The constraints on the generators and their parameters are the same for the PNAC as those for the FNAC described in Section 2.1.2.

2.1.4 The general case

The generally nested Arcimedean construction was originally treated by Joe (1997, chapter 4.2), and is also mentioned in Whelan (2004). However, Savu and Trede (2006) were the first to provide the notation for arbitrary nesting, and to show how to calculate the d-dimensional density in general.

Savu and Trede (2006) use the notation hierarchical Archimedean copula for the generally nested case. The idea is to build a hierarchy of Archimedean copulas. Assume that there are L levels. At each level l, there are n_l distinct objects (an object is either a copula or a variable). At level $l = 1$ the variables $u_1, \ldots, u_d$ are grouped into n_1 exchangeable multivariate Archimedean copulae. These copulae are in turn coupled into n_2 copulae at level $l = 2$, and so on.

Figure 3 shows an example. The nine-dimensional copula in the figure is given by

$$C(u_1, \ldots u_9) = C_{41}(C_{31}(C_{21}(C_{11}(u_1, u_2), u_3, u_4), u_5, u_6), C_{22}(u_7, C_{12}(u_8, u_9))).$$

At level one, there are two copulae. Both are two-dimensional EACs. The first, C_{11} joins the variables u_1 and u_2, while the other, C_{12}, joins u_8 and u_9. At the second level, there are also two copulae. The first, C_{21}, joins the copula C_{11} with the two variables u_3 and u_4, while the other, C_{22} joins C_{12} and u_7. At the third level there is only one copula, C_{31}, joining C_{21}, u_5 and u_6. Finally, at level four, the copula C_{41} joins the two copulae C_{31} and C_{22}.

The constraints on the generators and their parameters are the same in the general case as those for the FNAC described in Section 2.1.2.

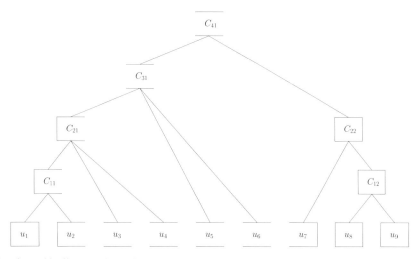

Figure 3. Hierarchically nested Archimedean construction.

2.1.5 Parameter estimation

Full estimation of a NAC should in principle consider the following three steps:

- the selection of a specific factorisation;
- the choice of pair-copula types; and
- the estimation of the copula parameters.

Hence, before estimating the parameters of the construction, one has to choose which variables to join at each level of the NAC as well as the parametric shapes of all pair-copulae involved. Due to the restrictions on the dependency parameters of the involved copulae described in Section 2.1.2, it is usually appropriate to join the variables that have the strongest tail dependence first. Very recently, there has been an attempt of formalising the procedure of determining the optimal structure of a NAC, see Okhrin, Okhrin, and Schmid (2007). Concerning the parametric shapes of the copulae, one may use one of the GOF tests described in Section 3.1 for determining the copula family that most appropriately fits the data. A problem with the NAC, however, is that many pairs have the same copula by construction. Hence, the choice of copula family for these pairs is not obvious.

Having determined the appropriate parametric shapes for each copula, all the parameters of the NAC may be estimated by maximum likelihood. However, not even for an EAC it is straightforward to derive the density in general for all parametric families. For instance, for the Gumbel family, one has to resort to a computer algebra system, such as Mathematica, or the function D in R, to derive the d-dimensional density. For the NAC it is even harder to obtain the density. Due to the complex structure of this construction, one has to use a recursive approach. One differentiates the d-dimensional top level copula with respect to its arguments using the chain rule. Hence, the number of computational steps needed to evaluate the density increases rapidly with the complexity of the copula, and parameter estimation becomes very time consuming in high dimensions. See Savu and Trede (2006) for more details.

2.1.6 Simulation

Simulating from the higher-dimensional constructions is a very important and central practical task. Simulating from an EAC is usually rather simple, and several algorithms exist. A popular algorithm utilizes the representation of the Archimedean copula generator using Laplace transform (Marshall and Olkin 1988). This algorithm can be briefly described as follows:

(1) Simulate a variate X with distribution function G such that the Laplace transform of G is the inverse of the generator.
(2) Simulate d independent, uniformly distributed variates $V_1, \ldots, V_d$.
(3) Return $U = (\phi^{-1}(-\log(V_1)/X), \ldots, \phi^{-1}(-\log(V_d)/X))$.

McNeil (2008) has recently generalised the idea of Marshall and Olkin (1988) to NACs. The basic idea of his algorithm is to apply the algorithm above iteratively. The problem with the algorithm of McNeil (2008) is however that it only works efficiently for the Gumbel family. The reason for this is the lack of knowledge of the inverse Laplace transforms of the generators that are required for this algorithm.

An alternative to the Laplace transform approach is the conditional distribution method described in e.g. Embrechts, Lindskog, and McNeil (2003) and Cherubini, Luciano, and Vecchiato (2004). This procedure, however, involves the $d - 1$ first derivatives of the copula function and, in most cases, numerical inversion. The higher-order derivatives are usually extremely complex expressions (see e.g. Savu and Trede (2006)). Hence, simulation is already a challenge for small dimensions, and may become very inefficient for high dimensions.

Finally, very recently, Hofert (2008) has presented algoritms for numerical inversion of Laplace transforms, that may make the algorithm given by McNeil (2008) efficient even for other copulae than the Gumbel.

2.2 The PCC

While the NAC constitutes a large improvement compared to the EAC, it still only allows for the specification of up to $d - 1$ copulae. An even more flexible construction, the PCC, allows for the free specification of $d(d - 1)/2$ copulae. This construction was orginally proposed by Joe (1996), and it has later been discussed in detail by Bedford and Cooke (2001, 2002), Kurowicka and Cooke (2006) (simulation) and Aas et al. (2007) (inference). Similar to the NAC, the PCC is hierarchical in nature. The modelling scheme is based on a decomposition of a multivariate density into $d(d - 1)/2$ bivariate copula densities, of which the first $d - 1$ are dependency structures of unconditional bivariate distributions, and the rest are dependency structures of conditional bivariate distributions.

While the NAC is defined through its distribution functions, the PCC is usually represented in terms of the density. Two main types of PCCs have been proposed in the literature; canonical vines and D-vines (Kurowicka and Cooke 2004). Here, we concentrate on the D-vine representation, for which the density is (Aas et al. 2007):

$$f(x_1, \ldots, x_d) = \prod_{k=1}^{d} f(x_k) \prod_{j=1}^{d-1} \prod_{i=1}^{d-j} c\{F(x_i|x_{i+1}, \ldots, x_{i+j-1}), F(x_{i+j}|x_{i+1}, \ldots, x_{i+j-1})\}. \quad (4)$$

Here, $c(\cdot, \cdot)$ is a bivariate copula density, and the conditional distribution functions are computed using (Joe 1996)

$$F(x|\boldsymbol{v}) = \frac{\partial C_{x,v_j|\boldsymbol{v}_{-j}}\{F(x|\boldsymbol{v}_{-j}), F(v_j|\boldsymbol{v}_{-j})\}}{\partial F(v_j|\boldsymbol{v}_{-j})}. \quad (5)$$

In (5), $C_{x,v_j|\boldsymbol{v}_{-j}}$ is the dependency structure of the bivariate conditional distribution of x and v_j conditioned on $\boldsymbol{v}_{-j}$, where the vector $\boldsymbol{v}_{-j}$ is the vector $\boldsymbol{v}$ excluding the component v_j.

To use the D-vine construction to represent a dependency structure through copulas, we assume that the univariate margins are uniform in [0, 1]. One four-dimensional case of (4) is then

$$c(u_1, u_2, u_3, u_4) = c_{11}(u_1, u_2) \cdot c_{12}(u_2, u_3) \cdot c_{13}(u_3, u_4)$$
$$\cdot c_{21}(F(u_1|u_2), F(u_3|u_2)) \cdot c_{22}(F(u_2|u_3), F(u_4|u_3))$$
$$\cdot c_{31}(F(u_1|u_2, u_3), F(u_4|u_2, u_3)),$$

where

$$F(u_1|u_2) = \partial C_{11}(u_1, u_2)/\partial u_2,$$
$$F(u_3|u_2) = \partial C_{12}(u_2, u_3)/\partial u_2,$$
$$F(u_2|u_3) = \partial C_{12}(u_2, u_3)/\partial u_3,$$
$$F(u_4|u_3) = \partial C_{13}(u_3, u_4)/\partial u_3,$$

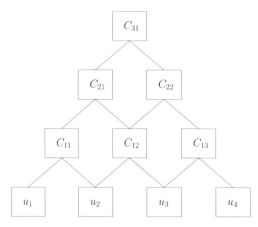

Figure 4. Pair-copula construction.

$$F(u_1|u_2, u_3) = \partial C_{21}(F(u_1|u_2), F(u_3|u_2))/\partial F(u_3|u_2),$$

$$F(u_4|u_2, u_3) = \partial C_{22}(F(u_4|u_3), F(u_2|u_3))/\partial F(u_2|u_3).$$

Hence, the conditional distributions involved at one level of the construction are always computed as partial derivatives of the bivariate copulae at the previous level. Since only bivariate copulae are involved, the partial derivatives may be obtained relatively easily for most parametric copula families. Figure 4 illustrates this construction.

The copulae involved in (4) do not have to belong to the same family. In contrast to the NAC they do not even have to belong to the same class. The resulting multivariate distribution will be valid even if we choose, for each pair of variables, the parametric copula that best fits the data. As seen from (4) the PCC consists of $d(d-1)/2$ bivariate copulae of known parametric families, of which $d-1$ are copulae of pairs of the original variables, while the remaining $(d-1)(d-2)/2$ are copulae of pairs of variables constructed using (5) recursively. This means that in contrast to the NAC, the unspecified bivariate margins will not belong to a known parametric family in general. However, it can be shown, that e.g. upper (lower) tail dependence on the bivariate copulae at the lowest level is a sufficient condition for all bivariate margins to have upper (lower) tail dependence.[2]

2.2.1 Parameter estimation

Full inference for a PCC should in principle consider the same three steps as described for the NAC in Section 2.1.5. First one has to choose which variables to join at the first level of the PCC. We then usually join the variables that have the strongest tail dependence. Having chosen the order of the variables at the first level, one has also determined which factorisation to use.

Given data and the chosen factorisation, one must then specify the parametric shape of each pair-copula involved. The parametric shapes may for instance be determined using the following procedure:

(1) Determine which copula families to use at level 1 by plotting the observations, and/or applying a GoF test (see Section 3.1 for suggestions of GoF tests).
(2) Estimate the parameters of the selected copulae.

(3) Determine the observations required for level 2 as the partial derivatives of the copulae from level 1.

(4) Determine which copula families to use at level 2 in the same way as at level 1.

(5) Repeat 1–3 for all levels of the construction.

This selection mechanism does not guarantee a globally optimal fit. Having determined the appropriate parametric shapes for each copulae, all parameters of the PCC are estimated by numerical optimization of the full likelihood. In contrast to the NAC, the density is explicitly given. However, also for this construction, a recursive approach is used (see Aas et al. (2007, Algorithm 4)). Hence, the number of computational steps to evaluate the density increases rapidly with the complexity of the copula, and parameter estimation becomes time consuming in high dimensions.

2.2.2 Simulation

The simulation algorithm for a D-vine is straightforward and simple to implement, see Aas et al. (2007, Algorithm 2). Like for the NAC, the conditional inversion method is used. However, to determine each of the conditional distribution functions involved, only the first partial derivative of a bivariate copula needs to be computed (see Aas et al. (2007)). Hence, the simulation procedure for the PCC is in general much simpler and faster than for the NAC.

2.3 Comparison

In this section we summarize the differences between the NAC and the PCC with respect to ease of interpretation, applicability and computational complexity.

First, the main advantage of the PCC is the increased flexibility compared to the NAC. While the NAC only allows for the free specification of $d - 1$ copulae, $d(d - 1)/2$ copulae may be specified in a PCC. Next, for the NAC there are restrictions on which Archimedean copulae that can be mixed, while the PCC can be built using copulae from different families and classes. Finally, the NAC has another even more important restriction in that $\varphi_{i+1,1} \circ \varphi_{i,1}^{-1}$ must have completely monotone derivatives for all levels i of the nesting. When looking for appropriate data sets for the applications in Section 3, it turned out to be quite difficult to find real-world data sets satisfying this restriction. Hence, this feature of the NAC might prevent it from being extensively used

Table 1. Summary of construction properties for the EAC, NAC and PCC constructions.

Construction	Maximum number of copulae	Constraints	Which families ?
EAC	1	None	Only one Archimedean copula
NAC	$d - 1$	Strict generators $\varphi_{i+1,1} \circ \varphi_{i,1}^{-1}$ must have completely monotone derivatives for all levels i of the construction	May combine different Archimedean families but under strong restrictions
PCC	$d(d - 1)/2$	None	May combine any copula families from any class

Table 2. Computational times in seconds for different constructions and copulae, fitted to the equity data in Section 3.3.

Method	Likelihood evaluation	Estimation	Simulation
	Gumbel		
NAC	0.32	34.39	0.02
PCC	0.04	5.09	7.56
	Frank		
NAC	0.12	5.34	64.83
PCC	0.02	1.22	5.82

in real-world applications. For the PCC, on the other hand, one is always guaranteed that all parameter combinations are valid. Table 1 summarizes these properties.

It is our opinion that another advantage of the PCC is that it is represented in terms of the density and hence easier to handle than the NAC that is defined through its distribution function. The PCC is also in general more computationally efficient than the NAC. Table 2 shows computational times in seconds using the statistical language R^3 for likelihood evaluation, parameter estimation and simulation for different constructions. The parameter estimation is done for the data set described in Section 3.3, and the simulation is performed using the parameters in Table 6 (based on 1000 samples). The values for NAC were computed using density expressions found in Savu and Trede (2006). General expressions may also easily be obtained symbolically using e.g. the function D in R. The estimation times in Table 2 are only indicative and included as examples since they are very dependent on size and structure of the data set. It is more appropriate to study the times needed to compute one evaluation of the likelihood given in the leftmost column. As can be seen from the table, the PCC is superior to the NAC for likelihood evaluation in both the Gumbel and the Frank case. Moreover, it is much faster for simulation in the Frank case, since one in this case must use the general conditional inversion algorithm with numerical inversion for the NAC. In the Gumbel case, however, one can perform much more efficient simulation from the NAC using the algorithms given in McNeil (2008). Hence, in this case, the NAC is faster than the PCC.

The multivariate distribution defined through a NAC will always by definition be an Archimedean copula (assuming that all requirements are satisfied), and all bivariate margins will belong to a known parametric family. This is not the case for the PCC, for which neither the multivariate distribution nor the unspecified bivariate marginal distributions will belong to a known parametric family in general. However, we do not view this as a problem, since both types of distributions are easily obtained by simulation.

3. Applications

The fit of the NAC and the PCC is assessed for two different four-dimensional data sets; precipitation values and equity returns. Appropriate modelling of precipitation is of great importance to insurance companies which are exposed to growth in damages to buildings caused by external water exposition. Modelling precipitation and valuing related derivative contracts is also indeed a frontier in the field of weather derivatives, see e.g. Musshoff, Odening, and Xu (2006). The dependencies within an equity portfolio can have enormous impacts on e.g. capital allocation and the pricing of collateralized debt obligations (CDOs). Most approaches for CDO pricing are based on the Merton model, in which default occurs if the asset value of a firm is lower than its debt (Merton 1974)). Before these two applications are further treated, we describe the tests used for GOF in our study.

3.1 *Goodness-of-fit*

To evaluate whether a copula or copula construction appropriately fits the data at hand, GOF testing is called upon. Lately, several procedures have been proposed. In a comparison study (Berg 2007) two procedures are shown to perform particularly well in most cases. Both approches are based on the empirical copula C_n introduced by Deheuvels (1979),

$$C_n(\mathbf{u}) = \frac{1}{n+1} \sum_{j=1}^{n} \mathbf{1}(U_{j1} \le u_1, \ldots, U_{jd} \le u_d), \quad \mathbf{u} = (u_1, \ldots, u_d) \in (0, 1)^d, \quad (6)$$

where $\mathbf{U}_j = (U_{j1}, \ldots, U_{jd})$ are the $U(0, 1)^d$ pseudo-observations, defined as normalized ranks.

The first procedure is based on the GOF process $\mathcal{V}_n = \sqrt{n}\{C_n - C_{\theta_n}\}$ where θ_n is some consistent estimator of θ. Basing a GOF procedure on $\mathcal{V}_n$ was originally proposed by Fermanian (2005), but there dismissed due to poor statistical properties. However, it has later been shown that it has the necessary asymptotic properties to be a justified GOF procedure (Quessy 2005; Genest and Rémillard 2005). Further, Genest, Rémillard, and Beaudoin (2008) and Berg (2007) have shown (by bootstrapping p-values) that it is a very powerful procedure in most cases.

We use the Cramér–von Mises statistic, defined by:

$$S_n = n \int_{[0,1]^d} \{C_n(\mathbf{u}) - C_{\theta_n}(\mathbf{u})\}^2 dC_n(\mathbf{u}) = \sum_{j=1}^{n} \{C_n(\mathbf{U}_j) - C_{\theta_n}(\mathbf{U}_j)\}^2. \quad (7)$$

Large values of S_n means a poor fit and leads to the rejection of the null hypothesis copula. In practice, the limiting distribution of S_n depends on θ. Hence, approximate p-values for the test must be obtained through a parametric bootstrap procedure. We adopt the procedure in Appendix 1 in Genest, Rémillard, and Beaudoin (2008), setting the bootstrap parameters m and N to 5000 and 1000, respectively. The validity of this bootstrap procedure was established in Genest and Rémillard (2005).

The second procedure is based on the GOF process $\mathcal{K}_n = \sqrt{n}\{K_n - K_{\theta_n}\}$, where

$$K_n(t) = \frac{1}{n+1} \sum_{j=1}^{n} \mathbf{1}(C_n(\mathbf{U}_j) \le t),$$

is the empirical distribution function of $C_n(\mathbf{u})$. See Genest, Quessy, and Rémillard (2006) for details. Also for this procedure we use the Cramér–von Mises statistic, i.e.

$$T_n = \int_{[0,1]^d} \{K_n(\mathbf{u}) - K_{\theta_n}(\mathbf{u})\}^2 dK_n(\mathbf{u}) = \sum_{j=1}^{n} \{K_n(\mathbf{U}_j) - K_{\theta_n}(\mathbf{U}_j)\}^2, \quad (8)$$

and the same parametric bootstrap procedure as described for S_n to obtain the p-values. For both procedures, we use a 5% significance level for all experiments in this section.

3.2 *Application 1: precipitation data*

In this section, we study daily precipitation data (mm) for the period 1 January 1990 to 31 December 2006 for four meteorological stations in Norway; Vestby, Ski, Nannestad and Hurdal, obtained from the Norwegian Meteorological Institute. According to Musshoff, Odening, and Xu (2006), the stochastic process of daily precipitation can be decomposed into a stochastic process of 'rainfall'/'no rainfall', and a distribution for the amount of precipitation given that it rains. Here, we are only interested in the latter. Hence, before further processing, we remove days with zero precipitation values for at least one station, resulting in 2065 observations for each variable. Figures 5 and 6 show the daily precipitation values and corresponding copulae for pairs of meteorological stations. Since we are mainly interested in estimating the dependence structure of the stations, the precipitation vectors are converted to uniform pseudo-observations before further modelling. In light of recent results due to Chen and Fan (2006), the method of maximum pseudo-likelihood is consistent even when time series models are fitted to the margins.

Based on visual inspection and preliminary GOF tests for bivariate pairs (the copulae taken into consideration in the GOF-tests were the Student, Clayton, survival Clayton, Gumbel and Frank copulae), we decided to examine Gumbel and Frank NACs, and Gumbel, Frank and Student PCCs for this data set.

3.2.1 *Hierarchically NAC*
We use the following NAC

$$C(u_1, u_2, u_3, u_4) = C_{21}(C_{11}(u_1, u_2), C_{21}(u_3, u_4)),$$

where the most appropriate ordering of the variates in the construction is found by comparing Kendall's tau values for all bivariate pairs. The Kendall's tau values are shown in Table 3. They

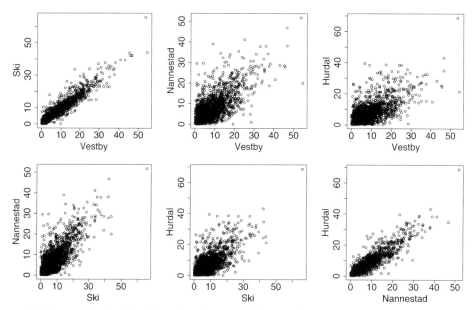

Figure 5. Daily precipitation (mm) for pairs of meteorological stations for the period 1 January 1990 to 31 December 2006, zeros removed.

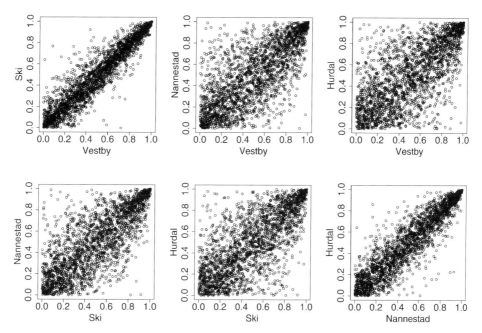

Figure 6. Pseudo-observations corresponding to Figure 5.

Table 3. Estimated Kendall's tau for pairs of variables.

Location	Ski	Nannestad	Hurdal
Vestby	0.79	0.49	0.47
Ski		0.56	0.53
Nannestad			0.71

confirm the intuition that the degree of dependence between the variables corresponds to the distances between the stations. Ski and Vestby are closely located, and so is Hurdal and Nannestad, while the distance from Ski/Vestby to Hurdal/Nannestad is larger. Based on the Kendall's tau values, we choose C_{11} and C_{12} to be the copulae of Vestby and Ski, and Nannestad and Hurdal, respectively, and C_{21} the copula of the remaining pairs.

The parameters of the Gumbel and Frank NACs are estimated using numerical optimization of the likelihood. The two leftmost columns of Table 4 show the estimated parameter values, resulting log-likelihoods, and estimated p-values for the two NACs. We see that both GOF procedures strongly reject the two NAC constructions. Hence we conclude that the NACs considered are not flexible enough to fit the precipitation data appropriately.

3.2.2 Pair-copula construction
We use the following PCC

$$c(u_1, u_2, u_3, u_4) = c_{11}(u_1, u_2) \cdot c_{12}(u_2, u_3) \cdot c_{13}(u_3, u_4) \cdot c_{21}(F(u_1|u_2), F(u_3|u_2))$$

$$\cdot c_{22}(F(u_2|u_3), F(u_4|u_3)) \cdot c_{31}(F(u_1|u_2, u_3), F(u_4|u_2, u_3)),$$

Table 4. Estimated parameters, log-likelihood and estimated p-values for NACs and PCCs fitted to the precipitation data.

Parameter	NAC		PCC		
	Gumbel	Frank	Gumbel	Frank	Student
$\theta_{11}\backslash\nu_{11}$	4.32	16.69	4.34	16.78	0.93\3.6
$\theta_{12}\backslash\nu_{12}$	3.45	13.01	2.24	7.10	0.78\6.7
$\theta_{13}\backslash\nu_{13}$	–	–	3.45	12.98	0.90\5.5
$\theta_{21}\backslash\nu_{21}$	1.97	5.96	1.01	0.08	0.01\9.6
$\theta_{22}\backslash\nu_{22}$	–	–	1.02	0.61	0.09\14.5
$\theta_{31}\backslash\nu_{31}$	–	–	1.03	0.27	0.04\17.3
Log-likelihood	4741.05	4561.72	4842.25	4632.19	4643.38
p-value of S_n	0.000	0.000	0.000	0.000	0.000
p-value of T_n	0.002	0.000	0.089	0.013	0.070

with three different parametric families for the copulae involved; Gumbel, Frank and Student. Like for the NACs the variables are ordered such that the copulae fitted at level 1 in the construction are those corresponding to the three largest Kendall's tau values. Hence, we choose c_{11} as the copula density of Vestby and Ski, c_{12} as the copula density of Ski and Nannestad, and c_{13} as the copula density of Ski and Hurdal. The parameters of the PCC are estimated by numerical optimization of the likelihood using Algorithm 4 in Aas et al. (2007).

The three rightmost columns of Table 4 show the estimated parameter values, resulting log-likelihoods and p-values for the Gumbel, Frank and Student PCCs. We see that, as for the NACs, all considered PCCs are strongly rejected by S_n. Hence, based on the GOF procedure S_n, we are not able to determine which of the two constructions that provides the best fit to the precipitation data. However, the procedure T_n rejects both NACs and the Frank PCC, but not the Gumbel and Student PCCs. Corresponding to the largest p-value, we conclude that the Gumbel PCC provides the best fit. However, since this construction was rejected by the S_n procedure, there might be need for further research to find constructions that captures the properties of the precipitation data even better.

3.3 Application 2: equity returns

In this section, we study an equity portfolio. The portfolio is comprised of four time series of daily log-return data from the period 14 August 2003 to 29 December 2006 (852 observations for each firm). The data set was downloaded from http://finance.yahoo.com. The firms are British Petroleum (BP), Exxon Mobile Corp (XOM), Deutsche Telekom AG (DT) and France Telecom (FTE). Financial log-returns are usually not independent over time. See descriptive statistics for the four time series in Appendix A. Hence, the original vectors of log-returns are processed by a GARCH filter before further modelling. We use the GARCH(1,1)-model (Bollerslev 1986):

$$r_t = c + \epsilon_t$$

$$E[\epsilon_t] = 0 \text{ and } \text{Var}[\epsilon_t] = \sigma_t^2 \qquad (9)$$

$$\sigma_t^2 = a_0 + a\epsilon_{t-1}^2 + b\sigma_{t-1}^2.$$

It has been known for a long time that GARCH models, coupled with the assumption of conditionally normally distributed errors are unable to fully account for the tails of the distributions of daily returns (Bollerslev 1987). Hence, we follow Venter and de Jongh (2002) and use the normal inverse Gaussian (NIG) distribution (Barndorff-Nielsen 1997) as the conditional distribution. In a study performed by Venter and de Jongh (2004) the NIG distribution outperforms a skewed Student's t-distribution and a non-parametric kernel approximation as the conditional distribution of a one-dimensional GARCH process. After filtering the original returns with (9) (estimated parameter values are shown in Appendix 1), the standardised residual vectors are converted to uniform pseudo-observations. Figures 7 and 8 show the filtered daily log-returns and pseudo-observations for each pair of assets.

Based on visual inspection and preliminary GOF tests for bivariate pairs (like for the precipitation data the copulae taken into consideration were the Student, Clayton, survival Clayton, Gumbel and Frank copulae), we decided to examine a Frank NAC and Frank and Student PCC's for this data set.

3.3.1 Hierarchically nested Archimedean construction

We use the following HNAC

$$C(u_1, u_2, u_3, u_4) = C_{21}(C_{11}(u_1, u_2), C_{21}(u_3, u_4)),$$

and also for this data set, the most appropriate ordering of the variates in the construction is found by comparing Kendall's tau values for all bivariate pairs. The Kendall's tau values are shown in Table 5. As expected, stocks within one industrial sector are more dependent than stocks from different sectors. Hence, we choose C_{11} as the copula of BP and XOM, C_{12} as the copula of DT and FTE, and C_{21} as the copula of the remaining pairs. The leftmost column of Table 6 shows

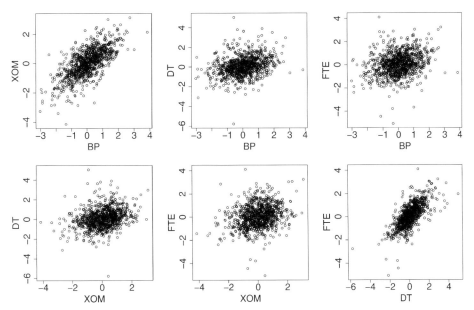

Figure 7. GARCH-filtered daily log-returns for our four stocks for the period from 14 August 2003 to 29 December 2006.

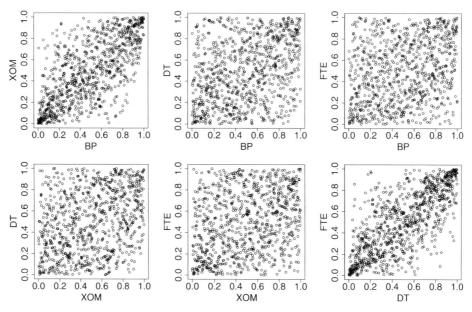

Figure 8. Pseudo-observations corresponding to Figure 7.

Table 5. Estimated Kendall's tau for pairs of variables for our four stocks.

Firm	XOM	DT	FTE
BP	0.45	0.19	0.20
XOM		0.23	0.17
DT			0.48

Table 6. Estimated parameters, log-likelihood and estimated p-values for NAC and PCCs fitted to the filtered equity data.

Parameter	NAC Frank	PCC	
		Frank	Student
$\theta_{11}\backslash\nu_{11}$	5.57	5.56	$0.70\backslash 13.8$
$\theta_{12}\backslash\nu_{12}$	6.34	1.89	$0.32\backslash 134.5$
$\theta_{13}\backslash\nu_{13}$	–	6.32	$0.73\backslash 6.4$
$\theta_{21}\backslash\nu_{21}$	1.78	0.91	$0.14\backslash 12.0$
$\theta_{22}\backslash\nu_{22}$	–	0.30	$0.06\backslash 20.6$
$\theta_{31}\backslash\nu_{31}$	–	0.33	$0.07\backslash 17.8$
Log-likelihood	616.45	618.63	668.49
p-value of S_n	0.006	0.008	0.410
p-value of T_n	0.385	0.385	0.697

the estimated parameter values, resulting log-likelihood and p-value for the Frank HNAC. Even though this construction is not rejected by T_n, the strong rejection by S_n suggests that the fit is not very good.

3.3.2 Pair-copula construction
We use the following PCC

$$c(u_1, u_2, u_3, u_4) = c_{11}(u_1, u_2) \cdot c_{12}(u_2, u_3) \cdot c_{13}(u_3, u_4)$$
$$\cdot c_{21}(F(u_1|u_2), F(u_3|u_2)) \cdot c_{22}(F(u_2|u_3), F(u_4|u_3))$$
$$\cdot c_{31}(F(u_1|u_2, u_3), F(u_4|u_2, u_3)).$$

Again, the most appropriate ordering of the variates in the construction is determined by the size of the Kendall's tau values. Hence, we choose c_{11} as the copula density of BP and XOM, c_{12} as the copula density of XOM and DT, and c_{13} as the copula density of DT and FTE. The parameters of the PCC are estimated by maximum likelihood, see Algorithm 4 in Aas et al. (2007). The two rightmost columns of Table 6 shows the estimated parameter values, resulting log-likelihood and estimated p-values for the Frank and Student PCCs. We see that the Frank PCC is rejected by S_n. Moreover, the p-value of T_n is equal to the one for the Frank NAC. The Student PCC, on the other hand, provides a very good fit and is not even rejected by S_n. Hence, we conclude that it fits the equity data very well.

3.4 Validation

With the increasing complexity of models there is always the risk of overfitting the data. To examine whether this is the case for the PCC, we validate it out-of-sample for the equity portfolio. More specifically, we use the GARCH-NIG-Student PCC described in Section 3.3.2 to determine the risk of the return distribution for an equally weighted portfolio of BP, XOM, DT and FTE over a one-day horizon. The equally-weighted portfolio is only meant as an example. In practice, the weights will fluctuate unless the portfolio is rebalanced every day.

The model estimated from the period 14 March 2003 to 29 December 2006 is used to forecast one-day VaR at different significance levels for each day in the period from 30 December 2006 to 11 June 2007 (110 days). The test procedure is as follows: For each day t in the test set:

(1) For each variable $j = 1, \ldots, 4$, compute the one-step ahead forecast of $\sigma_{j,t}$, given information up to time t.
(2) For each simulation $n = 1, \ldots, 10,000$
   - Generate a sample $u_1, \ldots, u_4$ from the estimated Student PCC.
   - Convert $u_1, \ldots, u_4$ to NIG(0,1)-distributed samples $z_1, \ldots, z_4$ using the inverses of the corresponding NIG distribution functions.
   - For each variable $j = 1, \ldots, 4$, determine the log-return $r_{j,t} = c_{j,t} + \sigma_{j,t} z_j$. (Here $c_{j,t}$ is computed as the mean of the last 100 observed log-returns.)
   - Compute the return of the portfolio as $r_{p,t} = \sum_{j=1}^{4}(1/4)r_{j,t}$.
(3) For significance levels $q \in \{0.005, 0.01, 0.05\}$
   - Compute the one-day VaR_t^q as the qth-quantile of the distribution of $r_{p,t}$.
   - If VaR_t^q is greater than the observed value of $r_{p,t}$ this day, a violation is said to occur.

Figure 9 shows the actual log-returns for the portfolio in the period 30 December 2006 to 11 June 2007 and the corresponding VaR levels obtained from the procedure described above. Further, the two upper rows of Table 7 gives the number of violations x, of VaR for each significance level and with the expected values, respectively. To test the significance of the differences between the

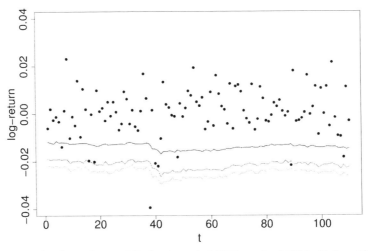

Figure 9. Log-returns for the equity portfolio for the period 30 December 2006 to 11 June 2007 along with 0.5%, 1%, 5% VaR simulated from the estimated GARCH-NIG-Student PCC.

Table 7. Number of violations of VaR, expected number of violations and p-values for the Kupiec test.

Significance level	0.005	0.01	0.05
Observed	1	2	9
Expected	0.55	1.1	5.5
P-value	0.13	0.44	0.16

observed and the expected values, we use the likelihood ratio statistic by Kupiec (1995). The null hypothesis is that the expected proportion of violations is equal to α. Under the null hypothesis, the likelihood ratio statistic given by

$$2 \ln \left(\left(\frac{x}{N} \right)^x \left(1 - \frac{x}{N} \right)^{N-x} \right) - 2 \ln \left(\alpha^x (1 - \alpha)^{N-x} \right),$$

where N is the length of the sample, is asymptotically distributed as $\chi^2(1)$. We have computed p-values of the null hypothesis for each quantile. The results are shown in the lower row of Table 7. If we use a 5% level for the Kupiec LR statistic, the null hypothesis is not rejected for any of the three quantiles. Hence, the GARCH-NIG-Student PCC seems to work very well out-of-sample.

A final comment to this validation is that VaR has been critisized as a measure of market risk of at least two reasons, see e.g. Artzner et al. (1997). First, it is not necessarily subadditive, and second it tells us nothing about the potential size of the loss given that a loss exceeding VaR has occurred. Several papers have therefore proposed using the Expected Shortfall as a risk measure instead. However, since VaR has become an industry standard for measuring risk (for instance in Basel II) we have chosen to use it here.

4. Summary and conclusions

In this paper, we have compared two constructions for modeling higher-dimensional dependence; the NAC and the PCC. For both constructions, a multivariate data set is modelled using a cascade of lower-dimensional copulae. They differ however in their construction of the dependence structure, the PCC being more flexible in that it allows for the free specification of $d(d-1)/2$ copulae, while the NAC only allows for $d-1$. In addition, the NAC has two important limitations. First, there are strong restrictions on the parameters of the construction. When looking for appropriate data sets for the applications in this paper, it turned out to be quite difficult to find real-world data sets satisfying these restrictions. Second, the NAC is restricted to the Archimedean class, and there are even restrictions on which Archimedean copulae that can be mixed. The PCC, on the other hand, can be built using copulas from any class and there are no constraints on the parameters of the construction.

Simulation and estimation techniques for the two constructions have been examined, and we have shown that the PCC in general both is more computationally efficient than the NAC, and provides a better fit to two different four-dimensional data sets; precipitation values and equity returns. Moreover, through VaR calculations we have shown that the PCC does not overfit the training data, but works very well also out-of-sample. Hence, the choice between a NAC and a PCC is not one between flexibility and efficiency. The PCC is generally both more flexible and more computationally efficient than the NAC. We therefore strongly recommend the PCC over the NAC.

Acknowledgements

Daniel Berg's work is supported by the Norwegian Research Council, grant number 154079/420 and Kjersti Aas' part is sponsored by the Norwegian fund Finansmarkedsfondet. We are very grateful to Cornelia Savu, Institute for Econometrics, University of Münster, Germany, for providing us with her code for the NAC's along with helpful comments. In addition we would like to express our deep gratitude for assistance on the GARCH-NIG filtration to Professor J.H. Venter, Centre of Business Mathematics and Informatics, North–West University, Potchefstroom, South Africa. We also thank two anonymous referees and Professor C.J. Adcock (the editor) for comments and suggestions that helped to improve the article. Finally, we thank participants at the conference on copulae and multivariate probability distributions at Warwick Business School in September 2007 for their valuable comments, in particular Professor Alexander McNeil.

Notes

1. The Laplace transform of a distribution function G on $\mathcal{R}^+$ satisfying $G(0) = 0$ is $\hat{G}(t) = \int_0^\infty e^{-tx}\,dG(x), \ \ t \geq 0$.
2. Personal communication with Harry Joe.
3. The experiments were run on an Intel(R) Pentium(R) 4 CPU 2.80 GHz PC.

References

Aas, K., C. Czado, A. Frigessi, and H. Bakken. 2009. Pair-copula constructions of multiple dependence. *Insurance: Mathematics and Economics* 44, no. 1.

Artzner, P., F. Delbaen, J.M. Eber, and D. Heat. 1997. Thinking coherently. *Risk* 10, no. 11: 68–71.

Barndorff-Nielsen, O.E. 1997. Normal inverse Gaussian distributions and stochastic volatility modelling. *Scandinavian Journal of Statistics* 24: 1–13.

Bedford, T., and R.M. Cooke. 2001. Probability density decomposition for conditionally dependent random variables modeled by vines. *Annals of Mathematics and Artificial Intelligence* 32: 245–68.

Bedford, T., and R.M. Cooke. 2002. Vines – a new graphical model for dependent random variables. *Annals of Statistics* 30: 1031–68.

Berg, D. 2007. Copula goodness-of-fit testing: An overview and power comparison. Working Paper, University of Oslo & Norwegian Computing Center.

Bollerslev, T. 1986. Generalized autoregressive conditional heteroskedasticity. *Journal of Econometrics* 31: 307–27.

Bollerslev, T. 1987. A conditionally heteroscedastic time series model for speculative prices and rates of return. *Review of Economics and Statistics* 69: 542–7.

Chen, X., and Y. Fan. 2006. Estimation and model selection of semi-parametric copula-based multivariate dynamic models under copula misspecification. *Journal of Econometrics* 135: 125–54.

Cherubini, U., E. Luciano, and W. Vecchiato. 2004. *Copula methods in finance*. West Sussex: Wiley.

Deheuvels, P. 1979. La fonction de d'ependance empirique et ses propriétés: Un test non paramétrique d'indépendence. *Acad. Royal Bel., Bull. Class. Sci., 5e série* 65: 274–92.

Embrechts, P., F. Lindskog, and A. McNeil. 2003. Modelling dependence with copulas and applications to risk management. In *Handbook of heavy tailed distributions in finance*, ed. S.T. Rachev, 329–384. North-Holland: Elsevier.

Fermanian, J.-D. 2005. Goodness-of-fit tests for copulas. *Journal of Multivariate analysis* 95: 119–52.

Genest, C., J.-F. Quessy, and B. Rémillard. 2006. Goodness-of-fit procedures for copula models based on the probability integral transform. *Scandinavian Journal of Statistics* 33: 337–66.

Genest, C., and B. Rémillard. 2005. Validity of the parametric bootstrap for goodness-offit testing in semiparametric models. Technical Report G-2005-51, GERAD, Montreal, Canada.

Genest, C., B. Rémillard, and D. Beaudoin. 2009. Omnibus goodness-of-fit tests for copulas: A review and a power study. *Insurance: Mathematics and Economics* 44, no. 1.

Hofert, M. 2008. Sampling Archimedean copulas. *Computational Statistics and Data Analysis* 52, no. 12: 5163–74.

Joe, H. 1996. Families of m-variate distributions with given margins and $m(m-1)/2$ bivariate dependence parameters. In *Distributions with fixed marginals and related topics*, ed. L. Rüschendorf, B. Schweizer, and M.D. Taylor, 120–141.

Joe, H. 1997. *Multivariate models and dependence concepts*. London: Chapman & Hall.

Kupiec, P. 1995. Techniques for verifying the accuracy of risk measurement models. *Journal of Derivatives* 2: 173–84.

Kurowicka, D., and R.M. Cooke. 2004. Distribution – free continuous Bayesian belief nets. Fourth International Conference on Mathematical Methods in Reliability Methodology and Practice, Santa Fe, New Mexico.

Kurowicka, D., and R.M. Cooke. 2006. *Uncertainty analysis with high dimensional dependence modelling*. New York: Wiley.

Marshall, A.W., and I. Olkin. 1988. Families of multivariate distributions. *The Journal of the American Statistical Association* 83: 834–41.

Mashal, R., and A. Zeevi. 2002. Beyond correlation: Extreme co-movements between financial assets. Technical Report, Columbia University.

McNeil, A.J. 2008. Sampling nested Archimedean copulas. *Journal of Statistical Computation and Simulation* 78: 567–81.

McNeil, A.J., R. Frey, and P. Embrechts. 2006. *Quantitative risk management: concepts, techniques and tools*. New Jersey: Princeton University Press.

Merton, R.C. 1974. On the pricing of corporate debt: The risk structure of interest rates. *Journal of Finance* 29: 449–70.

Morillas, P.M. 2005. A method to obtain new copulas from a given one. *Metrika* 61: 169–84.

Musshoff, O., M. Odening, and W. Xu. 2006. Modeling and hedging rain risk. Annual Meeting of the American Agricultural Economics Association (AAEA), July 23–26, Long Beach, USA.

Nelsen, R. 1999. *An introduction to copulas*. New York: Springer.

Okhrin, O., Y. Okhrin, and W. Schmid. 2007. Determining the structure and estimation of hierarchical archimedean copulae. Radon Workshop on Financial and Actuarial Mathematics for Young Researchers, Linz, Austria.

Quessy, J.-F. 2005. Théeorie et application des copules: Tests d'adéquation, tests d'indépendence et bornes pour la valeur-à-risque. PhD thesis, Universit'e Laval.

Savu, C., and M. Trede. 2006. Hierarchical Archimedean copulas. International Conference on High Frequency Finance, Konstanz, Germany, May.

Sibuya, M. 1960. Bivariate extreme statistics. *Annals of the Institute of Statistical Mathematics* 11: 195–210.

Venter, J.H., and P.J. de Jongh. 2002. Risk estimation using the normal inverse Gaussian distribution. *Journal of Risk* 4, no. 2: 1–24.

Venter, J.H., and P.J. de Jongh. 2004. Selecting an innovation distribution for garch models to improve efficiency of risk and volatility estimation. *Journal of Risk* 6, no. 3: 27–53.

Whelan, N. 2004. Sampling from Archimedean copulas. *Quantitative Finance* 4: 339–52.

Appendix 1. Financial return data set – more details

Table A1 shows the descriptive statistics for the log-returns of the four financial time series used in Section 3.3. For the Jarque–Bera test statistics for normality, the Ljung-Box test for white noise and the Lagrange multiplier (LM) test for ARCH effects, the p-values are reported. The p-values for the Ljung–Box test indicate that there are no autocorrelation in the log-returns. The null hypotheses of normality and no ARCH effects are rejected for the three time series XOM, DT and FTE. For BP, however, the p-values for the Jarque–Bera test and the LM-test indicate that the ARCH-effects are not very strong.

Table A2 shows the estimated parameters for the GARCH-NIG model used in Section 3.3. For further details of the estimation procedure see Venter and de Jongh (2002).

Table A1. Estimated GARCH and NIG parameters for our four stocks.

	BP	XOM	DT	FTE
Mean	0.0007	0.0010	0.0003	0.0002
Standard deviation	0.0114	0.0120	0.0127	0.0148
Kurtosis	0.2738	0.8482	2.6729	1.2967
Jarque–Bera	0.1565	0.0000	0.0000	0.0000
Ljung–Box	0.5684	0.7993	0.7563	0.3625
LM-test	0.9626	0.0000	0.0077	0.0246

Table A2. Estimated GARCH and NIG parameters for our four stocks.

Parameter	BP	XOM	DT	FTE
a_0	1.598e−06	1.400e−06	1.801e−06	1.231e−06
a	0.010	0.023	0.025	0.028
b	0.978	0.968	0.963	0.966
β	−0.357	−0.577	0.105	0.037
ψ	3.686	2.293	1.173	1.670

Dependency without copulas or ellipticity[†]

William T. Shaw and Asad Munir

Department of Mathematics, King's College London, The Strand, London WC2R 2LS, UK

The generation of multivariate probability distributions follows several approaches. Within financial applications the emphasis has mostly been on two methodologies. The first is the elliptical methodology, where the leap from univariate to multivariate has taken place by constructing density functions that are functions of quadratic forms of the marginals. The second is the copula philosophy, where the dependency structure is treated entirely separately from marginals. In financial applications one often needs to work with combinations of marginals of various distributional types, and the copula philosophy is very attractive as it copes well with heterogeneous marginals. However, with some notable exceptions, the copula approach does not normally correspond to any natural or *canonical* multivariate structure arising from some underlying dynamic.

This paper presents an approach to multivariate distribution theory that allows for heterogeneous marginals but without the limitations of the elliptical *ansatz* or the arbitrariness of the copula approach. The approach is to consider multivariate distributions as arising naturally from coupled stochastic differential equations (SDEs), and in this paper we consider a first step based on the equilibrium situation. The scope of this paper is where the marginals are one of the classic Pearson family of distributions, allowing for great diversity among the marginals. For simplicity we present details for the bivariate case. Using a recently developed quantile form of the Fokker–Planck equation it is first shown how the members of the Pearson family are associated with various types of one-dimensional SDE in a transparent manner. Then appropriate two-dimensional SDEs and the associated Fokker–Planck equations are considered. In the equilibrium limit these give solutions that are natural bivariate structures. Some examples with marginals drawn from Gaussian, Student and one-sided exponential are explored. Some possible generalizations are outlined.

1. Introduction

This paper presents an approach to multivariate distribution theory based on stochastic differential equations (SDEs), with a view towards financial applications. There are of course several existing approaches to the construction of multivariate densities. Many of these are surveyed in the text by Kotz, Balakrishnan, and Johnson (2000). Of particular note for this current work are the bivariate Pearson structures, as discussed by Elderton and Johnson (1969). Two approaches have stood out for applications to financial applications: the *elliptical* and *copula* philosophies.

The elliptical and meta-elliptical approaches, where the copula is elliptical, are well established in financial applications – see for example Embrechts, McNeil, and Straumann (2002) and McNeil,

[†]This paper (May 2008 update) is a revised and extended version of a presentation of the same name given at *Copulae and Multivariate Probability Distributions in Finance – Theory, Applications, Opportunities and Problems*, Warwick, UK, September 2007.

Frey, and Embrechts (2006) for discussions in the context of risk management. They are able to capture the phenomenon of asymptotic tail dependence observed in many financial data sets, and have the useful calibration enhancement of having tractable representations of parameters such as Kendall's tau (Lindskog, McNeil, and Schmock 2003). In the elliptical methodology the leap from univariate to multivariate has taken place, in simplified terms, by constructing density functions that are functions of quadratic forms of the marginals, with the dependency being encoded in the structure of the quadratic form. This is an elegant construction but is arguably *incomplete* as a characterization of multivariate structure, because unless the generator is exponential, when the distribution reduces to multivariate normal, the family thus generated will not include the case of independent marginals.

In the copula philosophy, the dependency structure is treated entirely separately from marginals, and the copula may arise from a real multivariate distribution or be posed in the abstract. Fundamentals are discussed by Nelsen (2006) and financial applications by Cherubini, Luciano, and Vecchiato (2004). In financial applications one often needs to work with combinations of marginals of various distributional types, and the copulas philosophy is very attractive as it copes well with heterogeneous marginals. However, it does not often enough correspond to any natural or *canonical* multivariate structure arising from a dynamic appreciation of a process. There are notable exceptions. The Marshall–Olkin copulas are associated with a system containing components that are subject to certain shocks leading to failure of either or both components (see Embrechts, McNeil, and Straumann 2003; Nelsen 2006). Some Archimedean copulas arise naturally in shared frailty models for dependent lifetimes, this being the origin of the Clayton (1978) copula in particular.

Recently, various attempts to work in a more natural and general setting have been made. These have thus far focused on specific problems with rather specific choices for the marginals. Baxter (2007) has considered an elegant dynamic gamma model for applications to the pricing of dependent credit products. The definition of the multivariate Student distribution has been extended outside the usual elliptical prescription, complete with simulation methods, by Shaw and Lee (2007). In the bivariate case new explicit forms for density and correlation functions have been obtained, and in the particular case of a bivariate Student–normal distribution we can write down canonical results for such exotica as a bivariate normal–Cauchy. A detailed analysis of highly correlated Student–normal distributions has also recently been given by Nadarajah (2007).

Our ability to create such constructions relies on having some way of creating the distributions in a natural way, without having to guess a Probability Density Function (PDF) or make arbitrary assumptions. This is not generally a straightforward task.

Many physical, biological and financial systems are well modelled by an underlying stochastic process, and the resulting distribution of variables is what we observe, or in modelling, simulate. So we shall consider an approach to multivariate distributions based on coupled SDEs. In general, this is a complicated time-dependent problem, but in this paper we will consider the equilibrium situation that will turn out to be rich enough to treat a large number of cases of diverse marginal distributions. The scope of this presentation is where all the marginals arise one of the classic Pearson family of distributions (Pearson 1916), but for simplicity we present details for the bivariate case, where each is still Pearson. The equilibrium case is considered for simplicity and as a first step towards a full dynamic theory. SDEs with a given cross-section distribution attained at some *finite* time may be obtained by the methods of Baudoin (2002), where the concept of a Brownian bridge is generalized to allow a given density to be targeted. We could also consider distributions still based on an SDE but that arise from other mechanisms than simply the distribution of the solution, for example, the generation of an inverse Gaussian distribution as the distribution of times at which a given level is crossed by a simple arithmetical Brownian motion. Similarly, we might also consider coupled Lévy processes, where we can link to generalized hyperbolic distributions, but in what follows we shall limit attention to the distribution of the solution for a standard SDE.

The first task is to associate SDEs with the Pearson family of "types". This can be made most transparent by using a recently developed "quantilized" form of the Fokker–Planck equation that we term the quantilized Fokker–Planck equation (QFPE). The equilibria associated with the QFPE link transparently to the differential characterization of distributions given by Pearson. The QFPE was introduced by Toscani and co-workers (see Carrillo and Toscani (2004) and references therein) and its elementary solutions and relationship to the Pearson family[1] has been elucidated by Steinbrecher and Shaw (2007).

Then we consider appropriate two-dimensional SDEs and the associated Fokker–Planck equations. In the equilibrium limit these give solutions that are natural bivariate structures. Some examples where one marginal is Gaussian or Student are explored.

2. The QFPE

If we wish to develop a natural multivariate distribution theory with marginals chosen from a large heterogeneous family we need a construction method that allows for such diversity. We shall base our approach on the theory of SDEs and use the notation of Steinbrecher and Shaw (2008). Consider first the univariate SDE

$$dx_t = \mu(x_t, t)dt + \Sigma(x_t, t)dW_t \tag{1}$$

where W_t is a standard Brownian motion. Let $f(x, t)$ denote the associated time-dependent probability density function. The quantile function $Q(u, t)$ associated with this density function is defined by the condition

$$\int_{-\infty}^{Q(u,t)} f(x, t)dx = u \tag{2}$$

and satisfies various conditions associated with the density function and the Fokker–Planck equation. The results we need are, first, the non-linear Ordinary Differential Equation (ODE)

$$\frac{\partial^2 Q(u, t)}{\partial u^2} = -\frac{\partial \log(f(Q(u, t), t))}{\partial Q} \left(\frac{\partial Q(u, t)}{\partial u} \right)^2 \tag{3}$$

and second, the QFPE in the form

$$\frac{\partial Q}{\partial t} = \mu(Q, t) - \frac{1}{2} \frac{\partial \Sigma^2}{\partial Q} + \frac{1}{2} \Sigma^2(Q, t) \left(\frac{\partial Q(u, t)}{\partial u} \right)^{-2} \frac{\partial^2 Q(u, t)}{\partial u^2}. \tag{4}$$

A detailed derivation of these relations is given by Steinbrecher and Shaw (2007).

3. Stochastic equilibria and the Pearson family

We shall say that the system defined by the SDE of Equation (1) is in stochastic equilibrium if the density is time independent. Then the quantile function is also time independent and satisfies the non-linear ODE arising from Equation (4) with the coefficients of the SDE also assumed to be time independent:

$$\left(\frac{\mathrm{d}Q}{\mathrm{d}u}\right)^{-2}\frac{\mathrm{d}^2 Q}{\mathrm{d}u^2} = \Sigma^{-2}(Q)\left(\frac{\mathrm{d}\Sigma^2}{\mathrm{d}Q} - 2\mu(Q)\right). \tag{5}$$

We write this in the form

$$\left(\frac{\mathrm{d}Q}{\mathrm{d}u}\right)^{-2}\frac{\mathrm{d}^2 Q}{\mathrm{d}u^2} = H(Q) \tag{6}$$

where from Equations (3) and (5) we know that

$$H(Q) = \Sigma^{-2}(Q)\left(\frac{\mathrm{d}\Sigma^2}{\mathrm{d}Q} - 2\mu(Q)\right) = -\frac{\partial \log(f(Q))}{\partial Q}. \tag{7}$$

Now we recall that Pearson's "types" (Pearson 1916) are linked to choices of density function for which, for constants a, b, c, m,

$$-\frac{\partial \log(f(Q))}{\partial Q} = \frac{Q - m}{a + bQ + cQ^2}. \tag{8}$$

Putting this all together, we are interested in that collection of SDEs for which

$$\Sigma^{-2}(Q)\left(\frac{\mathrm{d}\Sigma^2}{\mathrm{d}Q} - 2\mu(Q)\right) = \frac{Q - m}{a + bQ + cQ^2}. \tag{9}$$

We could of course have developed this from the ordinary Fokker–Planck equation, but it is much more transparent to see how this algebraic relationship emerges from the QFPE. We are now in a position to reconstruct distributions of Pearson's type(s) by writing down suitable forms for the functions in the SDE.

4. Reconstructing Pearson's types from the SDE

We now investigate the stochastic equilibria associated with Equation (9). We have a family of drift and volatility functions to consider compatible with the SDE. We shall start with the more familiar cases. It must be appreciated that merely writing down solutions of Equation (9) is necessary but not sufficient. Equation (9) is a differential constraint on allowable drift and volatility functions. It is necessary to find solutions of the constraint that furthermore will generate solutions of the equilibrium equations that are stable, and, for practical purposes, arise naturally from a variety of initial conditions. We would include starting off the SDE at a single point as a starting condition from which equilibrium should be achievable. It is desirable to have a theory of when this does and does not take place – in what follows we shall take a pragmatic approach.

We must note that the idea of a "Pearson diffusion" has recently been introduced by others (see e.g. the work of Forman and Sørensen (2007), and references contained therein). Forman and Sørensen postulate an SDE that is a specific solution to Equation (9) where the quantity Σ gis the square root of the quadratic in the denominator of the right side of Equation (9). There are many more possibilities for solving Equation (9), including as an obvious possibility solutions that arise from a change of time variable.

4.1 The Gaussian case: Pearson type 0

To treat the normal distribution in Pearson's scheme we set $b = c = 0$ and choose $a > 0$. We shall centre the distribution at zero at therefore take $m = 0$. The distribution will have unit variance if $a = 1$. The simplest way of realizing this in Equation (9) is to take Σ to be a constant Σ_0. So the underlying SDE is the Orenstein-Uhlenbeck process defined by

$$\mathrm{d}x_t = -\frac{1}{2}\Sigma_0^2 x_t \mathrm{d}t + \Sigma_0 \mathrm{d}W_t \tag{10}$$

and the solution to this with a given point start at x_0 is a standard result in the form

$$x_t = \exp(-\Sigma_0^2 t/2)\left(x_0 + \int_0^t \exp(\Sigma_0^2 s/2)\mathrm{d}W_s\right) \tag{11}$$

with an equilibrium limit distributed with zero mean and unit variance. The parameter Σ_0 fixes the time scale of convergence to the equilibrium. The parameters of the SDE are balanced such that this form of the OU process converges to a stable equilibrium.

4.2 The Student family: Pearson type VII

To treat the standard centred Student distribution with degrees of freedom v we set $b = 0 = m$ but now we have both a and c positive. After some algebra we make the following choice for the SDE:

$$\mathrm{d}x_t = -\frac{1}{2}\Sigma_0^2\left(1 - \frac{1}{v}\right)x_t \mathrm{d}t + \Sigma_0\sqrt{1 + \frac{x_t^2}{v}}\mathrm{d}W_t. \tag{12}$$

Inspection of the QFPE then shows that the equilibrium is a standard Student distribution when an equilibrium exists. This slightly contrived expression looks more natural when you consider it to be a simplified form of the SDE

$$\mathrm{d}x_t = -\frac{1}{2}\Sigma_0^2\left(1 - \frac{1}{v}\right)x_t \mathrm{d}t + \Sigma_0 \mathrm{d}W_t^1 + \frac{\Sigma_0}{v}x_t \mathrm{d}W_t^2 \tag{13}$$

which is OU extended to have a mixture on independent arithmetical and geometrical noise. Such a system arises naturally in plasma physics (Steinbrecher and Weyssow 2007) and also has a financial market microstructure motivation (Shaw 2008).

The details of the fully time-dependent solution require further investigation, but we can compute an ODE for the mean variance. When $x_0 = 0$ the mean remains zero and the variance reduces to

$$V(x_t) = \frac{v}{v - 2}\left(1 - \exp\left[-\Sigma_0^2(1 - 2/v)t\right]\right) \tag{14}$$

which we see converges to a limit if $v > 2$, which is also the requirement that the variance of a Student exists at all.

4.3 The one-sided exponential case: special Pearson type III

To treat the one-sided exponential case is interesting as the right side of Equation (9) is then a constant, so $m = c = a = 0$, and one can come up with diverse plausible choices for the drift and volatility. The reader is left to explore the possibilities, not all of which will generate a stable equilibrium. A natural choice is the SDE for the Cox–Ingersoll–Ross (CIR) interest rate model:

$$dx_t = \frac{1}{2}\Sigma_0^2(1 - \lambda x_t)dt + \Sigma_0\sqrt{x_t}dW_t \tag{15}$$

which has the remaining Pearson parameter is $b = \lambda^{-1}$, which is also the mean of the equilibrium exponential distribution, with density

$$f(x) = \lambda e^{-\lambda x}. \tag{16}$$

4.4 *The Gamma family: Pearson type III*

This is an easy generalization of the exponential case. For the gamma distribution with density

$$f(x) = \frac{x^{\alpha-1}e^{-x/\theta}}{\Gamma(\alpha)\theta^\alpha} \tag{17}$$

we employ the equilibrium limit of the SDE:

$$dx_t = \frac{1}{2}\Sigma_0^2\left(\alpha - \frac{x_t}{\theta}\right)dt + \Sigma_0\sqrt{x_t}dW_t. \tag{18}$$

5. Univariate computation

We now turn to the question of practical computation, and investigate whether the theoretically predicted behaviour is easily replicated in a simulation. Consider the simulation of the solution

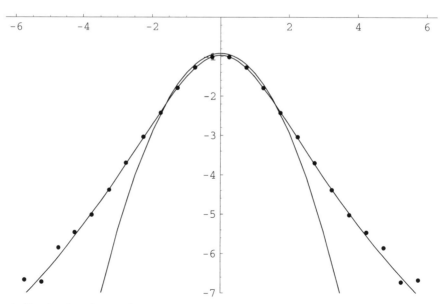

Figure 1. Simulated Student t with 5 degrees of freedom and analytical Student and Gaussian density functions.

of Equation (12). This was simulated in Mathematica with 30,000 paths (doubled up by antithetic method to be symmetric) starting at the origin. The parameters were as follows: degrees of freedom, 5; volatility, 100% per annum; 40 time steps per year in a simple Euler scheme run over 20 years to give it plenty of time to come to equilibrium. The resulting 60,000 terminal values were binned in lumps of 0.5 and normalized to compare with the theoretical density. Figure 1 shows the simulated and theoretical plot for the log Student density, with the log of the Gaussian density overlaid to demonstrate the relatively fat-tailed behaviour of the Student.

The density being recreated here is:

$$f_5(x) = \frac{8}{3\pi\sqrt{5}} \left(1 + \frac{t^2}{5}\right)^{-3}.$$
(19)

So the system is behaving even with a crude Euler scheme with no significant optimization of the method. This is not of course an optimal method for simulating the univariate system – the point is that we can generate a host of corresponding bivariate and multivariate systems in a similar natural manner.

6. The bivariate case and equilibrium PDE

It is self-evident that a natural means of construction of a bivariate or indeed multivariate system with any of the Pearson marginals is to write down a coupled set of SDEs where the dependency arises from the correlations in the underlying Brownian motions. So in the bivariate case we would consider the pair of SDEs

$$
\begin{aligned}
dx_{1t} &= \mu_1(x_{1t}, t)dt + \Sigma_1(x_{1t}, t)dW_t^1 \\
dx_{2t} &= \mu_2(x_{2t}, t)dt + \Sigma_2(x_{2t}, t)dW_t^2
\end{aligned}
$$
(20)

where

$$E[dW_t^1 dW_t^2] = \hat{\rho}dt$$
(21)

and $\hat{\rho}$ denotes the underlying correlation of the Brownian motions. The Fokker–Planck equation for the joint density function can be written down. Confining attention for now to the equilibrium case in dimension two, we have the two-dimensional PDE:

$$\frac{\partial}{\partial x_1}\left[-\mu_1 f + \frac{1}{2}\frac{\partial}{\partial x_1}(\Sigma_1^2 f)\right] + \frac{\partial}{\partial x_2}\left[-\mu_2 f + \frac{1}{2}\frac{\partial}{\partial x_2}(\Sigma_2^2 f)\right] + \frac{\partial}{\partial x_1}\frac{\partial}{\partial x_2}(\hat{\rho}\Sigma_1\Sigma_2 f) = 0 \quad (22)$$

6.1 *Recovering an old friend*

When we consider a pair of correlated OU processes the two-dimensional PDE reduces, making a simplification $\Sigma_1 = \Sigma_2$, to

$$\frac{\partial}{\partial x_1}\left[x_1 f + \frac{\partial f}{\partial x_1}\right] + \frac{\partial}{\partial x_2}\left[x_2 f + \frac{\partial f}{\partial x_2}\right] + 2\hat{\rho}\frac{\partial}{\partial x_1}\frac{\partial f}{\partial x_2} = 0$$
(23)

with a solution of the form

$$f \propto \exp\left\{-\frac{(x^2 + y^2 - 2\hat{\rho}xy)}{2(1 - \hat{\rho}^2)}\right\}$$
(24)

so we recover, as expected the standard dependent bivariate distribution. This is not remotely surprising. But what is interesting is that this derivation can now be applied to diverse combinations of marginals. We cannot go through all the possibilities even limited to marginals of Pearson type, but can go a little along the way.

7. Going fat tailed in one marginal: relaxing to the Student

This time we do something more novel, and ask what happens when one marginal is Gaussian and other is Student. This raises an interesting question for supporters of the copula approach. If one marginal is Gaussian and the other Student, should we use a Gaussian copula or a "t copula"? This question seems to highlight an essential arbitrariness in the copula philosophy.

The equilibrium PDE is now, taking the first variable to be Student, with degrees of freedom v

$$\frac{\partial}{\partial x_1}\left[\left(1 - \frac{1}{v}\right)x_1 f + \frac{\partial}{\partial x_1}\left(\left(1 + \frac{x_1^2}{v}\right)f\right)\right] + \frac{\partial}{\partial x_2}\left[x_2 f + \frac{\partial f}{\partial x_2}\right]$$

$$+ 2\hat{\rho}\frac{\partial}{\partial x_1}\frac{\partial}{\partial x_2}\left(f\sqrt{1 + \frac{x_1^2}{v}}\right) = 0 \tag{25}$$

and the associated SDE for simulation of the correlated system is

$$dx_{1t} = -\frac{1}{2}\Sigma_0^2\left(1 - \frac{1}{v}\right)x_{1t}dt + \Sigma_0\sqrt{1 + \frac{x_{1t}^2}{v}}dW_t^1$$

$$dx_{2t} = -\frac{1}{2}\Sigma_0^2 x_{2t}dt + \Sigma_0 dW_t^2 \tag{26}$$

and an explicit representation for simulation in an Euler scheme is

$$dW_t^1 = Z_1\sqrt{\Delta t}$$

$$dW_t^2 = \sqrt{\Delta t}(\hat{\rho}Z_1 + \sqrt{1 - \hat{\rho}^2}Z_2) \tag{27}$$

where the Z_i are independent standard normal variables. Again we wish to check that this makes sense. We consider identical parameters to that considered before for our univariate example, except that now we have an underlying correlation in the noise, which for testing we set to +0.5, and the second dimension has a Gaussian equilibrium rather than a Student. The first dimension remains Student with degrees of freedom five. We increase the number of sample points to 100,000 + antithetic reflection, in order to try to see the bivariate density clearly. Figure 2 shows the resulting scatter plot that demonstrates the relatively fat-tailed nature of the first variable compared with the second.

The contour plot of the log density implied by this is shown in Figure 3, and clearly demonstrates the non-elliptical nature of the density.

The distributions obtained in this way require comparison with those derived by Shaw and Lee (2008), where we claimed a canonical for the normal–Student case. A special type of highly correlated bivariate normal–Student distribution has also recently been introduced by Nadarajah (2007) and the links between all these definitions are of interest. The SDE approach is also capable of generating skew-Student distributions, as noted by Forman and Sørensen (2008), and the links between such a definition and others (see e.g. Aas and Haff (2006) and references contained therein) are also of considerable interest.

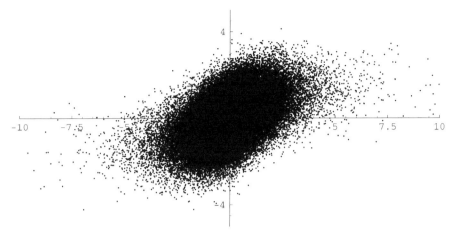

Figure 2. Simulated equilibrium Student–normal distribution; scatter plot.

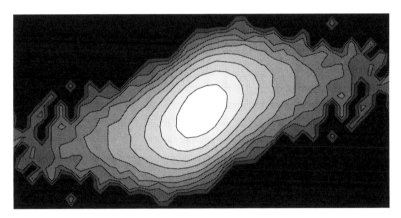

Figure 3. Simulated equilibrium Student–normal distribution; contour plot.

8. Multivariate exponential and related distributions

One of the more interesting dependency issues of the recent financial applications is the coupling together of two more one-sided exponential distributions to define the distributions associated with correlated default in credit applications. There are interesting existing candidates for bivariate exponential distributions, as discussed for example by Balakrishnan and Basu (1996). While it is premature to propose the equilibrium multivariate distributions here for the exponential distribution as the natural choice in such applications, we can certainly indicate how such a distribution may be simulated. The case of simulation of a multivariate gamma follows a similar path, in the sense that the SDE for Equation (18) is a simple generalization of Equation (15). However, the effective simulation of these systems presents some interesting matters of technical detail in the computation. The issue that arises is one that has been studied in the last few years in the matter of Monte Carlo simulation of CIR interest rate models, embodied by Equation (18),

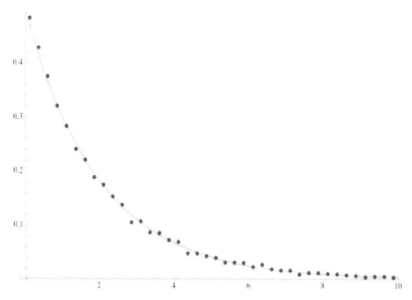

Figure 4. Simulated equilibrium exponential distribution and theoretical density.

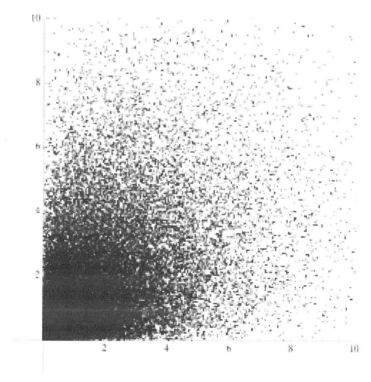

Figure 5. Simulated equilibrium bivariate exponential density.

which is of course the volatility SDE within the Heston model. The difficulty is that the simple Euler scheme

$$x_{t+\Delta t} - x_t = \frac{1}{2}\Sigma_0^2 (1 - \lambda x_t)\,\Delta t + \Sigma_0 \sqrt{x_t \Delta t} Z \qquad (28)$$

can produce negative samples at one stage in the evolution which at the next stage produces imaginary numbers. A survey of schemes for treating this problem has been given by Alfonsi (2005) in the CIR context. In what follows we shall employ the simple *reflection method* analysed by Diop (2003)

$$x_{t+\Delta t} = \left| x_t + \frac{1}{2}\Sigma_0^2 (1 - \lambda x_t)\,\Delta t + \Sigma_0 \sqrt{x_t \Delta t}\, Z \right|. \qquad (29)$$

This is straightforward to implement. As before, enough time is allowed for equilibrium to be attained, and the data are binned and compared with the theoretical density. We took parameters as follows: $\lambda = 0.5$, $\Sigma_0 = 0.4$, $x_0 = 1$, with 10,000 samples.

The resulting sampled density is compared, by elementary binning, with the theoretical univariate density in Figure 4.

As well as checking the appearance of such plots, one can check the basic statistical properties. The mean of the data behind Figure 4 is 1.982, against the theoretical value of 2. The variance is 3.94 (against 4) and the simulated kurtosis is 7.93 (against 9). The bivariate case may be treated as before, using correlated Brownian motions in a simple two-dimensional extension of Equation (29). The resulting simulated density and the associated copula are shown in Figures 5 and 6 for an underlying correlation of 0.5.

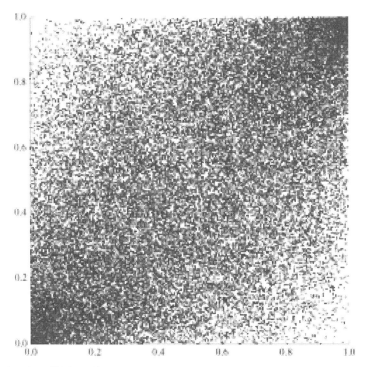

Figure 6. Simulated equilibrium bivariate exponential copula.

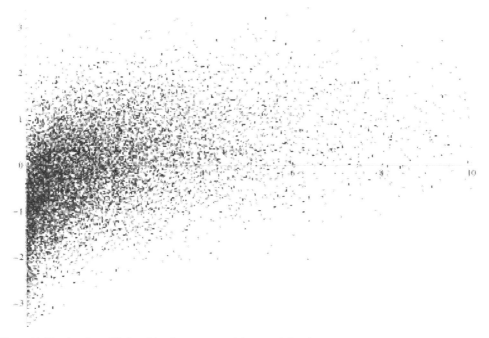

Figure 7. Simulated equilibrium bivariate exponential–normal density.

As before, we can build exotic hybrids. A hybrid exponential–Gaussian distribution with under-lying correlation 0.5 is simulated in Figure 7 (with similar parameters to Figure 5). The horizontal axis is exponential and the vertical is normal. This clearly demonstrates the power of the method to generate natural couplings between distributions of different types.

9.   Conclusions and further developments

This presentation is a small step on the way to building a theory of dependency based wholly on coupled stochastic processes. The equilibrium approach allows us to manage marginals based on members of the Pearson family, with dependency generated in a natural manner form correlations in the SDEs. There are 55 distinct bivariate distributions arising from combining marginals of the 10 distinct Pearson types. The use of the quantile form of the Fokker–Planck equation allows necessary conditions for creating a given marginal to be written down in a transparent manner. The simulation is conceptually straightforward in two or more dimensions, but is computationally demanding, and care may be needed with the numerical schemes.

Distributions generated in this way are not of course appropriate for all situations. Further work is needed to characterize the density and correlation structures and to develop computa-tional methods. An understanding of rank correlation measures is clearly desirable for calibration purposes.

The multivariate extensions of the finite-time approach given by Baudoin (2002) are also of considerable interest, with regard to both mathematical theory and computational implementation. Baudoin employs a combination of simple volatility with a complicated drift term in an SDE to bridge to a target distribution, and this raises questions related to computational efficiency, and also as to whether an independent financial motivation can be given for such drift functions. The X-factor information-based approach developed by Macrina (2006) and Brody, Hughston, and Macrina (2007) offers a natural approach to this. Work is proceeding on the relationships between all these topics, with the simulation in a parallel computer architecture. Computational work related to this area may be downloaded from: http://www.mth.kcl.ac.uk/~shaww/web_page/grid/external/.

Acknowledgements

We wish to acknowledge diverse contributions from K. Aas, L. Devroye, I.H. Haff, D. Hobson, E. Hoyle, A. Macrina, and S. Nadarajah. Particular thanks are due to A.J. McNeil for his detailed comments on an earlier version of this work.

Note

1. In this connection we note that the critical link to the Pearson family was based on an observation by Prof L. Devroye.

References

Aas, K., and I.H. Haff. 2006. The generalized hyperbolic skew Student's t-distribution. *Journal of Financial Econometrics* 4, no. 2: 275–309.

Alfonsi, A. 2005. On the discretization schemes for the CIR (and Bessel squared) processes. *Monte Carlo Methods and Applications* 11, no. 4: 355–84.

Balakrishnan, N., and A.P. Basu. 1996. *The exponential distribution; theory, methods and applications*. Boca Raton: CRC Press.

Baudoin, F. 2002. Conditioned stochastic differential equations: Theory, applications and application to finance. *Stochastic Processes and Their Applications* 100: 109–45.

Baxter, M. 2007. Gamma process dynamic modelling of credit. *RISK*, October 2007.

Brody, D.C., L.P. Hughston, and A. Macrina. 2007. Beyond hazard rates: A new framework for credit-risk modelling. In *Advances in mathematical finance, Festschrift volume in honour of DilipMadan*, eds. R. Elliott, M. Fu, R. Jarrow, and J.-Y. Yen. Basel: Birkhäuser.

Carrillo, J.A., and G. Toscani. 2004. *Wasserstein metric and large-time asymptotics of nonlinear diffusion equations, in new trends in mathematical physics*, 234–44. Hackensack, NJ: World Science Publication.

Cherubini, U., E. Luciano, and W. Vecchiato. 2004. *Copula methods in finance*. Hoboken: Wiley.

Clayton, D.G. 1978. A model for association in bivariate life tables and its application in epidemiological studies of familial tendency in chronic disease incidence. *Biometrika* 65: 141–51.

Diop, A. 2003. Sur la discrétisation et le comportement à petit bruit d'EDS multidimensionnelles dont les coefficients sont à dérivées singulières. PhD thesis, INRIA. http://www.inria.fr/rrrt/tu-0785.html.

Elderton, W.P., and N.L. Johnson. 1969. *Systems of frequency curves*. Cambridge: Cambridge University Press.

Embrechts, P., A.J. McNeil, and D. Straumann. 2002. Correlation and dependence in risk management: Properties and pitfalls. In *Risk management: Value at risk and beyond*, ed. M.A.H. Dempster, 176–223. Cambridge: Cambridge University Press.

Embrechts, P., F. Lindskog, and A.J. McNeil. 2003. Modelling dependence with copulas and applications to risk management. In *Handbook of heavy tailed distributions in finance*, ed. S. Rachev, 331–85. Amsterdam: Elsevier.

Forman, J.L., and M. Sørensen. 2008. The Pearson diffusions: A class of statistically tractable diffusion processes. *Scandinavian Journal of Statistics* 35, no. 3: 438–465. http://www.math.ku.dk/~michael/pearson.pdf.

Kotz, S., N. Balakrishnan, and N.L. Johnson. 2000. *Continuous multivariate distributions*. Vol. 1, *Models and applications*. 2nd ed. Hoboken: Wiley Series in Probability and Statistics.

Lindskog, F., A.J. McNeil, and U. Schmock. 2003. Kendall's tau for elliptical distributions. In *Credit risk-measurement, evaluation and management*, ed. G. Bol, G. Nakhaeizadeh, S.T. Rachev, T. Ridder, and K.-H. Vollmer. Heidelberg: Physica-Verlag.

Macrina, A. 2006. An information-based framework for asset pricing: X-factor theory and its applications. PhD thesis, King's College London. www.mth.kcl.ac.uk/finmath.

McNeil, A.J., R. Frey, and P. Embrechts. 2006. *Quantitative risk management*. Princeton: Princeton University Press.

Nadarajah, S. 2007. A bivariate distribution with normal and *t* marginals. *Journal of Computational Analysis and Applications* 9: 247–55.

Nelsen, R.B. 2006. *An introduction to copulas*. 2nd ed. Heidelberg: Springer.

Pearson, K. 1916. Second supplement to a memoir on skew variation. *Philosophical Transactions of the Royal Society of London, Series A* 216: 429–57.

Shaw, W.T. 2008. Share price movements in the post-credit-crunch environment. Working Paper, arxiv:0811.0182v2.

Shaw, W.T., and K.T.A. Lee. 2008. Bivariate student *t* distributions with variable marginal degrees of freedom and independence. *Journal of Multivariate Analysis* 99: 1276–1287, DOI:10.1016/j.jmva.2007.08.006.

Steinbrecher, G., and W.T. Shaw. 2008. Quantile mechanics. *European Journal of Applied Mathematics* 19, no. 2: 87–112. DOI:10.1017/S0956792508007341.

Steinbrecher, G., and B. Weyssow. 2007. Extreme anomalous particle transport at the plasma edge. Univ. of Craiova/Univ Libre de Bruxells Working Paper, May 2007.

Copula goodness-of-fit testing: an overview and power comparison

Daniel Berg

Department of Mathematics, University of Oslo & The Norwegian Computing Center, Oslo, Norway

Several copula goodness-of-fit approaches are examined, three of which are proposed in this paper. Results are presented from an extensive Monte Carlo study, where we examine the effect of dimension, sample size and strength of dependence on the nominal level and power of the different approaches. While no approach is always the best, some stand out and conclusions and recommendations are made. A novel study of p-value variation due to permutation order, for approaches based on Rosenblatt's transformation is also carried out. Results show significant variation due to permutation order for some of the approaches based on this transform. However, when approaching rejection regions, the additional variation is negligible.

1. Introduction

A copula contains all the information about the dependency structure of a continuous random vector $\mathbf{X} = (X_1, \ldots, X_d)$. Due to the representation theorem of Sklar (1959), every distribution function H can be written as $H(x_1, \ldots, x_d) = C\{F_1(x_1), \ldots, F_d(x_d)\}$, where $F_1, \ldots, F_d$ are the marginal distributions and $C : [0, 1]^d \to [0, 1]$ is the copula. This enables the modelling of marginal distributions and the dependence structure in separate steps. This feature in particular has motivated successful applications in areas such as survival analysis, hydrology, actuarial science and finance. For exhaustive and general introductions to copulae, the reader is referred to Joe (1997) and Nelsen (1999), and for introductions oriented to financial applications, Malevergne and Sornette (2006) and Cherubini, Luciano, and Vecchiato (2004). While the evaluation of univariate distributions is well documented, the study of goodness-of-fit (g-o-f) tests for copulas emerged only recently as a challenging inferential problem.

Let C be the underlying d-variate copula of a population. Suppose one wants to test the composite g-o-f hypothesis

$$\mathcal{H}_0 \colon C \in \mathcal{C} = \{C_\theta; \theta \in \Theta\} \quad vs. \quad \mathcal{H}_1 \colon C \notin \mathcal{C} = \{C_\theta; \theta \in \Theta\}, \tag{1}$$

where Θ is the parameter space. Recently, several contributions have been made to test this hypothesis, e.g., Genest and Rivest (1993), Shih (1998), Breymann, Dias, and Embrechts (2003), Malevergne and Sornette (2003), Scaillet (2005), Genest and Rémillard (2005), Fermanian (2005), Panchenko (2005), Berg and Bakken (2007), Genest, Quessy, and Rémillard (2006), Dobrić and

Schmid (2007), Quessy, Mesfioui, and Toipin (2007), Genest, Rémillard, and Beaudoin (2008), among others. However, general guidelines and recommendations are sparse.

For univariate distributions, the g-o-f assessment can be performed using, e.g., the well-known Anderson–Darling statistic (Anderson and Darling 1954), or less quantitatively using a QQ plot. In the multivariate domain, there are fewer alternatives. A simple way to build g-o-f approaches for multivariate random variables is to consider multidimensional chi-square approaches, as in Dobrić and Schmid (2005), for example. The problem with this approach, as with all binned approaches based on gridding the probability space, is that they will not be feasible for high-dimensional problems due to the curse of dimensionality. Another issue with binned approaches is that the grouping of the data is arbitrary and not trivial. Grouping too coarsely destroys valuable information and the ability to contrast distributions becomes very limited. On the other hand, too small groups lead to a highly irregular empirical cumulative distribution function (cdf) due to the limited amount of data. For these reasons, multivariate binned approaches are not considered in this study. Multivariate kernel density estimation (KDE) approaches such as the ones proposed by Fermanian (2005) and Scaillet (2005) are also excluded from this study as they will simply be too computationally exhaustive for high-dimensional problems. The author believes g-o-f to be most useful for high-dimensional problems since copulae are harder to conceptualize in such cases. Moreover, the consequences of poor model choice are often much greater in higher-dimensional problems, e.g., risk assessments for high-dimensional financial portfolios.

The class of dimension reduction approaches is a more promising alternative. Dimension reduction approaches reduce the multivariate problem to a univariate problem, and then apply some univariate test, leading to numerically efficient approaches even for high-dimensional problems. These approaches primarily differ in the way the dimension reduction is carried out. For the univariate test, it is common to apply standard univariate statistics such as Kolmogorov- or Cramér–von Mises (CvM)-type statistics. Examples include Breymann, Dias, and Embrechts (2003), Malevergne and Sornette (2003), Genest, Quessy, and Remillard (2006a), Berg and Bakken (2005), Quessy, Mesfioui, and Toupin (2007) and Genest and Remillard (2008) among others.

This paper is organized as follows. In Section 2, some preliminaries are presented. Section 3 gives an overview of the nine g-o-f approaches considered, including three new ones. In Section 4, results are presented from an extensive Monte Carlo study where we examine the effect of dimension, sample size and strength of dependence on the nominal level and power of the approaches. Several null and alternative hypothesis copulae are considered. Further, this section also presents results from a novel numerical study of the effect of permutation order for approaches based on Rosenblatt's transform. Finally, Section 5 discusses our findings and makes some recommendations for future research.

2. Preliminaries

For copula g-o-f testing one is interested in the fit of the copula alone. Typically, one does not wish to introduce any distributional assumptions for the marginals. Instead the testing is carried out using rank data. Suppose we have n independent samples $\mathbf{x}_1 = (x_{11}, \ldots, x_{1d}), \ldots, \mathbf{x}_n = (x_{n1}, \ldots, x_{nd})$ from the d-dimensional random vector $\mathbf{X}$. The inference is then based on the so-called pseudo-samples $\mathbf{z}_1 = (z_{11}, \ldots, z_{1d}), \ldots, \mathbf{z}_n = (z_{n1} \ldots, z_{nd})$ from the pseudo-vector $\mathbf{Z}$, where

$$\mathbf{z}_j = (z_{j1}, \ldots, z_{jd}) = \left(\frac{R_{j1}}{n+1}, \ldots, \frac{R_{jd}}{n+1} \right), \qquad (2)$$

where R_{ji} is the rank of x_{ji} amongst $(x_{1i}, \ldots, x_{ni})$. The denominator $(n + 1)$ is used instead of n to avoid numerical problems at the boundaries of $[0, 1]^d$. This transformation of each margin through their normalized ranks is often denoted the empirical marginal transformation. Given the independent samples $(\mathbf{x}_1, \ldots, \mathbf{x}_n)$, the pseudo-samples $(\mathbf{z}_1, \ldots, \mathbf{z}_n)$ can be considered to be samples from the underlying copula C. However, the rank transformation introduces dependence and $(\mathbf{z}_1, \ldots, \mathbf{z}_n)$ are no longer independent samples. The practical consequence is the need for parametric bootstrap procedures to obtain reliable P-value estimates. This is treated in more detail in Section 3.10.

2.1 *Rosenblatt's transformation*

The Rosenblatt transformation, proposed by Rosenblatt (1952), transforms a set of dependent variables into a set of independent $U[0,1]$ variables, given the multivariate distribution. The transformation is a universally applicable way of creating a set of i.i.d. $U[0,1]$ variables from any set of dependent variables with known distribution. Given a test for multivariate, independent uniformity, the transformation can be used to test the fit of any assumed model.

DEFINITION 2.1 (Rosenblatt's transformation) *Let* $\mathbf{Z} = (Z_1, \ldots, Z_d)$ *denote a random vector with marginal distributions* $F_i(z_i) = P(Z_i \leq z_i)$ *and conditional distributions* $F_{i|1,\ldots,i-1}(Z_i \leq z_i | Z_1 = z_1, \ldots, Z_{i-1} = z_{i-1})$ *for* $i = 1, \ldots, d$. *Rosenblatt's transformation of* $\mathbf{Z}$ *is defined as* $\mathcal{R}(\mathbf{Z}) = (\mathcal{R}_1(Z_1), \ldots, \mathcal{R}_d(Z_d))$ *where*

$$\mathcal{R}_1(Z_1) = P(Z_1 \leq z_1) = F_1(z_1),$$

$$\mathcal{R}_2(Z_2) = P(Z_2 \leq z_2 | Z_1 = z_1) = F_{2|1}(z_2|z_1),$$

$$\vdots$$

$$\mathcal{R}_d(Z_d) = P(Z_d \leq x_d | Z_1 = z_1, \ldots, Z_{d-1} = z_{d-1}) = F_{d|1,\ldots,d-1}(z_d|z_1, \ldots, z_{d-1}).$$

The random vector $\mathbf{V} = (V_1, \ldots, V_d)$, *where* $V_i = \mathcal{R}_i(Z_i)$, *is now i.i.d.* $U[0, 1]^d$.

A recent application of this transformation is multivariate g-o-f tests. The Rosenblatt transformation is applied to the samples $(\mathbf{x}_1, \ldots, \mathbf{x}_n)$, assuming a multivariate null hypothesis distribution. Under the null hypothesis, the resulting transformed samples $(\mathbf{v}_1, \ldots, \mathbf{v}_n)$ should be independent. Hence a test of multivariate independence is carried out. The null hypothesis is typically a parametric copula family. The parameters of this copula family need to be estimated before performing the transformation.

One advantage with Rosenblatt's transformation in a g-o-f setting is that the null and alternative hypotheses are the same, regardless of the distribution before the transformation. Hong and Li (2005) reported Monte Carlo evidence of multivariate tests using transformed variables outperforming tests using the original random variables. Chen, Fan, and Patton (2004) believe that a similar conclusion also applies to g-o-f tests for copulae.

A disadvantage with tests based on Rosenblatt's transformation is the lack of invariance with respect to the permutation of the variables since there are $d!$ possible permutations. However, as long as the permutation is decided randomly, the results will not be influenced in any particular direction. The practical implication of this disadvantage is studied in Section 4.2.

2.2 *Parameter estimation*

Testing the hypothesis in Equation (1) involves the estimation of the copula parameters θ by some consistent estimator $\hat{\theta}$. There are mainly two ways of estimating these parameters: the fully parametric method or a semi-parametric method. The fully parametric method, termed the inference functions for marginals (IFM) method (Joe 1997), relies on the assumption of parametric, univariate marginals. First, the parameters of the marginals are estimated and then each parametric margin is plugged into the copula likelihood which is then maximized with respect to the copula parameters. Since we treat the marginals as nuisance parameters we rather proceed with the pseudo-samples $(z_1, \ldots, z_n)$ and the semi-parametric method. This method is denoted the pseudo-likelihood (Demarta McNeil 2005) or the canonical maximum likelihood (CML) (Romano 2002) method, and is described in Genest, Ghoudi, and Rivest (1995) and in Shih and Louis (1995) in the presence of censorship. Having obtained the pseudo-samples $(z_1, \ldots, z_n)$ as described in Equation (2), the copula parameters can be estimated using either maximum likelihood (ML) or using the well-known relations to Kendall's tau.

For elliptical copulae in higher dimensions, we estimate pairwise Kendall's taus. These are inverted and give the components of the correlation and scale matrices for the Gaussian and Student copulae, respectively. For the Student copula, one must also estimate the degree-of-freedom parameter. We follow Mashal and Zeevi (2002) and Demarta and McNeil (2005), who proposed a two-stage approach in which the scale matrix is first estimated by inversion of Kendall's tau, and then the pseudo-likelihood function is maximized with respect to the degree-of-freedom ν, using the estimate of the scale matrix. For the Archimedean copulae the parameter is estimated by inversion of Kendall's tau. For dimension $d > 2$, we estimate the parameter as the average of the $d(d-1)/2$ pairs of Kendall's taus.

3. Copula g-o-f approaches

The following nine copula g-o-f approaches are examined:

$\mathcal{A}_1$: Based on Rosenblatt's transformation, proposed by Berg and Bakken (2005). This approach includes, as special cases, the approaches proposed by Malevergne and Sornette (2003), Breymann, Dias, and Embrechts (2003) and the second approach in Chen, Fan, and Patton (2004).

$\mathcal{A}_2$: Based on the empirical copula and the copula distribution function, proposed by Genest and Rémillard (2008).

$\mathcal{A}_3$: Based on approach $\mathcal{A}_2$ and the Rosenblatt transformation, proposed by Genest, Rémillard, and Beaudoin (2008).

$\mathcal{A}_4$: Based on the empirical copula and the cdf of the copula function, proposed by Genest and Rivest (1993), Wang and Wells (2000), Savu and Trede (2004) and Genest, Quessy, and Rémillard (2006a).

$\mathcal{A}_5$: Based on Spearman's dependence function, proposed by Quessy, Mesfioui, and Toupin (2007).

$\mathcal{A}_6$: A new approach that extends Shih's test (Shih 1998) for the bivariate Clayton model to arbitrary dimension.

$\mathcal{A}_7$: Based on the inner product between two vectors as a measure of their distance, proposed by Panchenko (2005).

$\mathcal{A}_8$: A new approach based on approach $\mathcal{A}_7$ and the Rosenblatt transformation.

$\mathcal{A}_9$: A new approach based on averages of the approaches above.

Approaches $\mathcal{A}_1$–$\mathcal{A}_5$ are all dimension reduction approaches, while $\mathcal{A}_6$ is a moment-based approach and $\mathcal{A}_7$ and $\mathcal{A}_8$ are denoted full multivariate approaches. For all the dimension reduction approaches, the study is restricted to the CvM statistic for the univariate test.

3.1 Approach $\mathcal{A}_1$

Berg and Bakken (2005) propose a generalization of the approaches proposed by Breymann, Dias, and Embrechts (2003) and Malevergne and Sornette (2003). The approach is based on Rosenblatt's transformation applied to the pseudo-samples $(\mathbf{z}_1, \ldots, \mathbf{z}_n)$ from Equation (2), assuming a null hypothesis copula $C_{\hat{\theta}}$. Under the null hypothesis, the resulting samples $(\mathbf{v}_1, \ldots, \mathbf{v}_n)$ are samples from the independence copula $C_\perp$. Since we are working with rank data this is only close to, but not exactly true. This issue is discussed in Section 3.10. Until then it is assumed that this holds.

The dimension reduction of approach $\mathcal{A}_1$ is based on the samples $(\mathbf{v}_1, \ldots, \mathbf{v}_n)$:

$$W_{1j} = \sum_{i=1}^{d} \Gamma\{v_{ji}; \boldsymbol{\alpha}\}, \quad j = \{1, \ldots, n\},$$

where Γ is any weight function used to weight the information in $(\mathbf{v}_1, \ldots, \mathbf{v}_n)$ and $\boldsymbol{\alpha}$ is the set of weight parameters. Any weight function may be used, depending on the use and the region of the unit hypercube one wishes to emphasize. Consider, for example, the special case $\Gamma\{v_{ji}; \boldsymbol{\alpha}\} = \Phi^{-1}(v_{ji})^2$ that corresponds to the approach proposed by Breymann, Dias, and Embrechts (2003). If the null hypothesis is the Gaussian copula, this is also equivalent with the approach proposed by Malevergne and Sornette (2003). Both of the latter studies apply the Anderson–Darling (Anderson and Darling 1954) statistic. Berg and Bakken (2005) show that the Anderson–Darling statistic with $\Gamma\{v_{ji}; \boldsymbol{\alpha}\} = |v_{ji} - 0.5|$ performs particularly well for testing the Gaussian null hypothesis. Hence, when performing the numerical studies in Section 4.1 the following two special cases of approach $\mathcal{A}_1$ are considered:

$$\mathcal{A}_1^{(a)}: \Gamma\{v_{ji}; \boldsymbol{\alpha}\} = \Phi^{-1}(v_{ji})^2 \quad \text{and} \quad \mathcal{A}_1^{(b)}: \Gamma\{v_{ji}; \boldsymbol{\alpha}\} = |v_{ji} - 0.5|.$$

For approach $\mathcal{A}_1^{(a)}$ it is easy to see that the distribution F_1 of W_{1j} is a χ_d^2 distribution for all j. Hence we can compare W_{1j} directly with the χ_d^2 distribution. However, for approach $\mathcal{A}_1^{(b)}$, and in general, the distribution of W_{1j} is not known and one must turn to a double bootstrap procedure (see Section 3.10) to approximate the cdf F_1 under the null hypothesis. The test observator S_1 of approach $\mathcal{A}_1$ is defined as the cdf of $F_1(W_1)$:

$$S_1(w) = P\{F_1(W_1) \le w\}, \quad w \in [0, 1].$$

Under the null hypothesis $S_1(w) = w$ for all j. The empirical version of the test observator can be computed as

$$\hat{S}_1(w) = \frac{1}{n+1} \sum_{j=1}^{n} I\{F_1(W_{1j}) \le w\}.$$

The appropriate version of the CvM statistic is (shown in Appendix 2):

$$\hat{T}_1 = n \int_0^1 \{\hat{S}_1(w) - S_1(w)\}^2 \, dS_1(w)$$

$$= \frac{n}{3} + \frac{n}{n+1} \sum_{j=1}^n \hat{S}_1 \left(\frac{j}{n+1}\right)^2 - \frac{n}{(n+1)^2} \sum_{j=1}^n (2j+1)\hat{S}_1 \left(\frac{j}{n+1}\right).$$

3.2 Approach $\mathcal{A}_2$

Genest and Rémillard (2008) propose to use the copula distribution function for the dimension reduction. The approach is based on the empirical copula process, introduced by Deheuvels (1979):

$$\hat{C}(\mathbf{u}) = \frac{1}{n+1} \sum_{j=1}^n I \left\{ Z_{j1} \le u_1, \ldots, Z_{jd} \le u_d \right\}, \tag{3}$$

where $\mathbf{Z}_j$ is given by Equation (2) and $\mathbf{u} = (u_1, \ldots, u_d) \in [0, 1]^d$. The empirical copula is the observed frequency of $P(Z_1 < u_1, \ldots, Z_d < u_d)$. The idea is to compare $\hat{C}(\mathbf{z})$ with an estimation $C_{\hat{\theta}}(\mathbf{z})$ of C_θ. This is a very natural approach for copula g-o-f testing considering that most univariate g-o-f tests are based on a distance between empirical and null hypothesis distribution functions. Genest, Rémillard, and Beaudoin (2008) state that, given that it is entirely non-parametric, $\hat{C}$ is the most objective benchmark for testing the copula g-o-f. A CvM statistic for approach $\mathcal{A}_2$ is (Genest, Rémillard, and Beaudoin 2008)

$$\hat{T}_2 = n \int_{[0,1]^d} \{\hat{C}(\mathbf{z}) - C_{\hat{\theta}}(\mathbf{z})\}^2 \, d\hat{C}(\mathbf{z}) = \sum_{j=1}^n \{\hat{C}(\mathbf{z}_j) - C_{\hat{\theta}}(\mathbf{z}_j)\}^2. \tag{4}$$

3.3 Approach $\mathcal{A}_3$

Genest, Rémillard, and Beaudoin (2008) propose to apply approach $\mathcal{A}_2$ to $\mathbf{V} = \mathcal{R}(\mathbf{Z})$. The idea is then to compare $\hat{C}(\mathbf{v})$ with the independence copula $C_\perp(\mathbf{v})$. A CvM statistic for approach $\mathcal{A}_3$ becomes (Genest, Rémillard, and Beaudoin 2008)

$$\hat{T}_3 = n \int_{[0,1]^d} \{\hat{C}(\mathbf{v}) - C_\perp(\mathbf{v})\}^2 \, d\hat{C}(\mathbf{v}) = \sum_{j=1}^n \{\hat{C}(\mathbf{v}_j) - C_\perp(\mathbf{v}_j)\}^2.$$

3.4 Approach $\mathcal{A}_4$

Genest and Rivest (1993), Wang and Wells (2000), Savu and Trede (2004) and Genest, Quessy, and Rémillard (2006a) propose to use Kendall's dependence function $K(w) = P(C(\mathbf{Z}) \le w)$ as a g-o-f approach. The test observator S_4 of approach $\mathcal{A}_4$ becomes

$$S_4(w) = P\{C(\mathbf{Z}) \le w\}, \quad w \in [0, 1],$$

where $\mathbf{Z}$ is the pseudo-vector. Under the null hypothesis, $S_4(w) = S_{4,\hat{\theta}}(w)$ which is copula-specific. The empirical version of the test observator S_4 equals

$$\hat{S}_4(w) = \frac{1}{n+1} \sum_{j=1}^n I\{\hat{C}(\mathbf{z}_j) \le w\}.$$

A CvM statistic for approach $\mathcal{A}_4$ is given by

$$\hat{T}_4 = n \int_0^1 \{\hat{S}_4(w) - S_{4,\hat{\theta}}(w)\}^2 \, \mathrm{d}\hat{S}_4(w) = \sum_{j=1}^n \left\{ \hat{S}_4 \left(\frac{j}{n+1} \right) - S_{4,\hat{\theta}} \left(\frac{j}{n+1} \right) \right\}^2.$$

3.5 Approach $\mathcal{A}_5$

Quessy, Mesfioui and Toupin (2007) proposed a g-o-f approach for bivariate copulae based on Spearman's dependence function $L_2(w) = P(Z_1 Z_2 \leq w)$. Notice that $L_2(w) = P(C_\perp(Z_1, Z_2) \leq w)$. A natural extension to arbitrary dimension d is then $L_d(w) = P(C_\perp(\mathbf{Z}) \leq w)$ and the test observator S_5 of approach $\mathcal{A}_5$ becomes

$$S_5(w) = P\{C_\perp(\mathbf{Z}) \leq w\}, \quad w \in [0, 1],$$

where $\mathbf{Z}$ is the pseudo-vector. Under the null hypothesis, $S_5(w) = S_{5,\hat{\theta}}(w)$, which is copula-specific. The empirical version of the test observator S_5 equals

$$\hat{S}_5(w) = \frac{1}{n+1} \sum_{j=1}^n I\{C_\perp(\mathbf{z}_j) \leq w\}.$$

A CvM statistic for approach A_5 is given by

$$\hat{T}_5 = n \int_0^1 \{\hat{S}_5(w) - S_{5,\hat{\theta}}(w)\}^2 \, \mathrm{d}\hat{S}_5(w) = \sum_{j=1}^n \left\{ \hat{S}_5 \left(\frac{j}{n+1} \right) - S_{5,\hat{\theta}} \left(\frac{j}{n+1} \right) \right\}^2.$$

3.6 Approach $\mathcal{A}_6$

Shih (1998) proposed a moment-based g-o-f test for the bivariate gamma frailty model, also known as Clayton's copula. Shih (1998) considered unweighted and weighted estimators of the dependency parameter θ via Kendall's tau and a weighted rank-based estimator, namely

$$\hat{\theta}_\tau = \frac{2\hat{\tau}}{1 - \hat{\tau}} \quad \text{and} \quad \hat{\theta}_W = \frac{\sum_{i<j} \Delta_{ij}/W_{ij}}{\sum_{i<j}(1 - \Delta_{ij})/W_{ij}},$$

where $\hat{\tau} = -1 + 4\sum_{i<j} \Delta_{ij}/\{n(n-1)\}$, $\Delta_{ij} = I\{(Z_{i1} - Z_{j1})(Z_{i2} - Z_{j2}) > 0\}$ and $W_{ij} = \sum_{k=1}^n I\{Z_{k1} \leq \max(Z_{i1}, Z_{j1}), Z_{k2} \leq \max(Z_{i2}, Z_{j2})\}$. Since $\hat{\theta}_\tau$ and $\hat{\theta}_W$ are both unbiased estimators of θ under the null hypothesis that $C = C_\theta$ for some $\theta \geq 0$, Shih (1998) proposed the g-o-f statistic

$$\hat{T}_{\text{Shih}} = \sqrt{n}\{\hat{\theta}_\tau - \hat{\theta}_W\}.$$

Shih (1998) showed that this statistic is asymptotically normal under the null hypothesis. Unfortunately, the variance provided by Shih (1998) was found to be wrong by Genest, Quessy, and Rémillard (2006b), where a corrected formula is provided.

One way of extending this approach to arbitrary dimension d is comparing each pairwise element of $\hat{\theta}_\tau$ and $\hat{\theta}_W$. The resulting vector of $d(d-1)/2$ statistics will tend, asymptotically, to a $d(d-1)/2$ dimensional normal vector with a non-trivial covariance matrix. The normalized version of the vector, i.e., the inverted square root of the covariance matrix multiplied with the vector of statistics, will be asymptotically standard normal and hence the sum of squares will now be chi-squared with $d(d-1)/2$ degrees of freedom. The covariance matrix of the vector of statistics remains to be computed and is deferred to future research. For now, we simply compute the non-normalized sum of squares and perform a parametric bootstrap (see Section 3.10) to estimate the P-value.

The test statistic for approach $\mathcal{A}_6$ then becomes

$$\hat{T}_6 = \sum_{i=1}^{d-1} \sum_{j=i+1}^{d} \{\hat{\theta}_{\tau,ij} - \hat{\theta}_{W,ij}\}^2.$$

$\hat{\theta}_W$, and hence approach $\mathcal{A}_6$ is constructed specifically for testing the Clayton copula and will not be considered for testing any other copula model.

3.7 Approach $\mathcal{A}_7$

Panchenko (2005) propose to test the entire data set in one step. The approach is based on the inner product of $\mathbf{Z}$ and $\mathbf{Z}_{\hat{\theta}}$, where $\mathbf{Z}$ is the pseudo-vector and $\mathbf{Z}_{\hat{\theta}}$ is the null hypothesis vector with $\hat{\theta}$ being a consistent estimator of the copula parameter. The inner product can be used as a measure of the distance between the two vectors. Now define the squared distance Q between the two vectors as

$$Q = \langle \mathbf{Z} - \mathbf{Z}_{\hat{\theta}} \, |\kappa_d| \, \mathbf{Z} - \mathbf{Z}_{\hat{\theta}} \rangle.$$

Here κ_d is a positive definite symmetric kernel such as the Gaussian kernel:

$$\kappa_d(\mathbf{Z}, \mathbf{Z}') = \exp\left\{-\|\mathbf{Z} - \mathbf{Z}'\|^2 / (2dh^2)\right\}$$

with $\|\cdot\|$ denoting the Euclidean norm in $\mathbb{R}^d$ and $h > 0$ being a bandwidth. Q will be zero if and only if $\mathbf{Z} = \mathbf{Z}_{\hat{\theta}}$. Suppose we have the random samples $(\mathbf{z}_1, \ldots, \mathbf{z}_n)$ from $\mathbf{Z}$. Now generate the random samples $(\mathbf{z}_1^*, \ldots, \mathbf{z}_n^*)$ from the null hypothesis vector $\mathbf{Z}_{\hat{\theta}}$. Following the properties of an inner product, Q can be decomposed as $Q = Q_{11} - 2Q_{12} + Q_{22}$. Each term of this decomposition is estimated using V-statistics (see Denker and Keller 1983) for an introduction to U- and V-statistics). The test statistic for approach $\mathcal{A}_7$ is given by

$$\hat{T}_7 = \frac{1}{n^2} \sum_{i=1}^{n} \sum_{j=1}^{n} \kappa_d(\mathbf{z}_i, \mathbf{z}_j) - \frac{2}{n^2} \sum_{i=1}^{n} \sum_{j=1}^{n} \kappa_d(\mathbf{z}_i, \mathbf{z}_j^*) + \frac{1}{n^2} \sum_{i=1}^{n} \sum_{j=1}^{n} \kappa_d(\mathbf{z}_i^*, \mathbf{z}_j^*).$$

3.8 Approach $\mathcal{A}_8$

Along the lines of approach $\mathcal{A}_3$, we propose a version of approach $\mathcal{A}_7$ based on $\mathbf{V} = \mathcal{R}(\mathbf{Z})$. Given the random samples $(\mathbf{v}_1^*, \ldots, \mathbf{v}_n^*)$, drawn from the independence copula, the statistic for approach $\mathcal{A}_8$ is simply

$$\hat{T}_8 = \frac{1}{n^2} \sum_{i=1}^{n} \sum_{j=1}^{n} \kappa_d(\mathbf{v}_i, \mathbf{v}_j) - \frac{2}{n^2} \sum_{i=1}^{n} \sum_{j=1}^{n} \kappa_d(\mathbf{v}_i, \mathbf{v}_j^*) + \frac{1}{n^2} \sum_{i=1}^{n} \sum_{j=1}^{n} \kappa_d(\mathbf{v}_i^*, \mathbf{v}_j^*).$$

For approaches $\mathcal{A}_7$ and $\mathcal{A}_8$, it may seem odd to base the deviance measure on one single sample from the null hypothesis and that an average over several repetitions would be more accurate. However, $\mathcal{A}_7$ is the approach in Panchenko (2005) and we include all approaches in their unaltered form. For approach $\mathcal{A}_8$, we wish to examine the effect of Rosenblatt's transformation on approach $\mathcal{A}_7$, so we stick to the deviance from one single sample.

3.9 *Approach* $\mathcal{A}_9$

One can imagine that the different approaches capture deviations from the null hypothesis in different ways. Hence, we propose to average several approaches in an attempt to capture these differences. The different approaches are not on the same scale, hence such averages should be taken over standardized variables, i.e., all approaches should be scaled appropriately. However, we include these averages in their simplest, non-standardized form, as suggestions for future research. Two specific averages are considered. First the average of all nine approaches and second the average of three approaches based on the empirical copula, namely $\mathcal{A}_2$, $\mathcal{A}_3$ and $\mathcal{A}_4$. The corresponding statistics are defined as

$$\hat{T}_9^{(a)} = \frac{1}{9}\left\{\hat{T}_1^{(a)} + \hat{T}_1^{(b)} + \sum_{j=2}^{8}\hat{T}_j\right\} \quad \text{and} \quad \hat{T}_9^{(b)} = \frac{1}{3}\left\{\hat{T}_2 + \hat{T}_3 + \hat{T}_4\right\}.$$

3.10 *Testing procedure*

In Section 3.1, it was assumed that $\mathbf{V} = \mathcal{R}(\mathbf{Z})$ is i.i.d. $U[0, 1]^d$. The use of ranks in the transformation of the marginals introduce sample dependence in $\mathbf{V}$. Thus $\mathbf{V}$ is only close to, but not exactly i.i.d. The consequence is that approximations of the limiting distributions of test statistics are inaccurate. In addition, the distributions depend on the value of the dependence parameter θ. Nevertheless, we can obtain reliable P-value estimates through a parametric bootstrap procedure. The parametric bootstrap procedure used in Genest, Quessy, and Rémillard (2006a) is adopted, the validity of which is established in Genest and Rémillard (2008). The asymptotic validity of the bootstrap procedure has only been proved so far for the approaches $\mathcal{A}_2$ and $\mathcal{A}_4$. However, results herein and in Berg and Bakken (2005) and Dobric and Schmid (2007) strongly indicate validity also for the other approaches.

Detailed test procedures for all approaches can be found in Berg (2007). Here, we restrict the presentation to approach $\mathcal{A}_2$:

(1) Extract the pseudo-samples $(\mathbf{z}_1, \dots, \mathbf{z}_n)$ by converting the sample data $(\mathbf{x}_1, \dots, \mathbf{x}_n)$ into normalized ranks according to Equation (2).
(2) Estimate the parameters θ with a consistent estimator $\hat{\theta} = \hat{\mathcal{V}}(\mathbf{z}_1, \dots, \mathbf{z}_n)$.
(3) Compute $\hat{C}(\mathbf{z})$ according to Equation (3).
(4) If there is an analytical expression for C_θ, compute the estimated statistic $\hat{T}_2$ by plugging $\hat{C}(\mathbf{z})$ and $C_{\hat{\theta}}(\mathbf{z})$ into Equation (4). Jump to step (5).

    If there is no analytical expression for C_θ then choose $N_b \geq n$ and carry out the following steps (double bootstrap):

    (i) Generate a random sample $(\mathbf{x}_1^*, \dots, \mathbf{x}_{N_b}^*)$ from the null hypothesis copula $C_{\hat{\theta}}$ and compute the associated pseudo-samples $(\mathbf{z}_1^*, \dots, \mathbf{z}_{N_b}^*)$ according to Equation (2).

    (ii) Approximate $C_{\hat{\theta}}$ by $C_{\hat{\theta}}^*(\mathbf{u}) = (1/(N_b + 1))\sum_{l=1}^{N_b} I\{\mathbf{z}_l^* \leq \mathbf{u}\}$, $\mathbf{u} \in [0, 1]^d$.

    (iii) Approximate the CvM statistic in Equation (4) by $\hat{T}_2 = \sum_{j=1}^{n}\{\hat{C}(\mathbf{z}_j) - C_{\hat{\theta}}^*(\mathbf{z}_j)\}^2$.

(5) For some large integer K, repeat the following steps for every $k \in \{1, \dots, K\}$ (parametric bootstrap):

    (a) Generate a random sample $(\mathbf{x}_{1,k}^0, \dots, \mathbf{x}_{n,k}^0)$ from the null hypothesis copula $C_{\hat{\theta}}$ and compute the associated pseudo-samples $(\mathbf{z}_{1,k}^0, \dots, \mathbf{z}_{n,k}^0)$ according to Equation (2).

    (b) Estimate the parameters θ^0 with a consistent estimator $\hat{\theta}_k^0 = \hat{\mathcal{V}}(\mathbf{z}_{1,k}^0, \dots, \mathbf{z}_{n,k}^0)$.

(c) Let $\hat{C}_k^0(\mathbf{u}) = (1/(n+1)) \sum_{j=1}^{n} I\{\mathbf{z}_{j,k}^0 \leq \mathbf{u}\}, \mathbf{u} \in [0,1]^d$.

(d) If there is an analytical expression for C_θ, let $\hat{T}_{2,k}^0 = \sum_{j=1}^{n}\{\hat{C}_k^0(\mathbf{z}_{j,k}^0) - C_{\hat{\theta}_k^0}(\mathbf{z}_{j,k}^0)\}^2$ and jump to step (6).

If there is no analytical expression for C_θ, then choose $N_b \geq n$ and proceed as follows:

(i) Generate a random sample $(\mathbf{x}_{1,k}^{0*}, \ldots, \mathbf{x}_{N_b,k}^{0*})$ from the null hypothesis copula $C_{\hat{\theta}_k^0}$ and compute the associated pseudo-samples $(\mathbf{z}_{1,k}^{0*}, \ldots, \mathbf{z}_{N_b,k}^{0*})$ according to Equation (2).

(ii) Approximate $C_{\hat{\theta}_k^0}$ by $C_{\hat{\theta}_k^0}^{0*}(\mathbf{u}) = (1/(N_b+1)) \sum_{l=1}^{N_b} I\{\mathbf{z}_{l,k}^{0*} \leq \mathbf{u}\}, \quad \mathbf{u} \in [0,1]^d$.

(iii) Approximate the CvM statistic in (4) by $\hat{T}_{2,k}^* = \sum_{j=1}^{n}\{\hat{C}_k^0(\mathbf{z}_{j,k}^0) - C_{\hat{\theta}_k^0}^{0*}(\mathbf{z}_{j,k}^0)\}^2$.

(6) An approximate P-value for approach $\mathcal{A}_2$ is then given by $\hat{p} = (1/(K+1)) \sum_{k=1}^{K} I\{\hat{T}_{2,k}^0 > \hat{T}_2\}$.

In this parametric bootstrap procedure, there are two parameters that need to be chosen, the sample size N_b for the double bootstrap step (step 4) and the number of replications K (step 5) for the estimation of P-values. In this paper, the number of replications $K = 1000$ while the double bootstrap sample size $N_b = 10,000$ for approach $\mathcal{A}_1$, and for approaches $\mathcal{A}_2, \mathcal{A}_4$ and $\mathcal{A}_5$ $N_b = 2500$ for dimensions $d = \{2,4\}$ and $N_b = 5000$ for dimension $d = 8$ (see Berg 2007 for details).

4. Numerical experiments

4.1 Size and power simulations

A large Monte Carlo study is performed to assess the properties of the approaches for various dimensions, sample sizes, levels of dependence and alternative dependence structures. The nominal levels and the power against fixed alternatives are of particular interest. The simulations are carried out according to the following factors:

- $\mathcal{H}_0$ copula (five choices: Gaussian, Student, Clayton, Gumbel, Frank),
- $\mathcal{H}_1$ copula (five choices: Gaussian, Student ($\nu = 6$), Clayton, Gumbel, Frank),
- Kendall's tau (two choices: $\tau = \{0.2, 0.4\}$),
- Dimension (three choices: $d = \{2, 4, 8\}$),
- Sample size (two choices: $n = \{100, 500\}$).

Due to extreme computational load, the Student copula is only considered as null hypothesis in the bivariate case. In each of the remaining 240 cases, a sample of dimension d and size n is drawn from the $\mathcal{H}_1$ copula with dependence parameter corresponding to τ. The statistics of the various g-o-f approaches are then computed under the null hypothesis $\mathcal{H}_0$, and P-values are estimated. This entire procedure is repeated 10,000 times in order to estimate the nominal level and power for each approach under consideration.

Since we apply a parametric bootstrap procedure in the estimation of P-values, critical values are obtained by simulating from the null hypothesis, and hence all reported powers are so-called size-adjusted powers and approaches can be compared appropriately (see, e.g., Hendry 2006 and Florax, Folmer, and Rey 2006 for size-adjustment suggestions).

A natural way of comparing approaches would be to rank their performance. However, an approach can be almost as good as the best approach in all cases but not necessarily the very best. For example, when testing the Gaussian copula where the alternative is the Gumbel copula for $d = 4$, $n = 500$ and $\tau = 0.40$, approach $\mathcal{A}_9^2$ will be ranked 1 with a power of 99.8 while approach $\mathcal{A}_5$ will be ranked number 5 with a power of 98.1. This small difference may not be statistically significant and purely due to Monte Carlo variation. Hence, we rather consider boxplots showing the differences in power from the best performing approach. We also present average powers for combinations of dimension and sample size, i.e., averaged over dependency levels and alternative copulae.

Sections 4.1.1–4.1.5 present power difference boxplots and average power tables for testing the Gaussian, Student, Clayton, Gumbel and Frank null hypotheses, respectively. Detailed tables with all power results are given in Appendix 3.

The critical values of each statistic under the true null hypothesis are tabulated for each dimension and sample size and for many levels of dependence. For the power simulations we used table look-up with linear interpolation to ensure comparison with the appropriate critical value. Despite the tabulation, this computationally exhaustive experiment would not have been feasible without access to the *Titan* computer grid at the University of Oslo, a cluster of (at the time) 1750 computing cores, 6.5 TB memory, 350 TB local disk and 12.5 Tflops.

4.1.1 *Testing the Gaussian hypothesis*

Let us first consider testing the Gaussian hypothesis under several fixed alternatives. The following summary can be read from Figure 1, Table 1 and the extensive results in Appendix 3, Table A.

- Nominal levels of all approaches match prescribed size of 5%.
- Power generally (but not always) increases with level of dependence.
- Power increases with sample size as it should for the approaches to be consistent.
- Power generally (but not always) increases with dimension, as expected. See, e.g., Chen, Fan, and Patton (2004) who show that the Kullbach–Leibler information criterion (a measure of distance between two copulae) between the Gaussian and Student copulae increases with dimension.

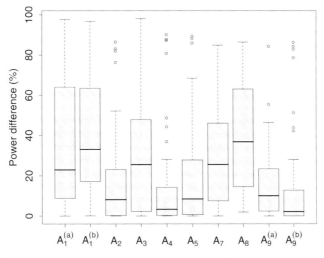

Figure 1. Power differences from the best approach for testing the Gaussian copula.

Table 1. Summary of rejection percentages (at 5% significance level). The results are averaged over sample size, dependency levels and alternative copulae.

$\mathcal{H}_0$	d	$\mathcal{A}_1^{(a)}$	$\mathcal{A}_1^{(b)}$	$\mathcal{A}_2$	$\mathcal{A}_3$	$\mathcal{A}_4$	$\mathcal{A}_5$	$\mathcal{A}_6$	$\mathcal{A}_7$	$\mathcal{A}_8$	$\mathcal{A}_9^{(a)}$	$\mathcal{A}_9^{(b)}$
Gauss	2	5.7	5.7	24.7	23.8	23.7	19.1	–	13.1	14.0	18.8	**26.6**
	4	22.1	16.3	37.4	32.1	43.4	39.5	–	27.3	20.8	42.7	**43.9**
	8	34.0	29.8	47.0	27.7	50.3	46.9	–	40.7	24.1	**52.2**	50.1
Student	2	5.2	5.2	23.5	17.1	23.9	19.5	–	12.3	12.1	20.6	**25.0**
Clayton	2	28.7	27.5	57.9	37.9	56.9	46.9	**58.4**	31.0	29.5	57.1	57.4
	4	54.6	42.2	69.0	32.4	70.9	69.2	71.8	46.3	34.2	**73.7**	71.1
	8	63.2	52.5	68.1	37.6	69.8	74.8	77.8	52.5	32.1	**78.3**	70.3
Gumbel	2	14.5	11.8	41.6	30.8	36.8	32.9	–	20.0	19.1	36.3	**39.4**
	4	39.2	35.7	65.7	57.2	65.6	59.0	–	46.4	23.0	64.9	**67.2**
	8	48.5	50.4	72.3	60.6	74.1	62.4	–	62.6	20.8	69.2	**74.6**
Frank	2	11.6	9.1	**33.9**	25.6	31.5	25.9	–	15.2	15.6	30.8	**33.9**
	4	23.9	25.7	58.6	50.1	58.2	51.6	–	32.6	22.3	59.9	**61.0**
	8	36.6	42.8	73.0	67.5	71.0	60.1	–	51.2	24.9	69.9	**73.3**

Note: Values in bold indicate the best performing approach.

- Approaches $\mathcal{A}_4$ and $\mathcal{A}_9^{(b)}$ perform very well and are recommended. However, there are exceptions and additions worth noting:
  - $\mathcal{A}_1$ and $\mathcal{A}_3$ perform particularly well for testing against heavy tails, i.e., the Student copula alternative.
  - $\mathcal{A}_2$ also perform very well for testing against Archimedean alternatives.
  - $\mathcal{A}_3$ performs particularly well for the Frank alternative in the bivariate case but very poor for higher dimensions. This illustrates the danger of concluding for higher dimensions based on bivariate results.

4.1.2 Testing the Student hypothesis
Next, we consider testing the Student copula hypothesis, for the bivariate case only. From Figure 2, Table 1 and the extensive results in Appendix 3, Table B, we can summarize:

- Nominal levels match prescribed size of 5%.
- Powers against Gaussian copula also match prescribed size. This is due to the Gaussian copula being a special case of the Student copula. The statistics are computed by estimating the parameters of the Student copula from the data, and hence the Student copula null hypothesis will include the Gaussian copula alternative through a large estimated value for the degree-of-freedom parameter.
- Approaches $\mathcal{A}_2$, $\mathcal{A}_4$ and, in particular, $\mathcal{A}_9^{(b)}$ perform very well and are recommended.
- $\mathcal{A}_1^{(a)}$, $\mathcal{A}_1^{(b)}$, $\mathcal{A}_7$ and $\mathcal{A}_8$ all perform rather poorly.
- For testing the Gaussian and Student hypotheses, powers are in general, as seen from Table 1, lower than for testing the Clayton, Gumbel and Frank hypotheses. This means that it is more difficult to test the elliptical than the Archimedean hypotheses.

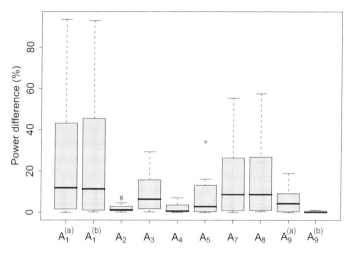

Figure 2. Distribution of power difference from the very best approach for testing the Student copula.

4.1.3 Testing the Clayton hypothesis

Figure 3, Table 1 and the extensive results in Appendix 3, Table C show the results of testing the Clayton copula hypothesis. We summarize:

- Nominal levels match prescribed size of 5%.
- Approaches $\mathcal{A}_2$, $\mathcal{A}_4$, $\mathcal{A}_9^{(b)}$ and, in particular, $\mathcal{A}_6$ perform very well and are recommended. $\mathcal{A}_9^{(a)}$ also performs very well but this is largely due to the good performance of $\mathcal{A}_6$ which dominates this average approach since its scale is much larger than that the of other approaches included in the average.
- $\mathcal{A}_7$, $\mathcal{A}_8$ and, in particular, $\mathcal{A}_3$ perform very poorly.

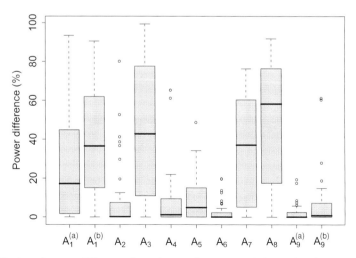

Figure 3. Distribution of power difference from the very best approach for testing the Clayton copula.

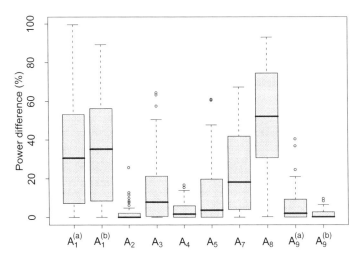

Figure 4. Distribution of power difference from the very best approach for testing the Gumbel copula.

- $\mathcal{A}_1^{(a)}$ and $\mathcal{A}_1^{(b)}$ also perform rather poorly.
- Powers are higher than for testing the Gaussian, Student and, as we will soon see, the Gumbel and Frank hypotheses, i.e., it is easier to test the Clayton hypothesis.

4.1.4 Testing the Gumbel hypothesis

We now test the Gumbel hypothesis. We summarize from Figure 4, Table 1 and the extensive results in Appendix 3, Table D:

- Nominal levels match prescribed size of 5%.
- Approaches $\mathcal{A}_2$, $\mathcal{A}_4$ and, in particular, $\mathcal{A}_9^{(b)}$, perform very well and are recommended.
- $\mathcal{A}_1^{(a)}$, $\mathcal{A}_1^{(b)}$ and, in particular, $\mathcal{A}_8$ perform very poorly.
- Powers are lower than for testing the Clayton hypothesis but higher than for testing the Gaussian, Student and, as we will soon see, the Frank hypotheses.

4.1.5 Testing the Frank hypothesis

Finally, we test the Frank hypothesis. From Figure 5, Table 1 and the extensive results in Appendix 3, Table E we summarize:

- Nominal levels match prescribed size of 5%.
- Approaches $\mathcal{A}_2$ and, in particular, $\mathcal{A}_9^{(b)}$ perform very well and are recommended.
- $\mathcal{A}_4$ and $\mathcal{A}_9^{(a)}$ also perform quite well.
- $\mathcal{A}_1^{(a)}$, $\mathcal{A}_1^{(b)}$ and, in particular, $\mathcal{A}_8$ perform very poorly.
- Powers are higher than for testing the Gaussian and Student hypotheses but lower than for testing the Clayton and Gumbel hypotheses.

4.2 Effect of permutation order for Rosenblatt's transform

Approaches $\mathcal{A}_1$, $\mathcal{A}_3$ and $\mathcal{A}_8$ are all based on Rosenblatt's transform and a consecutive test of independence. The lack of invariance to the order of permutation may pose a problem to these

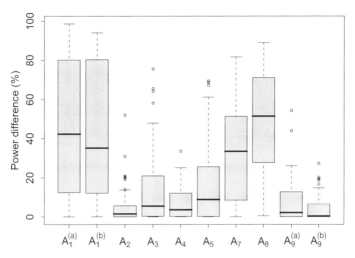

Figure 5. Distribution of power difference from the very best approach for testing the Frank copula.

approaches. The statistic for a given data set may prove very different depending on the permutation order. This is an undesirable feature of a statistical testing procedure. However, the practical consequence of this permutation invariance has not yet been investigated.

To examine this effect, we draw random samples from an alternative copula $\mathcal{H}_1$. We then compute a P-value, assuming a null copula $\mathcal{H}_0$. This is done for each approach and for each permutation of the variables. We then look at the mean and standard deviation over all permutations. We repeat

Table 2. Estimated mean P-values (mean of $d!$ permutations) for approaches based on Rosenblatt's transformation.

$\mathcal{H}_0$	$\mathcal{H}_1$	$\mathcal{A}_1^{(a)}$	$\mathcal{A}_1^{(b)}$	$\mathcal{A}_3$	$\mathcal{A}_8$
Gaussian	Gaussian	0.514 (0.000)	0.520 (0.263)	0.513 (0.287)	0.510 (0.290)
	Clayton	0.501 (0.000)	0.480 (0.239)	0.021 (0.038)	0.205 (0.201)
	Gumbel	0.479 (0.000)	0.460 (0.237)	0.549 (0.294)	0.294 (0.247)
	Frank	0.415 (0.000)	0.419 (0.232)	0.535 (0.311)	0.428 (0.287)
Clayton	Gaussian	0.003 (0.002)	0.008 (0.015)	0.312 (0.187)	0.248 (0.237)
	Clayton	0.520 (0.159)	0.535 (0.263)	0.519 (0.269)	0.501 (0.283)
	Gumbel	0.002 (0.002)	0.016 (0.024)	0.370 (0.222)	0.103 (0.139)
	Frank	0.008 (0.004)	0.040 (0.051)	0.424 (0.226)	0.265 (0.242)
Gumbel	Gaussian	0.082 (0.027)	0.095 (0.118)	0.109 (0.100)	0.390 (0.279)
	Clayton	0.035 (0.012)	0.214 (0.181)	0.000 (0.001)	0.101 (0.129)
	Gumbel	0.533 (0.110)	0.533 (0.270)	0.528 (0.264)	0.506 (0.287)
	Frank	0.113 (0.034)	0.340 (0.239)	0.417 (0.246)	0.463 (0.286)
Frank	Gaussian	0.242 (0.102)	0.129 (0.152)	0.104 (0.086)	0.380 (0.274)
	Clayton	0.536 (0.153)	0.400 (0.248)	0.000 (0.001)	0.173 (0.184)
	Gumbel	0.396 (0.135)	0.492 (0.265)	0.325 (0.227)	0.365 (0.267)
	Frank	0.509 (0.151)	0.508 (0.272)	0.506 (0.245)	0.486 (0.281)

Note: Applied to samples of size $n = 100$ for $d = 5$ dimensional copulae with dependence parameter $\tau = 0.5$.
The standard deviation over all permutations is given in parentheses. All quoted values are averaged over 1000 simulations.

Table 3. Estimated mean P-value (mean of $d!$ separate estimations based on the same data set) for approaches based on Rosenblatt's transformation.

$\mathcal{H}_0$	$\mathcal{H}_1$	$\mathcal{A}_1^{(a)}$	$\mathcal{A}_1^{(b)}$	$\mathcal{A}_3$	$\mathcal{A}_8$
Gaussian	Gaussian	0.514 (0.000)	0.530 (0.057)	0.523 (0.000)	0.510 (0.284)
	Clayton	0.501 (0.000)	0.483 (0.056)	0.021 (0.000)	0.205 (0.194)
	Gumbel	0.479 (0.000)	0.458 (0.052)	0.559 (0.000)	0.294 (0.239)
	Frank	0.415 (0.000)	0.416 (0.048)	0.551 (0.000)	0.432 (0.282)
Clayton	Gaussian	0.002 (0.000)	0.008 (0.003)	0.318 (0.000)	0.250 (0.216)
	Clayton	0.517 (0.000)	0.535 (0.056)	0.524 (0.000)	0.501 (0.275)
	Gumbel	0.002 (0.000)	0.013 (0.003)	0.382 (0.000)	0.105 (0.125)
	Frank	0.008 (0.000)	0.038 (0.007)	0.436 (0.000)	0.262 (0.218)
Gumbel	Gaussian	0.080 (0.000)	0.089 (0.023)	0.104 (0.000)	0.390 (0.268)
	Clayton	0.036 (0.000)	0.205 (0.036)	0.000 (0.000)	0.100 (0.123)
	Gumbel	0.527 (0.000)	0.531 (0.061)	0.532 (0.000)	0.508 (0.281)
	Frank	0.112 (0.000)	0.342 (0.050)	0.421 (0.000)	0.461 (0.278)
Frank	Gaussian	0.240 (0.000)	0.129 (0.031)	0.109 (0.000)	0.381 (0.263)
	Clayton	0.541 (0.000)	0.395 (0.055)	0.000 (0.000)	0.170 (0.174)
	Gumbel	0.391 (0.000)	0.489 (0.059)	0.320 (0.000)	0.366 (0.257)
	Frank	0.502 (0.000)	0.510 (0.063)	0.501 (0.000)	0.485 (0.274)

Note: Applied to samples of size $n = 100$ for $d = 5$ dimensional copulae with dependence parameter $\tau = 0.5$. The standard deviation over all permutations is given is parentheses. All quoted values are averaged over 1000 simulations.

this procedure 1000 times and report average values in Table 2. The study is restricted to dimension $d = 5$ for which there are $d! = 120$ different permutations, sample size $n = 100$ and dependence $\tau = 0.5$.

For some of the approaches, there are two sources of variation: permutation order and double bootstrap procedure (see Section 3.10). In order to see the effect of permutation order only, we report the same P-value variation results when the permutation is kept fixed (see Table 3).

From the two tables, one can see that the permutation order adds no variance for approach $\mathcal{A}_1^{(a)}$ when the null hypothesis is the Gaussian copula. This permutation invariance of approach $\mathcal{A}_1^{(a)}$ under the Gaussian null hypothesis is proved in Appendix 1. However, when using a different weight function or when the null hypothesis is different from the Gaussian copula, variation is added due to the permutation order. Note that in rejection regions or close to rejection regions, i.e., in cases where an approach has high power and the P-value is very small, the variation due to permutation order will not have a practical consequence as the conclusion will most probably be rejection of $\mathcal{H}_0$, regardless of the permutation order. We see the same for the other approaches. For approach $\mathcal{A}_1^{(a)}$ we see that the variation is in general lower than for the other approaches. Also note that for approach $\mathcal{A}_8$ the permutation order adds almost no variation in any case as the estimated P-value will vary heavily even when keeping the permutation order fixed. This is due to the construction of the approach where random samples from the null hypothesis copula are drawn in every computation of the statistic, inducing large variation.

5. Discussion and recommendations

An overview of six copula g-o-f approaches was given, along with the proposal of three new approaches. A large Monte Carlo study was presented, examining the nominal levels and the power against some fixed alternatives under several combinations of problem dimension, sample size and dependence. Finally, we investigated what effect the permutation order has in the Rosenblatt transformation.

Sections 4.1.1–4.1.5 summarize the findings of the Monte Carlo study and provide recommendations to which approach to use in each case. In general, we observe increasing power with dimension, sample size and dependence. While no approach strictly dominates the others in terms of power, approaches $\mathcal{A}_2$, $\mathcal{A}_4$ and, in particular, approach $\mathcal{A}_9^{(b)}$ perform very well, the latter being the overall best performing approach. However, when testing the Gaussian hypothesis against heavy tails, the otherwise poor approach $\mathcal{A}_1$ performs very well for high dimensions and large sample sizes. To decide which approaches to consider, a preliminary test of ellipticity (see, e.g., Huffera and Park 2007) may also be helpful. The strong performance of approach $\mathcal{A}_9^{(b)}$ is very interesting and further research into the properties and power of this and other average approaches should be carried out.

When doing model evaluation, it is recommended to also examine various diagnostic tests such as g-o-f plots, e.g., plotting $S_4(w)$ with simulated null hypothesis confidence bands as done in Genest, Quessy, and Rémillard (2006a). This may give valuable information on the fit of a copula. However, there is still an unsatisfied need for intuitive and informative diagnostic plots. Ideally such a plot should show, in some way and in case of rejection by the formal tests, which variable (i.e., which dimension) and/or which samples causes the rejection. Is it actually a deviation in the dependence structure between the variables or is the rejection due to some extreme samples? More research is needed on this topic.

Next, results were reported on the variation of the P-value estimates due to permutation order for approaches based on Rosenblatt's transformation. In general, one does not want a statistical testing procedure to give different values when running it several times on the same data set. However, for some of the approaches based on Rosenblatt's transformation, the estimated P-value will be different depending on which permutation order that is chosen for the variables. The practical consequence of this variation decreases as the P-value estimates approach critical/rejection levels. Hence, the author does not believe that the permutation effect is something to worry about. Also, as long as the permutation order is chosen in a random fashion, the results are not influenced in any particular direction.

The results concerning the permutation of variables also point in the direction of important future research. The variation of P-value estimates also depends on the bootstrap parameters M and N_b. These parameters are usually, in a rather arbitrary way, set to what is believed to be large values. This is also the case in this paper. However, there has been no study of the effect that these choices may have on the power, and even more importantly the nominal levels of an approach. Originally, in the power studies of Section 4.1, a double bootstrap parameter $N_b = 2500$ was chosen for all combinations of dimension, sample size, dependence and alternative copula. However, for dimension $d = 8$ we observed some peculiar results, e.g., decreasing power as sample size increased. These peculiarities vanished when increasing N_b to 5000 for dimension $d = 8$. Choosing appropriately large values for these parameters and thus achieving proper nominal levels is crucial for any study and/or application of these g-o-f approaches. Hence, a study of the effects of these parameters and required minimum values would be highly valuable.

The computational aspect also deserves some attention. An important quality of approaches based on Rosenblatt's transform is computational efficiency. Approaches $\mathcal{A}_2$, $\mathcal{A}_4$ and $\mathcal{A}_5$ need computationally intensive double-parametric bootstrap procedures to estimate P-values in some cases (e.g., for the elliptical copulae, in particular, for higher dimensions and large sample sizes). Approaches based on Rosenblatt's transformation do not, in general, need this double-bootstrap step, since after Rosenblatt's transformation, the null hypothesis is always the independence copula.

Finally, a word of warning. As emphasized in Genest, Rémillard, and Beaudoin (2008), the asymptotics of several of the procedures presented here are not known. Hence, one cannot know for sure whether a bootstrap procedure will converge in every case. However, all the results so far on the performance of the proposed approaches and bootstrap procedures are comforting and strongly indicate the validity of the test procedures. Keep in mind though, the original approach and test procedure proposed by Breymann, Dias, and Embrechts (2003), which showed terrible performance in the study of Dobrić and Schmid (2007). This shows how wrong it can all go if our test procedure is not valid. Approaches $\mathcal{A}_2$ and $\mathcal{A}_4$, that turned out to be among the best in our study, both have known asymptotics and the bootstrap procedures for these approaches are well established from Quessy (2005), Gnest, Quessy, and Rémillard (2006a) and Genest and Rémillard (2008).

Acknowledgments

I would like to thank my colleagues at the Norwegian Computing Center, in particular, Kjersti Aas and Xeni Kristine Dimakos. Credit is also due to my former colleague Henrik Bakken for fruitful discussions and collaboration in the early phase of this work. Finally, I would like to thank the editor, two anonymous referees and colleagues and participants at various workshops and conferences for valuable comments. I mention, in particular, Professors Christian Genest, Nils Lid Hjort, Jean-François Quessy and Mark Salmon. Partial funding in support of this work was provided by the Norwegian Research Council.

References

Anderson, T.W., and D.A. Darling. 1954. A test of goodness of fit. *Journal of the American Statistical Association* 49: 765–9.

Berg, D. 2007. Copula goodness-of-fit testing: An overview and power comparison. Technical Report, Statistical research report no. 5, ISSN 0806-3842, University of Oslo.

Berg, D., and H. Bakken. 2005. A goodness-of-fit test for copulae based on the probability integral transform. Technical Report, Statistical research report no. 10, ISSN 0806-3842, University of Oslo.

Breymann, W., A. Dias, and P. Embrechts. 2003. Dependence structures for multivariate high-frequency data in finance. *Quantitative Finance* 1: 1–14.

Chen, X., Y. Fan, and A. Patton. 2004. Simple tests for models of dependence between multiple financial time series, with applications to U.S. equity returns and exchange rates. Discussion Paper 483, Financial Markets Group, London School of Economics, Revised July 2004.

Cherubini, U., E. Luciano, and W. Vecchiato. 2004. *Copula methods in finance*. Wiley.

Deheuvels, P. 1979. La fonction de dépendance empirique et ses propriétés: Un test non paramétrique d'indépendence. *Académie Royal de Belegique. Bullatin de la Class des Sciences.* 5$_e$ série 65: 274–92.

Demarta, S., and A.J. McNeil. 2005. The t copula and related copulas. *International Statistical Review* 73 no. 1: 111–129.

Denker, M., and G. Keller. 1983. On u-statistics and v. mises' statistics for weakly dependent processes. *Zeitschrift für Wahrscheinlichkeitstheorie und Verwandte Gebiete* 64: 505–22.

Dobrić, J., and F. Schmid. 2005. Testing goodness-of-fit for parametric families of copulas-application to financial data. *Communications in Statistics: Simulation and Computation* 34 no. 4: 1053–68.

Dobrić, J., and F. Schmid. 2007. A goodness of fit test for copulas based on Rosenblatt's transformation. *Computational Statistics & Data Analysis* 51 no. 9: 4633–42.

Fermanian, J. 2005. Goodness of fit tests for copulas. *Journal of Multivariate Analysis* 95: 119–52.

Florax, R.J.G.M., H. Folmer, and S.J. Rey. 2006. A comment on specification searches in spatial econometrics: The Relevance of Hendry's methodology: A reply. *Regional Science and Urban Economics* 36: 300–8.

Genest, C., and B. Rémillard. 2008. Validity of the parametric bootstrap for goodness-of-fit testing in semiparametric models. *Annales Henri Poincaré* 44: 1096–1127.

Genest, C., and L.-P. Rivest. 1993. Statistical inference procedures for bivariate Archimedean copulas. *Journal of the American Statistical Association*, 88, no. 423: 1034–43.

Genest, C., K. Ghoudi, and L. Rivest. 1995. A semi-parametric estimation procedure of dependence parameters in multivariate families of distributions. *Biometrika* 82: 543–52.

Genest, C., J.-F. Quessy, and B. Rémillard. 2006a. Goodness-of-fit procedures for copula models based on the probability integral transform. *Scandinavian Journal of Statistics* 33: 337–66.

Genest, C., J.-F. Quessy, and B. Rémillard. 2006b. On the joint asymptotic behavior of two rank-based estimators of the association parameter in the gamma frailty model. *Statistics Probability Letters* 76: 10–18.

Genest, C., B. Rémillard, and D. Beaudoin. In press. Omnibus goodness-of-fit tests for copulas: A review and a power study. *Insurance: Mathematics and Economics* 42.

Hendry, D.F. 2006. Specification searches in spatial econometrics: The relevance of Hendry's methodology. *Regional Science and Urban Economics* 36: 309–12.

Hong, Y., and H. Li. 2005. Nonparametric specification testing for continuous-time models with application to spot interest rates. *Reviews of Financial Studies* 18: 37–84.

Huffera, F.W., and C. Park. 2007. A test for elliptical symmetry. *Journal of Multivariate Analysis* 98, no. 2: 256–81.

Joe, H. 1997. *Multivariate models and dependence concepts*. London: Chapman & Hall.

Malevergne, Y., and D. Sornette. 2003. Testing the gaussian copula hypothesis for financial assets dependence. *Quantitative Finance* 3: 231–50.

Malevergne, Y., and D. Sornette. 2006. *Extreme financial risks: From dependence to risk management*. Berlin:Springer.

Mashal, R., and A. Zeevi. 2002. Beyond correlation: Extreme co-movements between financial assets. Technical Report, Columbia University.

Nelsen, R.B. 1999. *An introduction to copulas*. New York: Springer Verlag.

Panchenko, V. 2005. Goodness-of-fit test for copulas. *Physica A* 355, no. 1: 176–182.

Quessy, J.-F. 2005. *Théorie et application des copules: Tests d'adéquation, tests d'indépendance et bornes pour la valeur-à-risque*. PhD thesis, Université Laval.

Quessy, J.-F., M. Mesfioui, and M.-H. Toupin. 2007. A goodness-of-fit test based on Spearmans dependence function. Working Paper, Université du Québec à Trois-Rivières.

Romano, C. 2002. Calibrating and simulating copula functions: An application to the Italian stock market. Working Paper No. 12, CIDEM, Universit'a degli Studi di Roma "La Sapienza".

Rosenblatt, M. 1952. Remarks on a multivariate transformation. *The Annals of Mathematical Statistics* 23: 470–72.

Savu, C., and M. Trede. 2008. Goodness-of-fit tests for parametric families of Archimedean copulas. *Quantitave Finance* 8, no. 2: 109–116.

Scaillet, O. 2005. Kernel based goodness-of-fit tests for copulas with fixed smoothing parameters. FAME Research Paper Series rp145, International Center for Financial Asset Management and Engineering. http://ideas.repec.org/p/fam/rpseri/rp145.html

Shih, J.H. 1998. A goodness-of-fit test for association in a bivariate survival model. *Biometrika* 85: 189–200.

Shih, J.H. and T.A. Louis. 1995. Inferences on the association parameter in copula models for bivariate survival data. *Biometrics* 51: 1384–99.

Sklar, A. 1959. Fonctions de répartition à n dimensions et leurs marges. *Publications de Institut Statistique de l'Universite de Paris* 8: 299–31.

Wang, W., and M.T. Wells. 2000. Model selection and semiparametric inference for bivariate failure-time data. *Journal of the American Statistical Association* 95: 62–72.

Appendix 1. Proof of permutation invariance of $\mathcal{A}_1^{(a)}$ under Gaussian copula null hypothesis

To prove that approach $\mathcal{A}_1^{(a)}$ is permutation-invariant under the Gaussian copula null hypothesis, let us first look at how Rosenblatt's transformation is carried out. For the Gaussian copula null hypothesis, this transformation is easily computed using the Cholesky decomposition of the covariance matrix. Let $\mathbf{X} \sim \mathcal{N}(\boldsymbol{\mu}, \boldsymbol{\Sigma})$ be a d-dimensional vector, where $\boldsymbol{\mu} = \mathbb{E}(\mathbf{X})$ and $\boldsymbol{\Sigma}$ is the $d \times d$ positive-definite covariance matrix.

Since $\boldsymbol{\Sigma}$ is positive definite, it can be written as $\boldsymbol{\Sigma} = \mathbf{A}^{\mathrm{T}}\mathbf{A}$, where $\mathbf{A}$ is a lower triangular matrix and $\mathbf{A}^{\mathrm{T}}$ denotes its transpose. Next, it is well known that $\mathbf{X}$ can be expressed as $\mathbf{X} = \boldsymbol{\mu} + \mathbf{A}^{\mathrm{T}}\mathbf{Y}$, where $\mathbf{Y} \sim \mathcal{N}(0, \boldsymbol{I})$ and $\boldsymbol{I}$ is the d-dimensional identity matrix, that is, $\mathbf{Y}$ is a vector of d i.i.d. standard normally distributed variables. Solving for $\mathbf{Y}$ gives $\mathbf{Y} = (\mathbf{A}^{\mathrm{T}})^{-1}(\mathbf{X} - \boldsymbol{\mu})$. We now see that the vector $\mathbf{V} = \Phi(\mathbf{Y})$ is i.i.d. $U(0,1)^d$ under the Gaussian null hypothesis.

For approach $\mathcal{A}_1^{(a)}$ we now need to compute $W_1 = \sum_{i=1}^{d} \Phi^{-1}(V_i)^2 = \sum_{i=1}^{d} Y_i^2 = \mathbf{Y}^{\mathrm{T}}\mathbf{Y}$. We now proceed with the bivariate setting for simplicity but the proof can easily be extended to arbitrary dimension d. Consider the Cholesky

85

decomposition of the covariance matrix $\Sigma = \mathbf{A}^{\mathrm{T}}\mathbf{A}$ in detail:

$$\Sigma^1 = \begin{pmatrix} \sigma_1^2 & \sigma_{12} \\ \sigma_{12} & \sigma_2^2 \end{pmatrix} = \begin{pmatrix} a_{11} & a_{12} \\ 0 & a_{22} \end{pmatrix} \begin{pmatrix} a_{11} & 0 \\ a_{12} & a_{22} \end{pmatrix} = \begin{pmatrix} a_{11}^2 + a_{12}^2 & a_{12}a_{22} \\ a_{12}a_{22} & a_{22}^2 \end{pmatrix},$$

where the superscript 1 in Σ^1 denotes permutation order 1. We see now that $a_{11} = \sqrt{\sigma_1^2\sigma_2^2 - \sigma_{12}^2}/\sigma_2$, $a_{12} = \sigma_{12}/\sigma_2$ and $a_{22} = \sigma_2$. Next, we see that

$$(\mathbf{A}^{\mathrm{T}})^{-1} = \begin{pmatrix} \dfrac{1}{a_{11}} & -\dfrac{a_{12}}{a_{11}a_{22}} \\ 0 & \dfrac{1}{a_{22}} \end{pmatrix}$$

and that

$$\mathbf{Y} = (\mathbf{A}^{\mathrm{T}})^{-1}(\mathbf{X} - \mu) = \begin{pmatrix} \dfrac{1}{a_{11}}(X_1 - \mu_1) - \dfrac{a_{12}}{a_{11}a_{22}}(X_2 - \mu_2) \\ \dfrac{1}{a_{22}}(X_2 - \mu_2) \end{pmatrix}.$$

Now to compute $W_1^1 = \mathbf{Y}^{\mathrm{T}}\mathbf{Y}$, superscript 1 denoting permutation order 1, we get

$$W_1^1 = \frac{(X_1 - \mu_1)^2}{a_{11}^2} + \frac{a_{12}^2}{a_{11}^2 a_{22}^2}(X_2 - \mu_2)^2 - \frac{2a_{12}}{a_{11}^2 a_{22}}(X_1 - \mu_1)(X_2 - \mu_2) + \frac{(X_2 - \mu_2)^2}{a_{22}^2}$$

$$= \frac{(X_1 - \mu_1)^2\sigma_2^2 + (X_2 - \mu_2)^2\sigma_1^2 - 2(X_1 - \mu_1)(X_2 - \mu_2)\sigma_{12}}{\sigma_1^2\sigma_2^2 - \sigma_{12}^2}$$

by inserting σ's for the a's.

By doing the same exercise with permutation order 2, we first get

$$\Sigma^2 = \begin{pmatrix} \sigma_2^2 & \sigma_{12} \\ \sigma_{12} & \sigma_1^2 \end{pmatrix}$$

and $a_{11} = \sqrt{\sigma_1^2\sigma_2^2 - \sigma_{12}^2}/\sigma_1$, $a_{12} = \sigma_{12}/\sigma_1$ and $a_{22} = \sigma_1$. Next, in the same manner as above, it is easily shown that

$$W_1^2 = \frac{(X_2 - \mu_2)^2\sigma_1^2 + (X_1 - \mu_1)^2\sigma_2^2 - 2(X_1 - \mu_1)(X_2 - \mu_2)\sigma_{12}}{\sigma_1^2\sigma_2^2 - \sigma_{12}^2} = W_1^1.$$

Hence, we have shown that approach $\mathcal{A}_1^{(a)}$ is permutation-invariant under the Gaussian copula null hypothesis. This is not so for other weight functions or other null hypothesis copulae. The invariance stems from the use of Φ^{-1} which cancels out with the Φ in $\mathbf{V} = \Phi(\mathbf{Y})$ and the squaring $\Phi(V_i)^2$.

Appendix 2. Derivation of a CvM statistic

Consider the CvM statistic

$$T = n \int_0^1 \{\hat{F}(w) - F(w)\}^2 \, \mathrm{d}F(w),$$

where $\hat{F}(w) = (1/(n+1))\sum_{j=1}^n I(X_j \le t)$ is the empirical distribution function. Given a random sample $(x_1, \ldots, x_n)$, the empirical version $\hat{T}$ of the CvM statistic can be derived as follows.

$$\hat{T} = n \int_0^1 \{\hat{F}(w) - F(w)\}^2 \mathrm{d}F(w)$$

$$= n \int_0^1 \hat{F}(w)^2 \mathrm{d}F(w) - 2n \int_0^1 \hat{F}(w)F(w)\mathrm{d}F(w) + n \int_0^1 F(w)^2\mathrm{d}F(w).$$

Since $\hat{F}(w)$ is constant and equal to $\hat{F}(j/(n+1))$ between $j/(n+1)$ and $(j+1)/(n+1)$ for $j = 1, \ldots, n$, the first two integrals can be split into n smaller integrals:

$$\hat{T} = n \sum_{j=1}^{n} \int_{j/(n+1)}^{(j+1)/(n+1)} \hat{F}\left(\frac{j}{n+1}\right)^2 dF(w) - 2n \sum_{j=1}^{n} \int_{j/(n+1)}^{(j+1)/(n+1)} \hat{F}\left(\frac{j}{n+1}\right) F(w) dF(w) + \frac{n}{3}\left[F(w)^3\right]_0^1$$

$$= \frac{n}{3} + n \sum_{j=1}^{n} \hat{F}\left(\frac{j}{n+1}\right)^2 \left\{ F\left(\frac{j+1}{n+1}\right) - F\left(\frac{j}{n+1}\right) \right\} - n \sum_{j=1}^{n} \hat{F}\left(\frac{j}{n+1}\right) \left\{ F\left(\frac{j+1}{n+1}\right)^2 - F\left(\frac{j}{n+1}\right)^2 \right\}.$$

For approach $\mathcal{A}_1$ the test observator $S_1(w)$ is $U[0, 1]$ under the null hypothesis. Hence $F(w) = w$ and we easily see that $\hat{T}$ reduces to

$$\hat{T}' = \frac{n}{3} + \frac{n}{n+1} \sum_{j=1}^{n} \hat{F}\left(\frac{j}{n+1}\right)^2 - \frac{n}{(n+1)^2} \sum_{j=1}^{n} (2j+1)\hat{F}\left(\frac{j}{n+1}\right).$$

Appendix 3. Power results from numerical experiments

Table A. Percentage of rejections (at 5% significance level) of the Gaussian copula:

d	n	τ	True copula	$\mathcal{A}_1^{(a)}$	$\mathcal{A}_1^{(b)}$	$\mathcal{A}_2$	$\mathcal{A}_3$	$\mathcal{A}_4$	$\mathcal{A}_5$	$\mathcal{A}_6$	$\mathcal{A}_7$	$\mathcal{A}_8$	$\mathcal{A}_9^{(a)}$	$\mathcal{A}_9^{(b)}$
2	100	0.2	Gaussian	5.3	5.0	5.0	4.6	5.4	5.7	–	4.7	5.2	5.0	5.1
			Student ($\nu = 6$)	0.9	4.2	7.0	**8.8**	6.1	5.3	–	5.6	6.0	3.3	6.4
			Clayton	2.6	5.0	19.7	19.6	19.9	15.6	–	7.1	6.9	10.6	**24.0**
			Gumbel	1.9	4.6	10.7	3.6	**11.6**	8.4	–	6.2	5.9	4.9	9.7
			Frank	3.4	3.2	6.0	**7.4**	6.0	6.2	–	5.4	5.5	3.4	6.1
		0.4	Gaussian	5.2	5.0	4.7	5.4	4.8	4.7	–	5.0	4.7	5.0	4.9
			Student ($\nu = 6$)	1.3	2.4	5.9	**11.6**	4.8	3.9	–	5.3	5.8	2.3	6.4
			Clayton	1.1	2.5	57.4	59.6	49.7	33.7	–	14.9	15.8	22.2	**63.9**
			Gumbel	1.3	2.6	**19.1**	5.0	18.5	8.2	–	7.0	7.9	4.1	16.2
			Frank	0.8	1.2	10.6	11.6	10.1	8.9	–	6.1	6.3	1.5	**11.8**
	500	0.2	Gaussian	4.7	4.9	5.2	4.8	5.2	5.1	–	5.1	4.9	4.9	5.0
			Student ($\nu = 6$)	19.5	16.9	10.0	16.9	8.4	8.5	–	10.3	9.8	**21.4**	10.0
			Clayton	2.0	5.8	72.5	71.3	71.9	57.2	–	23.8	20.3	56.5	**79.5**
			Gumbel	2.5	6.9	33.2	8.5	33.9	25.8	–	12.3	11.1	21.2	**34.3**
			Frank	2.2	2.9	11.4	**21.9**	11.1	9.9	–	7.6	8.1	5.8	14.5
		0.4	Gaussian	5.0	5.0	4.6	5.4	4.9	4.8	–	4.9	5.5	5.1	4.8
			Student ($\nu = 6$)	23.8	12.5	8.2	**30.5**	6.6	6.9	–	10.1	12.6	20.6	12.0
			Clayton	6.8	4.3	99.8	**100**	99.6	96.2	–	78.1	84.3	99.0	99.9
			Gumbel	8.8	6.0	**65.3**	18.9	62.9	39.8	–	26.4	32.4	42.3	**65.3**
			Frank	15.1	12.2	36.9	**60.7**	33.4	26.4	–	17.0	20.6	36.9	52.1
4	100	0.2	Gaussian	4.8	5.0	4.6	4.8	4.8	5.3	–	5.6	5.0	5.0	4.9
			Student ($\nu = 6$)	5.1	6.5	8.9	**15.4**	8.5	7.0	–	6.7	6.6	7.5	9.7
			Clayton	1.1	5.0	45.6	30.5	52.5	19.2	–	9.4	7.0	20.2	**55.9**
			Gumbel	1.2	3.1	12.8	0.7	42.5	**56.4**	–	13.9	8.8	13.2	34.9
			Frank	2.0	1.4	1.8	3.0	12.2	**19.6**	–	7.5	6.8	2.0	8.4
		0.4	Gaussian	4.5	4.8	5.2	5.4	5.1	5.1	–	4.9	5.3	4.9	5.3
			Student ($\nu = 6$)	9.2	3.7	8.6	**24.4**	6.1	5.3	–	6.9	7.1	7.5	8.1
			Clayton	1.1	1.8	**90.8**	80.4	84.0	45.6	–	27.9	18.3	48.8	90.1
			Gumbel	1.5	1.7	41.0	3.6	**52.0**	48.7	–	25.8	15.4	17.1	50.1
			Frank	1.6	2.2	10.1	7.3	**23.6**	20.6	–	12.6	8.3	5.6	21.2

(Continued)

Continued.

d	n	τ	True copula	$\mathcal{A}_1^{(a)}$	$\mathcal{A}_1^{(b)}$	$\mathcal{A}_2$	$\mathcal{A}_3$	$\mathcal{A}_4$	$\mathcal{A}_5$	$\mathcal{A}_6$	$\mathcal{A}_7$	$\mathcal{A}_8$	$\mathcal{A}_9^{(a)}$	$\mathcal{A}_9^{(b)}$
	500	0.2	Gaussian	*5.8*	*5.3*	*5.3*	*5.0*	*4.8*	*4.9*	–	*5.0*	*5.5*	*4.9*	*4.7*
			Student ($\nu = 6$)	**98.5**	71.8	16.5	47.1	11.2	12.6	–	13.6	15.0	96.5	15.7
			Clayton	4.3	7.7	99.0	94.4	98.0	88.4	–	39.3	22.2	94.6	**99.2**
			Gumbel	8.0	5.9	84.2	48.0	97.7	**98.5**	–	70.3	34.7	92.3	98.0
			Frank	3.6	6.6	25.4	5.0	64.3	**66.2**	–	20.3	17.2	39.1	63.8
		0.4	Gaussian	*4.7*	*4.7*	*4.8*	*4.9*	*4.7*	*4.8*	–	*5.1*	*5.0*	*4.4*	*4.6*
			Student ($\nu = 6$)	**98.1**	67.5	11.6	72.1	8.0	8.8	–	16.4	18.7	94.0	13.8
			Clayton	44.3	13.2	**100**	**100**	**100**	99.9	–	97.2	91.2	**100**	**100**
			Gumbel	63.2	34.7	98.9	70.1	99.6	98.1	–	95.5	77.4	99.4	**99.8**
			Frank	79.3	74.2	73.2	19.5	88.6	74.5	–	61.2	40.7	**97.4**	90.6
8	100	0.2	Gaussian	*5.0*	*5.2*	*5.9*	*4.7*	*5.8*	*5.2*	–	*5.3*	*5.2*	*5.4*	*5.7*
			Student ($\nu = 6$)	**40.4**	16.4	9.8	15.0	12.3	7.7	–	7.9	6.9	35.9	12.4
			Clayton	0.7	4.1	48.7	24.3	**66.0**	1.2	–	11.8	6.6	19.5	65.5
			Gumbel	0.6	1.7	22.0	2.3	61.5	**98.3**	–	56.9	13.8	14.0	56.1
			Frank	0.4	0.6	3.8	1.3	7.3	**56.0**	–	14.4	7.2	0.6	4.7
		0.4	Gaussian	*5.1*	*5.2*	*5.0*	*4.6*	*5.3*	*5.7*	–	*5.5*	*5.1*	*5.3*	*5.1*
			Student ($\nu = 6$)	**51.7**	16.1	8.3	17.6	7.4	6.1	–	8.0	8.5	39.2	7.8
			Clayton	1.6	2.4	**96.6**	49.2	93.3	28.1	–	40.4	19.9	59.9	95.0
			Gumbel	16.2	10.1	70.5	2.7	78.4	**92.8**	–	67.9	28.1	52.7	78.6
			Frank	4.8	8.3	19.6	2.9	**28.7**	23.9	–	26.7	7.5	14.6	25.7
	500	0.2	Gaussian	*5.5*	*4.8*	*4.4*	*5.1*	*4.8*	*5.4*	–	*5.2*	*5.1*	*4.6*	*4.8*
			Student ($\nu = 6$)	**100**	99.9	23.7	56.4	19.1	11.8	–	21.7	20.9	**100**	21.3
			Clayton	11.8	12.9	**100**	74.3	99.7	84.8	–	50.5	13.6	97.2	99.9
			Gumbel	30.0	13.4	**100**	71.7	**100**	**100**	–	**100**	63.0	99.9	**100**
			Frank	22.9	38.3	99.8	10.5	98.4	**99.9**	–	69.6	19.4	90.7	99.8
		0.4	Gaussian	*4.9*	*5.4*	*4.9*	*5.2*	*5.4*	*5.1*	–	*4.7*	*5.9*	*5.1*	*5.2*
			Student ($\nu = 6$)	**100**	99.8	16.9	71.5	12.2	10.6	–	21.4	32.0	**100**	13.7
			Clayton	78.0	52.6	**100**	99.8	**100**	**100**	–	99.2	81.5	**100**	**100**
			Gumbel	**100**	98.7	**100**	33.9	**100**	**100**	–	**100**	94.7	**100**	**100**
			Frank	99.5	99.5	**100**	1.9	99.8	95.6	–	97.3	37.7	**100**	**100**

Note: Values in italics are nominal levels and should correspond to the size of 5%. Values in bold indicate the best performing approach.

Table B. Percentage of rejections (at 5% significance level) of the Student copula:

d	n	τ	True copula	$\mathcal{A}_1^{(a)}$	$\mathcal{A}_1^{(b)}$	$\mathcal{A}_2$	$\mathcal{A}_3$	$\mathcal{A}_4$	$\mathcal{A}_5$	$\mathcal{A}_6$	$\mathcal{A}_7$	$\mathcal{A}_8$	$\mathcal{A}_9^{(a)}$	$\mathcal{A}_9^{(b)}$
2	100	0.2	Gaussian	**5.7**	5.4	4.9	4.0	5.0	5.2	–	5.6	5.3	5.6	4.8
			Student ($\nu = 6$)	*4.4*	*4.6*	*4.8*	*4.1*	*5.1*	*4.8*	–	*5.1*	*5.0*	*4.6*	*4.8*
			Clayton	4.8	5.3	19.2	11.0	20.1	17.2	–	7.3	6.8	15.4	**21.3**
			Gumbel	4.7	5.1	9.2	4.9	**10.5**	7.0	–	5.9	5.8	7.6	10.1
			Frank	4.9	5.4	6.0	4.4	6.6	**7.1**	–	5.8	5.7	6.5	6.6
		0.4	Gaussian	4.7	5.4	4.9	4.0	5.2	5.4	–	**5.7**	4.9	5.2	4.8
			Student ($\nu = 6$)	*4.1*	*4.5*	*4.2*	*4.4*	*4.8*	*5.1*	–	*4.9*	*4.9*	*4.4*	*4.4*
			Clayton	4.2	4.9	55.0	31.7	53.3	41.1	–	15.4	14.8	39.9	**57.3**

(*Continued*)

Continued.

d	n	τ	True copula	$\mathcal{A}_1^{(a)}$	$\mathcal{A}_1^{(b)}$	$\mathcal{A}_2$	$\mathcal{A}_3$	$\mathcal{A}_4$	$\mathcal{A}_5$	$\mathcal{A}_6$	$\mathcal{A}_7$	$\mathcal{A}_8$	$\mathcal{A}_9^{(a)}$	$\mathcal{A}_9^{(b)}$
			Gumbel	4.4	5.0	17.2	6.1	**18.7**	9.1	–	7.2	7.4	10.5	17.5
			Frank	2.9	3.4	11.8	5.3	**12.5**	10.5	–	7.5	6.3	6.9	11.6
	500	0.2	Gaussian	5.8	5.8	5.1	5.1	5.0	5.6	–	5.8	5.5	**6.0**	5.3
			Student ($\nu = 6$)	*5.1*	*5.1*	*4.5*	*4.5*	*4.5*	*5.3*	–	*5.1*	*5.2*	*4.8*	*4.6*
			Clayton	5.6	4.8	69.9	60.4	72.4	61.3	–	22.0	19.9	65.7	**77.5**
			Gumbel	5.2	5.3	28.6	18.6	30.0	19.7	–	11.0	10.0	23.5	**33.2**
			Frank	5.2	6.3	12.3	8.3	12.7	12.6	–	7.4	7.8	11.6	**13.4**
		0.4	Gaussian	**5.6**	5.2	4.5	5.3	5.0	5.5	–	5.2	4.9	5.4	5.0
			Student ($\nu = 6$)	*4.9*	*4.6*	*5.3*	*4.4*	*4.5*	*4.8*	–	*4.7*	*5.0*	*4.7*	*4.6*
			Clayton	6.4	7.0	99.8	99.6	99.6	97.7	–	74.6	78.4	99.5	**99.9**
			Gumbel	4.5	5.1	61.7	40.0	61.2	34.1	–	22.4	24.1	49.2	**68.3**
			Frank	11.6	5.9	41.2	15.4	40.4	31.7	–	17.2	14.2	36.0	**44.8**

Note: Values in italics are nominal levels and should correspond to the size of 5%. Values in bold indicate the best performing approach.

Table C. Percentage of rejections (at 5% significance level) of the Clayton copula:

d	n	τ	True copula	$\mathcal{A}_1^{(a)}$	$\mathcal{A}_1^{(b)}$	$\mathcal{A}_2$	$\mathcal{A}_3$	$\mathcal{A}_4$	$\mathcal{A}_5$	$\mathcal{A}_6$	$\mathcal{A}_7$	$\mathcal{A}_8$	$\mathcal{A}_9^{(a)}$	$\mathcal{A}_9^{(b)}$
2	100	0.2	Gaussian	7.5	7.3	21.3	6.6	**23.2**	14.5	20.9	7.3	6.9	20.8	22.4
			Student ($\nu = 6$)	8.0	8.5	23.8	8.4	**24.1**	16.3	15.9	7.5	7.0	21.0	23.7
			Clayton	*4.9*	*5.1*	*5.0*	*5.2*	*5.0*	*5.2*	*4.5*	*5.2*	*5.2*	*5.0*	*5.1*
			Gumbel	6.2	9.4	46.7	13.0	**47.3**	32.3	40.4	12.4	11.1	41.2	47.1
			Frank	7.0	6.9	24.6	6.4	27.1	16.3	**30.3**	8.6	7.4	25.1	25.8
		0.4	Gaussian	24.0	26.7	58.9	26.4	58.2	33.7	62.1	16.6	15.3	**66.5**	60.6
			Student ($\nu = 6$)	13.4	19.0	**60.6**	16.0	58.4	35.1	53.6	15.4	13.7	58.2	57.3
			Clayton	*4.4*	*4.8*	*4.8*	*5.4*	*4.9*	*4.9*	*4.8*	*4.7*	*4.8*	*4.6*	*4.8*
			Gumbel	29.7	38.9	91.6	41.2	90.6	70.1	90.2	34.9	31.7	**92.0**	90.2
			Frank	24.1	19.2	64.8	24.2	66.2	35.6	**84.3**	19.3	16.5	77.0	65.6
	500	0.2	Gaussian	20.6	13.3	78.7	44.8	70.2	52.9	**85.9**	24.0	20.5	68.5	75.3
			Student ($\nu = 6$)	26.9	23.3	**82.1**	33.4	73.7	64.8	68.5	26.1	22.2	76.1	77.6
			Clayton	*5.2*	*5.1*	*5.0*	*4.8*	*5.1*	*5.4*	*5.1*	*5.3*	*4.5*	*4.8*	*5.2*
			Gumbel	12.6	23.2	**99.2**	84.9	97.9	94.0	99.0	60.1	52.0	97.2	98.6
			Frank	18.8	9.0	86.6	42.9	82.2	63.4	**97.6**	30.4	22.7	78.3	84.8
		0.4	Gaussian	94.8	85.6	**100**	99.5	99.7	95.5	**100**	77.7	82.3	99.9	99.9
			Student ($\nu = 6$)	65.3	71.4	**99.9**	89.7	99.6	97.3	99.8	74.7	74.9	99.8	99.8
			Clayton	*5.3*	*5.1*	*5.0*	*5.2*	*4.7*	*4.8*	*4.9*	*4.7*	*4.4*	*5.0*	*4.7*
			Gumbel	98.4	97.8	**100**	**100**	**100**	**100**	**100**	99.4	99.5	**100**	**100**
			Frank	97.8	69.9	**100**	99.4	99.9	96.7	**100**	84.6	86.8	**100**	**100**
4	100	0.2	Gaussian	10.8	10.6	37.4	3.2	38.5	39.1	**49.8**	10.6	6.5	49.2	37.9
			Student ($\nu = 6$)	27.1	21.3	48.4	17.8	37.7	42.2	37.7	10.1	7.3	**57.2**	42.5
			Clayton	*4.7*	*5.1*	*5.3*	*5.6*	*5.2*	*5.1*	*4.6*	*6.3*	*4.7*	*5.0*	*5.2*
			Gumbel	8.8	12.0	64.4	3.0	91.1	**94.1**	81.5	31.9	14.0	88.4	88.6
			Frank	7.7	6.5	36.0	1.4	**74.7**	68.9	73.0	15.1	7.2	72.8	68.8

(Continued)

Continued.

d	n	τ	True copula	$\mathcal{A}_1^{(a)}$	$\mathcal{A}_1^{(b)}$	$\mathcal{A}_2$	$\mathcal{A}_3$	$\mathcal{A}_4$	$\mathcal{A}_5$	$\mathcal{A}_6$	$\mathcal{A}_7$	$\mathcal{A}_8$	$\mathcal{A}_9^{(a)}$	$\mathcal{A}_9^{(b)}$
		0.4	Gaussian	78.3	65.7	89.8	3.0	83.0	73.9	91.6	31.0	16.7	**95.2**	84.3
			Student ($\nu = 6$)	53.9	45.7	**92.9**	6.1	82.6	76.0	86.2	29.9	15.8	92.2	85.6
			Clayton	*5.2*	*4.7*	*5.6*	*5.5*	*5.2*	*5.1*	*4.5*	*5.3*	*4.9*	*5.1*	*5.3*
			Gumbel	79.1	62.1	99.3	4.9	99.8	99.8	99.8	80.8	40.1	**99.9**	99.8
			Frank	68.7	37.9	91.4	3.2	97.0	84.8	**99.6**	52.4	15.1	99.3	96.3
	500	0.2	Gaussian	89.6	38.1	99.4	18.1	97.0	91.2	**99.9**	38.8	23.0	99.4	98.0
			Student ($\nu = 6$)	93.7	76.9	99.9	89.7	95.8	94.5	97.9	44.1	30.8	**100**	98.7
			Clayton	*4.8*	*4.7*	*5.2*	*5.6*	*5.6*	*4.7*	*5.0*	*4.8*	*5.3*	*5.1*	*5.6*
			Gumbel	71.1	37.8	**100**	80.3	**100**	**100**	**100**	97.8	83.4	**100**	**100**
			Frank	82.6	11.8	99.8	14.5	**100**	99.9	**100**	67.9	24.8	**100**	**100**
		0.4	Gaussian	**100**	**100**	**100**	99.7	**100**	99.9	**100**	97.4	95.5	**100**	**100**
			Student ($\nu = 6$)	**100**	99.8	**100**	80.0	**100**	**100**	**100**	96.9	90.1	**100**	**100**
			Clayton	*4.9*	*5.2*	*5.3*	*5.7*	*5.6*	*5.2*	*5.6*	*4.8*	*5.5*	*5.1*	*5.4*
			Gumbel	**100**	**100**	**100**	**100**	**100**	**100**	**100**	**100**	**100**	**100**	**100**
			Frank	**100**	99.0	**100**	99.9	**100**	**100**	**100**	**100**	93.6	**100**	**100**
8	100	0.2	Gaussian	14.3	12.6	29.9	9.9	21.4	53.5	**82.6**	8.1	6.6	74.2	22.3
			Student ($\nu = 6$)	57.8	61.0	44.3	40.9	20.2	54.3	65.9	9.3	8.6	**85.5**	24.4
			Clayton	*5.5*	*5.0*	*5.2*	*5.5*	*5.6*	*5.4*	*4.3*	*4.7*	*5.2*	*5.1*	*5.5*
			Gumbel	7.6	10.5	63.2	52.6	91.9	**100**	98.0	68.7	26.5	97.0	90.8
			Frank	3.2	6.0	16.6	4.2	74.8	96.5	**96.7**	20.4	6.3	93.4	68.9
		0.4	Gaussian	97.5	91.7	96.9	2.5	87.1	89.0	98.2	34.8	10.9	**99.1**	90.2
			Student ($\nu = 6$)	86.3	80.5	**98.4**	29.5	86.1	89.4	96.0	32.4	10.7	97.7	91.4
			Clayton	*5.7*	*5.4*	*4.8*	*5.1*	*4.7*	*4.8*	*4.6*	*5.3*	*5.0*	*4.7*	*4.7*
			Gumbel	93.0	82.2	99.8	19.9	**100**	**100**	**100**	97.3	43.4	**100**	**100**
			Frank	85.2	62.8	93.7	0.6	99.6	97.7	**100**	76.5	8.1	**100**	99.6
	500	0.2	Gaussian	**100**	71.6	**100**	24.9	98.9	97.4	**100**	41.8	17.0	**100**	99.5
			Student ($\nu = 6$)	**100**	**100**	**100**	99.3	96.7	98.1	**100**	50.8	32.0	**100**	99.3
			Clayton	*5.3*	*4.8*	*5.0*	*4.8*	*4.9*	*5.3*	*4.6*	*5.3*	*5.4*	*5.4*	*4.7*
			Gumbel	98.3	40.7	**100**	96.6	**100**	**100**	**100**	**100**	96.8	**100**	**100**
			Frank	99.9	11.0	**100**	3.7	**100**	**100**	**100**	92.8	15.5	**100**	**100**
		0.4	Gaussian	**100**	**100**	**100**	96.1	**100**	**100**	**100**	98.7	84.4	**100**	**100**
			Student ($\nu = 6$)	**100**	**100**	**100**	93.2	**100**	**100**	**100**	98.7	78.1	**100**	**100**
			Clayton	*4.5*	*4.8*	*4.8*	*4.9*	*4.9*	*5.2*	*5.1*	*5.5*	*4.9*	*4.8*	*4.8*
			Gumbel	**100**	**100**	**100**	88.5	**100**	**100**	**100**	**100**	**100**	**100**	**100**
			Frank	**100**	**100**	**100**	69.5	**100**	**100**	**100**	**100**	76.0	**100**	**100**

Note: Values in italics are nominal levels and should correspond to the size of 5%. Values in bold indicate the best performing approach.

Table D. Percentage of rejections (at 5% significance level) of the Gumbel copula:

d	n	τ	True copula	$\mathcal{A}_1^{(a)}$	$\mathcal{A}_1^{(b)}$	$\mathcal{A}_2$	$\mathcal{A}_3$	$\mathcal{A}_4$	$\mathcal{A}_5$	$\mathcal{A}_6$	$\mathcal{A}_7$	$\mathcal{A}_8$	$\mathcal{A}_9^{(a)}$	$\mathcal{A}_9^{(b)}$
2	100	0.2	Gaussian	7.7	6.6	9.9	7.3	9.6	9.6	–	6.4	6.6	**10.2**	9.8
			Student ($\nu = 6$)	7.1	6.2	**11.2**	9.8	9.0	7.6	–	5.9	6.2	8.8	10.4
			Clayton	5.9	6.5	45.8	31.1	44.0	35.1	–	12.3	10.8	33.1	**47.5**

(*Continued*)

Continued.

d	n	τ	True copula	$\mathcal{A}_1^{(a)}$	$\mathcal{A}_1^{(b)}$	$\mathcal{A}_2$	$\mathcal{A}_3$	$\mathcal{A}_4$	$\mathcal{A}_5$	$\mathcal{A}_6$	$\mathcal{A}_7$	$\mathcal{A}_8$	$\mathcal{A}_9^{(a)}$	$\mathcal{A}_9^{(b)}$
			Gumbel	*5.3*	*5.1*	*5.1*	*4.9*	*5.1*	*5.1*	–	*5.1*	*5.3*	*5.1*	*4.9*
			Frank	6.7	5.2	12.1	8.0	11.3	**13.3**	–	7.4	6.8	10.4	11.7
		0.4	Gaussian	11.4	11.2	17.5	8.9	16.4	13.7	–	8.1	7.2	**19.1**	17.6
			Student ($\nu = 6$)	5.8	6.2	**20.2**	15.2	16.1	11.3	–	7.5	6.7	13.9	19.7
			Clayton	8.1	14.0	**92.6**	75.4	89.8	75.3	–	34.7	31.4	83.4	**92.6**
			Gumbel	*4.8*	*4.6*	*4.8*	*5.1*	*4.9*	*4.7*	–	*4.7*	*5.2*	*4.8*	*5.0*
			Frank	8.1	7.1	**28.7**	9.4	24.8	24.3	–	10.3	9.0	20.9	25.7
	500	0.2	Gaussian	19.9	9.8	**37.0**	23.9	29.2	26.9	–	11.7	10.2	31.4	33.1
			Student ($\nu = 6$)	16.6	11.6	**39.1**	33.7	25.2	17.3	–	11.8	10.2	27.7	30.8
			Clayton	8.4	10.3	**99.6**	98.5	98.5	95.9	–	57.5	51.5	97.1	99.3
			Gumbel	*4.7*	*4.6*	*5.1*	*4.8*	*4.6*	*5.1*	–	*5.0*	*4.6*	*4.6*	*4.6*
			Frank	16.0	7.4	**53.9**	30.7	38.5	42.6	–	16.2	12.7	37.1	44.3
		0.4	Gaussian	49.9	32.4	**74.1**	38.4	61.6	46.8	–	25.4	28.9	73.8	67.7
			Student ($\nu = 6$)	9.0	10.8	**74.1**	56.7	57.3	36.0	–	20.9	21.1	53.0	68.4
			Clayton	43.6	57.8	**100**	**100**	**100**	**100**	–	99.3	99.6	**100**	**100**
			Gumbel	*5.4*	*4.9*	*5.2*	*5.5*	*5.0*	*5.0*	–	*4.8*	*5.2*	*5.0*	*4.9*
			Frank	45.3	13.8	**95.5**	47.8	85.1	82.2	–	44.4	42.1	86.2	89.2
4	100	0.2	Gaussian	6.8	13.0	54.7	43.4	51.1	24.0	–	14.9	7.5	41.6	**57.3**
			Student ($\nu = 6$)	24.9	24.8	56.8	55.7	52.8	21.1	–	13.0	8.8	58.7	**60.1**
			Clayton	3.4	15.1	89.6	85.4	97.1	82.2	–	29.9	10.1	90.6	**97.2**
			Gumbel	*5.0*	*4.9*	*5.0*	*4.5*	*5.0*	*5.3*	–	*5.0*	*5.6*	*4.8*	*5.0*
			Frank	4.6	5.4	22.2	13.1	29.2	**30.6**	–	12.6	5.5	18.6	30.0
		0.4	Gaussian	29.7	36.6	66.7	44.0	59.9	33.7	–	28.8	9.2	**70.5**	65.0
			Student ($\nu = 6$)	15.1	22.0	68.0	66.1	60.7	30.2	–	26.2	9.9	60.0	**68.9**
			Clayton	26.8	29.9	99.9	99.1	**100**	98.8	–	82.4	32.8	99.8	**100**
			Gumbel	*5.0*	*5.0*	*5.0*	*5.2*	*5.1*	*5.1*	–	*5.0*	*5.4*	*5.5*	*5.0*
			Frank	17.8	9.0	51.4	12.5	54.3	**56.1**	–	26.2	7.3	46.5	53.7
	500	0.2	Gaussian	75.9	59.1	**99.4**	98.5	98.3	96.0	–	68.4	19.5	**99.4**	99.2
			Student ($\nu = 6$)	92.0	88.5	99.1	99.7	97.7	94.5	–	67.4	27.3	**100**	99.2
			Clayton	34.2	64.9	**100**	**100**	**100**	**100**	–	98.1	53.3	**100**	**100**
			Gumbel	*4.7*	*4.8*	*4.8*	*4.6*	*4.7*	*5.0*	–	*4.7*	*4.2*	*4.6*	*4.7*
			Frank	47.7	10.0	86.6	47.5	92.7	**98.1**	–	58.0	9.8	93.2	94.0
		0.4	Gaussian	99.9	98.2	**100**	99.7	99.6	97.6	–	95.9	54.8	**100**	99.9
			Student ($\nu = 6$)	86.1	91.3	**100**	**100**	99.6	97.1	–	93.9	60.2	**100**	**100**
			Clayton	**100**	95.7	**100**	**100**	**100**	**100**	–	**100**	99.8	**100**	**100**
			Gumbel	*4.7*	*5.1*	*4.9*	*5.3*	*5.1*	*4.8*	–	*4.6*	*5.1*	*4.8*	*5.2*
			Frank	99.4	31.8	99.9	58.9	99.8	**100**	–	93.0	23.7	**100**	99.9
8	100	0.2	Gaussian	1.0	30.0	89.8	73.2	87.1	29.9	–	37.6	6.7	50.0	**90.4**
			Student ($\nu = 6$)	52.3	70.3	89.4	76.6	86.2	30.9	–	36.1	8.3	**91.9**	89.9
			Clayton	0.2	29.9	93.6	95.4	**99.8**	81.2	–	53.3	8.6	89.3	99.7
			Gumbel	*5.4*	*5.1*	*4.1*	*4.8*	*4.9*	*4.8*	–	*4.6*	*5.1*	*5.1*	*4.8*
			Frank	0.3	4.3	14.6	10.3	**40.4**	19.4	–	28.4	5.5	3.6	36.8
		0.4	Gaussian	36.8	68.2	**98.1**	72.3	90.2	50.3	–	70.1	6.8	93.7	93.7
			Student ($\nu = 6$)	45.3	65.7	**97.8**	83.8	90.8	51.8	–	65.0	11.7	94.1	94.6
			Clayton	38.5	45.9	**100**	99.6	**100**	99.9	–	98.2	42.0	**100**	**100**
			Gumbel	*5.2*	*5.1*	*5.3*	*5.1*	*5.3*	*5.4*	–	*5.0*	*5.5*	*5.2*	*5.4*
			Frank	16.0	8.7	54.3	9.6	**67.1**	63.5	–	53.4	4.9	42.5	66.2

(Continued)

Continued.

d	n	τ	True copula	$\mathcal{A}_1^{(a)}$	$\mathcal{A}_1^{(b)}$	$\mathcal{A}_2$	$\mathcal{A}_3$	$\mathcal{A}_4$	$\mathcal{A}_5$	$\mathcal{A}_6$	$\mathcal{A}_7$	$\mathcal{A}_8$	$\mathcal{A}_9^{(a)}$	$\mathcal{A}_9^{(b)}$
	500	0.2	Gaussian	99.9	99.1	**100**	**100**	**100**	**100**	–	99.2	14.8	**100**	**100**
			Student ($v=6$)	**100**	**100**	**100**	**100**	**100**	**100**	–	98.9	31.7	**100**	**100**
			Clayton	79.4	98.9	**100**	**100**	**100**	**100**	–	**100**	33.0	**100**	**100**
			Gumbel	*5.1*	*4.9*	*4.1*	*4.8*	*5.1*	*5.2*	–	*4.3*	*4.8*	*5.2*	*5.0*
			Frank	78.6	18.6	90.1	36.7	99.9	**100**	–	93.7	7.0	99.2	99.9
		0.4	Gaussian	**100**	**100**	**100**	**100**	**100**	**100**	–	**100**	37.5	**100**	**100**
			Student ($v=6$)	**100**	**100**	**100**	**100**	**100**	**100**	–	**100**	67.5	**100**	**100**
			Clayton	**100**	99.9	**100**	**100**	**100**	**100**	–	**100**	99.7	**100**	**100**
			Gumbel	*5.3*	*4.9*	*5.1*	*5.3*	*5.2*	*5.4*	–	*4.9*	*5.0*	*5.2*	*5.1*
			Frank	**100**	48.8	**100**	35.6	**100**	**100**	–	99.8	9.5	**100**	**100**

Note: Values in italics are nominal levels and should correspond to the size of 5%. Values in bold indicate the best performing approach.

Table E. Percentage of rejections (at 5% significance level) of the Frank copula:

d	n	τ	True copula	$\mathcal{A}_1^{(a)}$	$\mathcal{A}_1^{(b)}$	$\mathcal{A}_2$	$\mathcal{A}_3$	$\mathcal{A}_4$	$\mathcal{A}_5$	$\mathcal{A}_6$	$\mathcal{A}_7$	$\mathcal{A}_8$	$\mathcal{A}_9^{(a)}$	$\mathcal{A}_9^{(b)}$
2	100	0.2	Gaussian	5.8	5.5	6.0	**7.5**	6.9	6.6	–	4.9	5.1	6.2	7.4
			Student ($v=6$)	10.6	8.4	8.8	9.9	8.9	7.9	–	6.0	5.7	**11.9**	10.1
			Clayton	5.1	5.3	24.4	21.3	26.2	18.5	–	7.9	7.4	17.4	**29.4**
			Gumbel	5.2	6.0	13.5	8.8	14.2	11.4	–	6.3	6.3	10.0	**14.9**
			Frank	*5.8*	*5.6*	*5.5*	*7.3*	*5.6*	*5.4*	–	*5.4*	*4.8*	*5.7*	*5.9*
		0.4	Gaussian	12.2	9.1	9.4	9.2	9.5	6.8	–	5.6	6.5	**13.1**	10.7
			Student ($v=6$)	8.2	6.4	13.7	10.4	13.3	9.4	–	6.2	7.1	12.0	**14.7**
			Clayton	6.8	5.2	65.4	47.5	62.4	34.6	–	15.9	16.9	46.6	**68.2**
			Gumbel	6.5	6.0	**29.1**	9.6	26.0	15.7	–	8.4	9.1	18.0	26.6
			Frank	*5.9*	*4.8*	*4.9*	*6.3*	*5.2*	*4.7*	–	*4.1*	*5.1*	*5.3*	*5.3*
	500	0.2	Gaussian	7.6	6.7	11.2	**15.3**	10.3	10.3	–	6.7	7.3	10.3	11.8
			Student ($v=6$)	47.8	26.9	28.0	20.5	26.5	25.2	–	12.4	13.4	**48.0**	29.2
			Clayton	7.6	7.1	87.7	81.0	84.2	66.4	–	27.5	27.5	74.3	**87.8**
			Gumbel	11.4	10.3	**55.6**	31.9	44.5	41.8	–	15.1	15.9	41.1	49.2
			Frank	*5.5*	*4.9*	*4.5*	*7.2*	*5.4*	*5.1*	–	*4.6*	*5.4*	*4.9*	*5.5*
		0.4	Gaussian	30.3	23.1	42.5	35.1	32.7	23.2	–	14.0	14.9	**47.5**	42.2
			Student ($v=6$)	20.9	14.5	**68.5**	28.6	57.1	46.2	–	22.3	21.5	58.9	63.8
			Clayton	11.9	9.5	**100**	99.9	**100**	97.6	–	83.9	85.2	99.9	**100**
			Gumbel	9.9	12.2	**95.2**	47.5	85.8	77.3	–	41.7	41.2	81.2	89.9
			Frank	*6.0*	*4.8*	*4.2*	*6.4*	*4.7*	*4.0*	–	*4.6*	*5.0*	*4.9*	*5.0*
4	100	0.2	Gaussian	4.8	9.3	27.6	27.0	24.8	10.3	–	6.9	6.9	18.2	**29.8**
			Student ($v=6$)	44.0	25.9	40.0	41.1	36.8	20.3	–	8.2	7.7	**59.2**	44.5
			Clayton	6.5	8.5	68.0	75.0	87.1	41.9	–	13.2	8.5	71.9	**88.4**
			Gumbel	10.2	5.3	19.6	3.9	33.8	**50.5**	–	11.2	7.2	27.3	31.1
			Frank	*5.5*	*5.3*	*4.5*	*4.9*	*4.8*	*4.7*	–	*5.2*	*5.1*	*5.2*	*4.8*

(*Continued*)

Continued.

d	n	τ	True copula	$\mathcal{A}_1^{(a)}$	$\mathcal{A}_1^{(b)}$	$\mathcal{A}_2$	$\mathcal{A}_3$	$\mathcal{A}_4$	$\mathcal{A}_5$	$\mathcal{A}_6$	$\mathcal{A}_7$	$\mathcal{A}_8$	$\mathcal{A}_9^{(a)}$	$\mathcal{A}_9^{(b)}$
		0.4	Gaussian	14.1	29.4	30.1	33.1	31.3	18.4	–	10.8	7.6	**43.9**	37.3
			Student ($\nu = 6$)	18.5	16.7	47.4	53.0	43.3	29.2	–	13.0	9.3	49.8	**53.6**
			Clayton	4.5	9.8	95.5	97.5	98.0	62.1	–	47.1	19.4	93.8	**98.8**
			Gumbel	9.7	5.1	58.0	7.2	54.7	**65.3**	–	21.3	9.1	44.0	56.6
			Frank	*5.6*	*4.8*	*5.4*	*5.4*	*5.3*	*5.7*	–	*5.2*	*4.6*	*5.4*	*5.5*
	500	0.2	Gaussian	13.4	38.1	**86.1**	79.1	66.0	57.7	–	19.8	15.9	77.3	76.2
			Student ($\nu = 6$)	99.0	90.2	97.4	95.7	88.3	88.7	–	34.3	27.9	**99.9**	95.2
			Clayton	11.2	31.1	**100**	**100**	**100**	99.7	–	66.7	37.3	**100**	**100**
			Gumbel	26.6	7.8	84.7	22.0	91.9	**97.5**	–	56.8	25.5	91.2	92.5
			Frank	*5.6*	*5.4*	*5.1*	*4.9*	*4.4*	*5.6*	–	*4.9*	*5.0*	*5.8*	*4.5*
		0.4	Gaussian	78.9	93.7	98.3	95.3	90.9	74.2	–	58.9	40.3	**99.9**	95.7
			Student ($\nu = 6$)	72.0	78.8	99.9	99.6	98.6	95.8	–	72.2	52.2	**100**	99.6
			Clayton	8.0	36.9	**100**	**100**	**100**	**100**	–	99.9	96.5	**100**	**100**
			Gumbel	35.0	6.9	**99.9**	51.9	99.7	**99.9**	–	91.5	54.4	99.7	99.8
			Frank	*4.9*	*5.1*	*5.3*	*6.0*	*5.0*	*5.1*	–	*5.7*	*4.8*	*5.0*	*5.3*
8	100	0.2	Gaussian	1.0	20.5	**81.2**	68.2	60.8	12.5	–	11.2	6.3	26.9	72.6
			Student ($\nu = 6$)	75.6	68.9	84.6	73.1	69.2	27.1	–	12.6	7.9	**94.3**	79.5
			Clayton	2.6	15.5	83.6	94.6	**97.7**	36.5	–	22.7	8.6	79.5	97.4
			Gumbel	20.3	5.0	35.7	22.2	63.2	**87.7**	–	39.8	7.8	43.7	60.4
			Frank	*4.5*	*5.1*	*4.7*	*5.2*	*4.8*	*4.8*	–	*5.5*	*5.1*	*4.9*	*4.8*
		0.4	Gaussian	11.7	62.0	**93.6**	81.4	60.1	24.2	–	25.7	8.2	78.1	73.4
			Student ($\nu = 6$)	47.8	55.9	**95.2**	91.3	74.1	38.4	–	28.3	10.8	90.9	86.2
			Clayton	1.3	18.1	98.7	99.8	**99.9**	69.4	–	81.0	39.4	98.5	**99.9**
			Gumbel	26.5	7.9	72.8	29.5	74.7	**93.7**	–	50.3	11.0	67.6	77.0
			Frank	*5.0*	*4.8*	*4.6*	*5.2*	*5.1*	*5.5*	–	*4.7*	*4.4*	*4.9*	*5.0*
	500	0.2	Gaussian	47.7	94.1	**100**	**100**	99.8	99.0	–	66.6	15.1	**100**	**100**
			Student ($\nu = 6$)	**100**	**100**	**100**	**100**	**100**	**100**	–	77.4	32.3	**100**	**100**
			Clayton	6.3	82.8	**100**	**100**	**100**	**100**	–	93.7	35.8	**100**	**100**
			Gumbel	71.4	6.0	95.9	74.3	**100**	**100**	–	98.5	34.1	98.9	**100**
			Frank	*4.5*	*4.8*	*4.3*	*5.1*	*5.2*	*5.3*	–	*5.6*	*5.3*	*5.5*	*5.1*
		0.4	Gaussian	**100**	**100**	**100**	**100**	99.9	93.1	–	97.6	37.9	**100**	**100**
			Student ($\nu = 6$)	**100**	**100**	**100**	**100**	**100**	99.7	–	98.6	61.5	**100**	**100**
			Clayton	8.3	83.7	**100**	**100**	**100**	**100**	–	**100**	99.6	**100**	**100**
			Gumbel	93.3	16.3	**100**	95.1	**100**	**100**	–	99.9	62.5	**100**	**100**
			Frank	*5.0*	*4.6*	*4.7*	*4.9*	*4.6*	*4.2*	–	*5.3*	*4.7*	*4.4*	*4.6*

Note: Values in italics are nominal levels and should correspond to the size of 5%. Values in bold indicate the best performing approach.

Asymmetric dependence patterns in financial time series

Manuel Ammann and Stephan Süss

Swiss Institute of Banking and Finance, University of St. Gallen, Rosenbergstrasse 52, CH-9000 St. Gallen, Switzerland

This article proposes a new copula-based approach to test for asymmetries in the dependence structure of financial time series. Simply splitting observations into subsamples and comparing conditional correlations lead to spurious results due to the well-known conditioning bias. Our suggested framework is able to circumvent these problems. Applying our test to market data, we statistically confirm the widespread notion of significant asymmetric dependence structures between daily changes of the VIX, VXN, VDAXnew, and VSTOXX volatility indices and their corresponding equity index returns. A maximum likelihood method is used to perform a likelihood ratio test between the ordinary t-copula and its asymmetric extension. To the best of our knowledge, our study is the first empirical implementation of the skewed t-copula to generate meta-skewed Student's t-distributions. Its asymmetry leads to significant improvements in the description of the dependence structure between equity returns and implied volatility changes.

1. Introduction

This study uses the copula theory to construct a likelihood ratio-based test for asymmetric dependence structures. As an application, we confirm the well-known empirical property of rising dependence between daily changes of implied volatility and equity market returns during periods of financial market turmoil. This is shown for Chicago Board Options Exchange's implied volatility index VIX, the VXN, Germany's VDAXnew, and the VSTOXX and daily returns of their corresponding equity indices. The dynamics of option implied volatility has been widely studied (see e.g. Fleming, Ostdiek, and Whaley 1995; Moraux, Navatte, and Villa 1998; Whaley 2000; Blair, Poon, and Taylor 2001; Simon 2003; Corrado and Miller 2005). One of the main findings is that in periods of heightened equity market volatility, correlations between returns and implied volatility changes increase in magnitude. The usually applied approach to test for unstable correlations is to condition the estimated correlation coefficient on ex post realizations of equity market returns. An implementation of this research design comprises several drawbacks, however. First, Boyer, Gibson, and Loretan (1999), Longin and Solnik (2001), Forbes and Rigobon (2002), as well as Ang and Chen (2002) note that conditional correlation is highly nonlinear in the volatility of the returns on which it is conditioned. This finding became known as the 'conditioning bias' For illustration purposes, consider the simple introductory example of Boyer, Gibson, and Loretan (1999): let x and y be two normally distributed univariate random variables with means μ_x and μ_y, respectively, standard deviations of σ_x and σ_y, and a correlation coefficient of ρ_{xy} ($= \sigma_{xy}/\sigma_x\sigma_y$).

Using a Cholesky decomposition, these can be written as

$$x = \mu_x + \sigma_x u,$$
$$y = \mu_y + \rho_{xy}\sigma_y u + \sqrt{1 - \rho_{xy}}\sigma_y v,$$
(1)

where $u, v \sim N(0, 1)$. Now consider an event $x \in \mathcal{A}$ for any $\mathcal{A} \subset \mathbb{R}$ with $0 < \text{Prob}(\mathcal{A}) < 1$. The conditional correlation coefficient is now calculated as

$$\rho_{\mathcal{A}} = \frac{\text{Cov}(x, y \mid x \in \mathcal{A})}{\sqrt{\text{Var}(x \mid x \in \mathcal{A})}\sqrt{\text{Var}(y \mid x \in \mathcal{A})}}.$$
(2)

Inserting Equation (1) and rearranging leads to

$$\rho_{\mathcal{A}} = \rho_{xy}\left[\rho_{xy}^2 + (1 - \rho_{xy}^2)\frac{\sigma_x^2}{\text{Var}(x \mid x \in \mathcal{A})}\right]^{-1/2}.$$
(3)

As such, simply splitting samples of ex post return realizations can yield misleading results, due to the dependence of $\rho_{\mathcal{A}}$ on $\text{Var}(x \mid x \in \mathcal{A})$.

Second, the empirical estimation of the conditional correlations causes serious biases. Its results are severely dependent upon the point of the sample split. With the cut-off frontier moving further into the tails of the distribution, fewer observations are included in the estimation and the weight of single outliers might distort the estimation. Conversely, moving the cut-off frontier toward the core of the distribution sharply increases the observation number. Yet, the correlation coefficient is now dominated by the bulk of the observations in the center and is unable to capture the behavior of the dependence pattern in the tails.

Finally, it is a well-known fact that empirical distributions of financial market variables such as equity returns or interest rates typically exhibit strong non-Gaussian features. They are usually leptokurtic and skewed with one heavy and one Gaussian-like tail.[1] Using correlation coefficients to measure dependence is only appropriate when the joint distribution of the time series is multivariate normal and therefore cannot properly account for these patterns.[2] Several authors have proposed methods to circumvent these problems.[3] Ang and Bekaert (2002), for example, implement an asymmetric generalized autoregressive heteroscedasticity (GARCH) model with time-varying volatilities and constant correlation. They conclude that these specifications cannot properly account for the asymmetry in the dependence structure. Longin and Solnik (2001) use multivariate extreme value theory. Ang and Bekaert (2002) and Das and Uppal (2004) implement regime-switching models for modeling time-varying dependence patterns in the time series. All of these studies reject symmetric correlation patterns in equity return time series.

The first contribution of this article is a formal test for asymmetric dependence patterns in multivariate distributions. As copulas isolate the dependence pattern from the marginal distributions, we are able to alleviate the biases deriving from the conditioning of observations. An attractive feature of our methodology is that it is not specific to any model of the marginal time series processes and therefore to the marginal distributions. The idea is simple: we fit a skewed t-copula by pseudo-maximum likelihood independently of the univariate marginal time series models.[4] Setting all its skewness parameters equal to zero results in the ordinary t-copula as a special case. A pseudo-likelihood ratio test between the skewed t-copula and its symmetric counterpart therefore provides a simple tool to test for asymmetric dependence structures.

The specification of the skewed Student's t-distribution we apply in our framework is mentioned by Prause (1999), Barndorff-Nielsen and Shephard (2001), Jones and Faddy (2003), and Mencía and Sentana (2004). Little, however, is known about its behavior in practical situations. Aas and Haff (2006) and Hu (2006) outline its first empirical implementations for risk management applications. Demarta and McNeil (2005) derive its copula. To the best of our knowledge, our study constitutes the first implementation of its copula to generate meta-skewed Student's t-distributions. The estimation procedure is based on an augmented version of the expectation maximization (EM) algorithm outlined in Demarta and McNeil (2005) and McNeil, Frey, and Embrechts (2005).

The empirical contribution of this article is to apply our framework to test for asymmetric dependence patterns in the dynamics between the VIX, VXN, VDAXnew, and VSTOXX implied volatility changes and the returns of their corresponding equity indices. Our concept is related to GARCH type models with asymmetric conditional volatility distributions. These specifications have become popular in the literature during the past decade. The connection to our setting can intuitively be seen in Equation (3). Introducing skewness increases the conditional variance in the tails. This in turn leads to higher absolute conditional correlation values. The main disadvantage of these settings is the close connection between the shape of the univariate distributions and the dependence structure. Using copula theory, we are able to separate the variance distribution from the dependence structure.

Our findings strongly confirm the general impression of rising negative dependence between both time series during equity market turmoils.

The article is organized as follows: Section 2 outlines the construction principle of our test for asymmetric dependence structures. The subsequent Section 3 provides an empirical implementation to test for rising dependence between daily S&P 500 equity returns and VIX level changes. Section 4 concludes. The EM algorithm to estimate parameters of the skewed t-copula is illustrated in the appendix.

2. A model to test for asymmetric conditional dependence

This section develops a copula-based framework to test for asymmetry in the dependence structure between two random variables. For excellent introductions into this topic, we recommend Joe (1997), Nelsen (1999), and Embrechts, McNeil, and Straumann (2002).

Our suggested setting is similar to the bivariate GARCH models of Patton (2006), Jondeau and Rockinger (2006), and Hu (2006). It is most related to that of Fortin and Kusmics (2002), who found comovements of extreme stock return pairs.

We fit parametric copula families using a two-stage procedure, as proposed in Oakes (1994), Genest, Ghoudi, and Rivest (1995), and Shih and Louis (1995). This approach comprises the transformation of univariate time series into uniformly distributed vectors. Then, the dependence parameters are estimated by the maximization of a pseudo-log-likelihood function.

The general idea of the test does not depend on a specific model for the univariate marginal processes. For ease of exposition, we estimate auto-regressive GARCH(1, 1) models for the time series of equity index returns and volatility index level changes. Consider a d-dimensional time series sample of length T. Specify for each univariate time series $j \in \{1, \ldots, d\}$ the model

$$x_{j,t} = \alpha_j + \sum_{k=1}^{K_j} \phi_{j,k} x_{j,t-k} + \sigma_{j,t} \tilde{\varepsilon}_{j,t}$$

$$\sigma_{j,t}^2 = \omega_j + \beta_j \varepsilon_{j,t-1}^2 + \gamma_j \sigma_{j,t-1}^2, \tag{4}$$

where $\tilde{\varepsilon}_{j,t}$ follows an iid Student's t-distribution with ν_j degrees of freedom, i.e. $\varepsilon \sim t_{\nu_j}(0, 1)$. K_j is determined by optimizing the Bayesian information criterion. Using the probability integral transform, we can infer for the jth marginal distribution $\hat{u}_{j,t} = \hat{F}^t_{\nu_j}(x_{j,t})$, where F^t_ν denotes the univariate t-distribution with ν degrees of freedom. Assuming $\hat{u}_j$ to be iid, we can form the vectors $\hat{\mathbf{u}}_t = (\hat{F}_{t,1}, \ldots, \hat{F}_{t,d})'$, $\forall t = 1, \ldots, T$ and estimate the considered copula parameters by maximizing the pseudo-log-likelihood function

$$\ln \mathscr{L} = \sum_{t=1}^{T} \ln c(\hat{\mathbf{u}}_1, \ldots, \hat{\mathbf{u}}_d, \theta), \tag{5}$$

where $c(\hat{\mathbf{u}}_1, \ldots, \hat{\mathbf{u}}_d) = \partial C^d(\hat{\mathbf{u}}_1, \ldots, \hat{\mathbf{u}}_d)/\partial \hat{\mathbf{u}}_1 \cdots \partial \hat{\mathbf{u}}_d$ denotes the copula density and θ the collection of parameters required to determine the dependence structure.

As already mentioned, our study applies the Student's t and the skewed t-copula. For a brief outline of both dependence patterns, we consider their mixture representations.

$\mathbf{X} = (t_\nu^{-1}(u_1), \ldots, t_\nu^{-1}(u_d))'$ is said to follow a t-distribution with ν degrees of freedom, if

$$\mathbf{X} \sim \mu + \sqrt{W}\mathbf{Z}, \tag{6}$$

where $\mathbf{Z} \sim N(\mathbf{0}, \boldsymbol{\Sigma})$ and W is independent of $\mathbf{Z}$, satisfying $\nu/W \sim \chi^2_\nu$. The d-dimensional t-distribution can be written as

$$F^t_{\nu, \boldsymbol{\Sigma}}(x_1, \ldots, x_d)$$
$$= \int_{-\infty}^{x_1} \cdots \int_{-\infty}^{x_d} \frac{\Gamma((\nu + d)/2)}{\Gamma(\nu/2)\sqrt{(\pi\nu)^d|\boldsymbol{\Sigma}|}} \left(1 + \frac{(\mathbf{X} - \mu)'\boldsymbol{\Sigma}^{-1}(\mathbf{X} - \mu)}{\nu}\right)^{-(\nu+d)/2} dx_1 \ldots dx_d,$$

where Γ denotes Euler's gamma function.

A random vector $\mathbf{X}$ has a skewed t-distribution if

$$\mathbf{X} \sim \mu + \gamma W + \sqrt{W}\mathbf{Z}, \tag{7}$$

where $\mathbf{Z} \sim N(\mathbf{0}, \boldsymbol{\Sigma})$ and W has the inverse gamma distribution $I(\nu/2, \ldots, \nu/2)$. The corresponding distribution function can be written as

$$F^t_{\nu, \boldsymbol{\Sigma}, \gamma}(x_1, \ldots, x_d) = \int_{-\infty}^{x_1} \cdots \int_{-\infty}^{x_d} f^t_{\nu, \boldsymbol{\Sigma}, \gamma}(\mathbf{X})dx_1 \ldots dx_d, \tag{8}$$

where

$$f^t_{\nu, \boldsymbol{\Sigma}, \gamma}(\mathbf{X}) = c\frac{K_{(\nu+d)/2}\left(\sqrt{(\nu + (\mathbf{X} - \mu)'\boldsymbol{\Sigma}^{-1}(\mathbf{X} - \mu))\gamma'\boldsymbol{\Sigma}^{-1}\gamma}\right)\exp((\mathbf{X} - \mu)'\boldsymbol{\Sigma}^{-1}\gamma)}{\left(\sqrt{(\nu + (\mathbf{X} - \mu)'\boldsymbol{\Sigma}^{-1}(\mathbf{X} - \mu))\gamma'\boldsymbol{\Sigma}^{-1}\gamma}\right)^{-(\nu+d)/2}\left(1 + \frac{(\mathbf{X}-\mu)'\boldsymbol{\Sigma}^{-1}(\mathbf{X}-\mu)}{\nu}\right)^{(\nu+d)/d}}. \tag{9}$$

K_λ denotes the modified Bessel function of the third kind. The normalizing constant c is defined as

$$c = \frac{2^{(2-(\nu+d))/2}}{\Gamma(\nu/2)(\pi\nu)^{d/2}|\boldsymbol{\Sigma}|^{1/2}}.$$

Due to the strict monotonicity of the (skewed) t-distribution, we can infer the d-dimensional copula function applying Sklar's theorem by

$$C_{\nu,\Sigma,(\gamma)}^{t}(\hat{u}_{1,t},\ldots,\hat{u}_{d,t}) = F_{\nu,\Sigma,(\gamma)}^{t}\left(\left(\hat{F}_{\nu}^{t}(\hat{u}_{1,t})\right)^{-1},\ldots,\left(\hat{F}_{\nu}^{t}(\hat{u}_{d,t})\right)^{-1}\right), \qquad (10)$$

where $(\hat{F}_{\nu}^{t}(\hat{u}_{j,t}))^{-1}$ denotes the inverse Student's t-distribution function. Note that Equation (8) nests the Student's t dependence structure as $\gamma \to \mathbf{0}$. The Gaussian case is obtained by additionally letting $\nu \to \infty$.

With this setting we can control for tail dependence by altering the degrees of freedom. Furthermore, we are able to account for asymmetries in the dependence structure by varying the skewness vector γ. A simple 'pseudo-likelihood ratio test' between the ordinary t-copula and its generalization is able to test for the significance of these asymmetries.

3. The asymmetric dependence structure between volatility index level changes and equity index returns

There has been a large amount of empirical research investigating the rising return dependence of different equity markets during periods of financial market turmoil. This section highlights a comparable, yet negative, relationship between volatility indices and their 'underlying' equity indices, which was first mentioned by Whaley (2000).

3.1 *Data*

Data for this study are distributed over several time periods and equity markets. Our observations of daily VIX closing levels and returns of its corresponding S&P 500 index spread from 2 January 1990 to 29 September 2007. Although the dissemination of the new VIX calculation took place on 22 September 2003 daily historical values are available since the beginning of 1990.[5] After the exclusion of non-trading days, our sample contains a total of 4475 closing index values for both time series.

The high success of the VIX as an accepted measure of implied market volatility led to the introduction of several different volatility indices. On 2 February 2001, CBOE additionally launched VXN, tracking implied volatility figures of Nasdaq 100 equity index options. Consideration of the entire history of daily closing levels and Nasdaq 100 returns leads to sample lengths of 1672 observations each.

On 5 December 1994, the German Futures and Options Exchange (DTB) launched VDAX, currently termed VDAXnew after a change in its calculation method. It tracks implied volatility of DAX index options. Our study includes daily observations of DAX and VDAXnew closing levels for the 2 January 1992 to 29 September 2007, period.[6] The exclusion of non-trading days leads to a total of 3983 observations for each time series.

Finally, we investigate the European-implied volatility index VSTOXX that was introduced on 4 January 1999. It tracks the implied volatility levels of DJ Euro STOXX 50 index options. Daily equity index log-returns and closing levels have series lengths of 2233 observations.

Figure 1 illustrates scatter plots of the four samples. The strong negative linear dependence with unconditional correlation coefficients of $\rho(r_{S\&P500}, \Delta VIX) = -0.7374$, $\rho(r_{Nasdaq100}, \Delta VXN) = -0.6063$, $\rho(r_{DAX}, \Delta VDAXnew) = -0.6615$, and $\rho(r_{DJEuroSTOXX50}, \Delta VSTOXX) = -0.7650$ is clearly observable in each graph. This is in line with the results first mentioned by Whaley (1993). High equity returns are typically accompanied by negative changes in volatility index

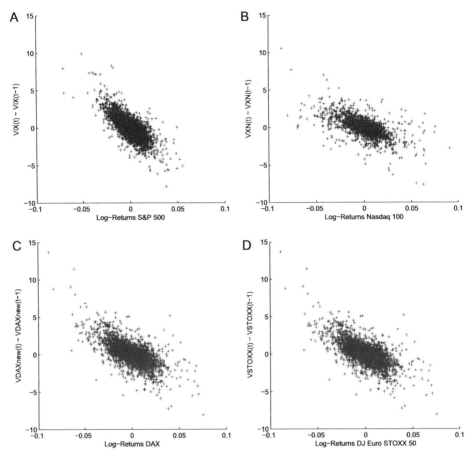

Figure 1. Scatter plot of daily equity index log-returns and changes in the corresponding volatility index levels. (a) A scatter plot of daily VIX index level changes and S&P 500 log-returns for the period from 3 January 1990, until 29 September 2007. After the exclusion of non-trading days, the sample comprises a total of 4474 observations for each time series. (b) The respective plot for the Nasdaq 100/VXN time series. The sample covers the period from 5 February 2001, until 29 September 2007, with a total of 1671 observations. (c) The scatter plot of the DAX/VDAXnew time series combination for the 3 January 1992, to 29 September 2007, period with a total of 3982 data points for each time series after the exclusion of non-trading days. (d) The scatter plot of daily DJ Euro STOXX 50 returns versus the corresponding level changes of the VSTOXX volatility index. Our sample covers the period from 5 January 1999, to 29 September 2007, resulting in 2232 data point combinations.

levels, whereas huge upward spikes of the latter are most likely observable during equity market downturns. The clustering of observations is less tight in the tails than in the core of the distribution. Therefore, calculated correlation coefficients might be distorted, especially due to positive outliers of volatility index level changes.

Daily volatility index closing levels and the corresponding equity log-returns are displayed in Figure 2. In Figure 2a, CBOE's VIX reveals several periods of relatively high levels, usually initiated by a sharp upward spike in connection with large squared S&P 500 log-returns. These include the period of the first Gulf War from mid-1990 until the beginning of 1991, the Asian currency crises in 1997, the period of the Russian restructuring started on August 1998 in combination with

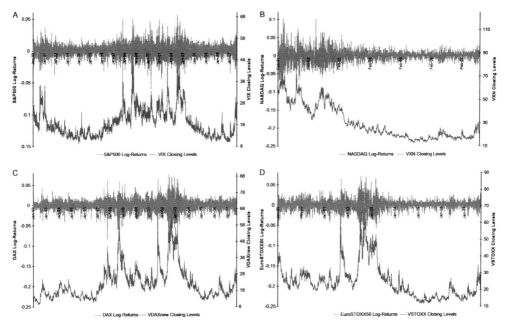

Figure 2. Time series plots of equity index log-returns and the corresponding volatility index levels. (a) Daily VIX index closing levels and the corresponding S&P 500 log-returns for the period from 3 January 1990 until 29 September 2007. The VIX values of the period until the calculation amendment on 23 September 2003, are backfilled. (b) The illustration for the Nasdaq 100 log-return/VXN time series. The sample covers the period from 5 February 2001 until 29 September 2007. (c) The respective plot of the DAX log-return/VDAXnew time series combination for the 3 January 1992, to 29 September 2007, period. (d) The plot of daily DJ Euro STOXX 50 returns and the corresponding levels of the VSTOXX volatility index. The sample covers the period from 5 January 1999 to 29 September 2007.

the restructuring of Long-Term Capital Management shortly thereafter, the successive bursting of the dotcom bubble in 2000–2001, the terrorist attack on 11 September 2001, and the period of the American invasion of Iraq in March 2003. Similar patterns can be seen in the behavior of the other three sample time series. Typically, high market returns are accompanied by negative changes in implied volatility levels, whereas pronounced equity market downturns lead to huge upward spikes in volatility.

Descriptive statistics of all sample time series are given in Table 1. Regarding equity index log-returns, we find mean and median values to be of very small magnitude. Skewness parameters are typically negative, ranging from −0.085 for the DJ Euro STOXX 50 to −0.252 for DAX returns. An exemption from this finding is the positive skewness of 0.105 for Nasdaq 100 returns during our sample period. Jarque–Bera and augmented Dickey–Fuller tests can be rejected for all four time series to a significance level of 1%.

Closing levels of implied volatility indices have averages ranging from 18.933 for VIX levels to 29.695 for VXN levels. The distributions typically have a positive skewness, reflecting the existence of positive outliers that can also be detected in the time series plots of Figure 2. Jarque–Bera tests can be rejected for all four time series to a level of 1%.

Our study uses implied volatility level changes rather than closing index values. It is well known in the literature that implied volatility indices are highly persistent and hence have a low degree of mean reversion.[7] The characteristic polynomial of their processes typically has a root close to unity. Therefore, their processes are frequently referred to be 'near-integrated'.

Table 1. Descriptive statistics of the sample time series.

	Parameters of S&P 500 and VIX			Parameters of Nasdaq 100 and VXN		
	$r_{S\&P500}$	VIX	ΔVIX	$r_{Nasdaq100}$	VXN	ΔVXN
Mean	0.000	18.933	0.000	0.000	29.695	−0.020
Median	0.000	17.620	−0.040	0.001	23.580	−0.070
Standard deviation	0.010	6.404	1.212	0.019	14.661	1.333
Skewness	−0.120	0.990	0.554	0.105	0.857	0.270
Kurtosis	6.868	3.809	9.275	6.315	2.456	8.976
Jarque–Bera	2799.974	853.209	7568.833	768.258	225.297	2507.170
p-value	(0.000)	(0.000)	(0.000)	(0.000)	(0.000)	(0.000)
Augmented D.F. test statistic	−67.409	−4.048	−24.514	−31.377	−2.210	−19.351
p-value	(0.000)	(0.001)	(0.000)	(0.000)	(0.203)	(0.000)
1% critical value	−3.432	−3.432	−3.432	−3.434	−3.434	−3.434
Number of lags	0	11	10	1	5	5
	Parameters of DAX 30 and VDAX			Parameters of STOXX 50 and VSTOXX		
	r_{DAX}	VDAX	ΔVDAX	$r_{STOXX50}$	VSTOXX	ΔVSTOXX
Mean	0.000	22.353	0.001	0.000	24.433	−0.004
Median	0.001	19.900	−0.060	0.000	22.790	−0.075
Standard deviation	0.014	9.609	1.271	0.014	9.766	1.481
Skewness	−0.252	1.521	0.887	−0.085	1.314	1.304
Kurtosis	6.613	5.244	12.964	5.845	4.630	19.909
Jarque–Bera	2208.209	2371.060	16994,600	755.617	889.881	27221.710
p-value	(0.000)	(0.000)	(0.000)	(0.000)	(0.000)	(0.000)
Augmented DF test statistic	−63.731	−3.753	−49.631	−48.324	−3.235	−36.783
p-value	(0.000)	(0.004)	(0.000)	(0.000)	(0.018)	(0.000)
1% critical value	−3.432	−3.432	−3.432	−3.433	−3.433	−3.433
Number of lags	0	2	1	0	2	1

Note: This table provides descriptive statistics of the four sample time series pairs S&P 500/VIX, Nasdaq 100/VXN, DAX 30/VDAXnew, and DJ Euro STOXX 50/VSTOXX.
r indicates the time series of log-returns, Δ denotes the time series of first order level differences. All figures are expressed on a daily basis. Augmented Dickey–Fuller test statistics for the presence of unit roots and their respective 1% critical values are given for all time series. The tests are based on the regressions

$$\Delta X_{j,t} = \mu_j + \gamma_j X_{j,t-1} + \sum_{k=1}^{N_j} \psi_j \Delta X_{j,t-k} + \tilde{\varepsilon}_{j,t},$$

where $X_{j,t}$ denotes the time t observation of series j. μ_j, γ_j, and ψ_j are constants and $\tilde{\varepsilon}_{j,t}$ is the error term. The optimum lag lengths N_j of the specifications are determined by the Schwarz information criterion (SIC).

This is confirmed by our sample: Table 1 outlines the statistics of augmented Dickey–Fuller tests for implied volatility index closing levels. Although they can be rejected for the VIX and DAX series to a level of 1%, the statistics are very close to the 1% critical values. The corresponding test for VXN and VSTOXX closing levels cannot be rejected with p-values of 0.203 and 0.018, respectively. Therefore, we use implied volatility level changes for our study rather than closing levels.[8] Descriptive statistics for these time series are also outlined in Table 1. Difference means and medians have values around zero for all the four time series. Daily VXN level changes show the lowest average value of -0.020. This finding can mainly be attributed to the negative index trend during the short sample observation period. This can also be seen in Figure 2. All four series have a positive skewness, ranging between 0.270 for the VXN to 1.304 for the VSTOXX. Jarque–Bera tests for normality and augmented Dickey–Fuller tests for the presence of unit roots can convincingly be rejected for all four time series.

3.2 *Estimating the asymmetry in the dependence pattern*

Before we turn to the implementation of our copula test, we estimate the correlation structure of return exceedances. These are defined with cut-off frontiers ϑ. Subsamples for the calculation of conditional correlations include all observations $\mathbf{X}_\vartheta$ with $r_{\text{Equity Index}}(\mathbf{X}_\vartheta) \in (-\infty, \vartheta]$, $\forall \vartheta \leq 0$ and $r_{\text{Equity Index}}(\mathbf{X}_\vartheta) \in [\vartheta, \infty)$, $\forall \vartheta > 0$, respectively. The estimated values are illustrated in Figure 3.

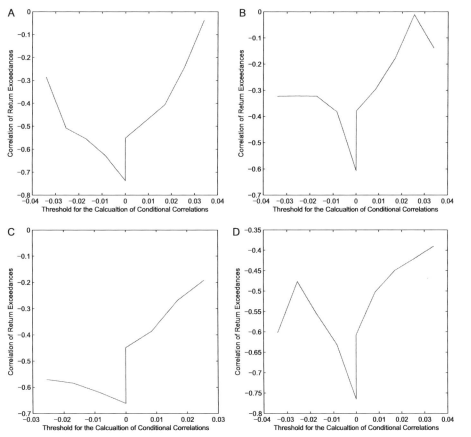

Figure 3. Correlation structure between volatility index level changes and equity index log-return exceedances. This figure illustrates the correlation structure of volatility index level differences and the corresponding log-return exceedances. All calculations are based on subsamples including all observations $\mathbf{X}_\vartheta$ with $r_{\text{Equity Index}}(\mathbf{X}_\vartheta) \in (-\infty, \vartheta]$, $\forall \vartheta \leq 0$ and $r_{\text{Equity Index}}(\mathbf{X}_\vartheta) \in [\vartheta, \infty)$, $\forall \vartheta > 0$, respectively, where r defines the equity index log-return and ϑ the respective threshold level. The correlation structures are shown for the S&P 500/VIX (a), the Nasdaq 100/VXN (b), DAX/VDAXnew (c), and DJ Euro STOXX 50/VSTOXX (d) time series combinations.

Table 2. Parameter estimates for the univariate marginal distributions.

Parameters for daily S&P 500 log-returns and first VIX level differences

$$r_{\text{S\&P500},t} = \underset{(0.000)}{5.63} \times 10^{-4} + \tilde{\varepsilon}_{r_{\text{S\&P500}},t}(\nu_{\tilde{\varepsilon}} = 7.157)$$

$$\sigma^2_{r_{\text{S\&P500}},t} = \underset{(0.005)}{3.74} \times 10^{-7} + \underset{(0.000)}{0.059}\, \varepsilon^2_{r_{\text{S\&P500}},t-1} + \underset{(0.000)}{0.947}\, \sigma^2_{r_{\text{S\&P500}},t-1}$$

$$\Delta\text{VIX}_t = \underset{(0.440)}{-0.002} - \underset{(0.000)}{0.085}\, \Delta\text{VIX}_{t-1} - \underset{(0.000)}{0.098}\, \Delta\text{VIX}_{t-2}$$

$$- \underset{(0.000)}{0.071}\, \Delta\text{VIX}_{t-3} - \underset{(0.000)}{0.067}\, \Delta\text{VIX}_{t-4} + \tilde{\varepsilon}_{\Delta\text{VIX},t}(\nu_{\tilde{\varepsilon}} = 4.762)$$

$$\sigma^2_{\Delta\text{VIX},t} = \underset{(0.000)}{0.025} + \underset{(0.000)}{0.143}\, \varepsilon^2_{\Delta\text{VIX},t-1} + \underset{(0.000)}{0.854}\, \sigma^2_{\Delta\text{VIX},t-1}$$

Parameters for daily Nasdaq 100 log-returns and first VXN level differences

$$r_{\text{Nasdaq100},t} = \underset{(0.041)}{5.07} \times 10^{-4} + \tilde{\varepsilon}_{r_{\text{Nasdaq100}},t}(\nu_{\tilde{\varepsilon}} = 14.389)$$

$$\sigma^2_{r_{\text{Nasdaq100}},t} = \underset{(0.056)}{5.95} \times 10^{-7} + \underset{(0.000)}{0.043}\, \varepsilon^2_{r_{\text{Nasdaq100}},t-1} + \underset{(0.000)}{0.954}\, \sigma^2_{r_{\text{Nasdaq100}},t-1}$$

$$r_{\Delta\text{VXN},t} = \underset{(0.061)}{-0.033} + \tilde{\varepsilon}_{\Delta\text{VXN},t}(\nu_{\tilde{\varepsilon}} = 6.127)$$

$$\sigma^2_{\Delta\text{VXN},t} = \underset{(0.016)}{0.012} + \underset{(0.000)}{0.080}\, \varepsilon^2_{\Delta\text{VXN},t-1} + \underset{(0.000)}{0.916}\, \sigma^2_{\Delta\text{VXN},t-1}$$

Parameters for daily DAX log-returns and first VDAXnew level differences

$$r_{\text{DAX},t} = \underset{(0.303)}{8.09} \times 10^{-5} + \tilde{\varepsilon}_{r_{\text{DAX}},t}(\nu_{\tilde{\varepsilon}} = 7.832)$$

$$\sigma^2_{r_{\text{DAX}},t} = \underset{(0.000)}{1.04} \times 10^{-5} + \underset{(0.000)}{0.317}\, \varepsilon^2_{r_{\text{DAX}},t-1} + \underset{(0.000)}{0.645}\, \sigma^2_{r_{\text{DAX}},t-1}$$

$$\Delta\text{VDAX}_t = \underset{(0.101)}{-0.013} - \underset{(0.000)}{0.065}\, \Delta\text{VDAX}_{t-1} - \underset{(0.000)}{0.054}\, \Delta\text{VDAX}_{t-2}$$

$$- \underset{(0.008)}{0.038}\, \Delta\text{VDAX}_{t-3} + \tilde{\varepsilon}_{\Delta\text{VDAX},t}(\nu_{\tilde{\varepsilon}} = 4.573)$$

$$\sigma^2_{\Delta\text{VDAX},t} = \underset{(0.001)}{7.10} \times 10^{-3} + \underset{(0.000)}{0.106}\, \varepsilon^2_{\Delta\text{VDAX},t-1} + \underset{(0.000)}{0.901}\, \sigma^2_{\Delta\text{VDAX},t-1}$$

Parameters for daily DJ Euro STOXX 50 log-returns and first VSTOXX level differences

$$r_{\text{STOXX50},t} = \underset{(0.004)}{6.06} \times 10^{-4} + \tilde{\varepsilon}_{r_{\text{STOXX50}},t}(\nu_{\tilde{\varepsilon}} = 13.120)$$

$$\sigma^2_{r_{\text{STOXX50}},t} = \underset{(0.001)}{1.23} \times 10^{-6} + \underset{(0.000)}{0.078}\, \varepsilon^2_{r_{\text{STOXX50}},t-1} + \underset{(0.000)}{0.917}\, \sigma^2_{r_{\text{STOXX50}},t-1}$$

$$\Delta\text{VSTOXX}_t = \underset{(0.007)}{-0.045} - \underset{(0.009)}{0.050}\, \Delta\text{VSTOXX}_{t-1} - \underset{(0.001)}{0.064}\, \Delta\text{VSTOXX}_{t-2} + \tilde{\varepsilon}_{\Delta\text{VSTOXX},t}(\nu_{\tilde{\varepsilon}} = 5.013)$$

$$\sigma^2_{\Delta\text{VSTOXX},t} = \underset{(0.012)}{0.018} + \underset{(0.000)}{0.117}\, \varepsilon^2_{\Delta\text{VSTOXX},t-1} + \underset{(0.000)}{0.883}\, \sigma^2_{\Delta\text{VSTOXX},t-1}$$

Note: This table illustrates the parameter estimates of the marginal distributions. All univariate processes j are specified as auto-regressive GARCH(1,1) models that can be written as:

$$x_{j,t} = \alpha_j + \sum_{k=1}^{K_j} \phi_{j,k} x_{j,t-k} + \sigma_{j,t}\tilde{\varepsilon}_{j,t}, \qquad \sigma^2_{j,t} = \omega_j + \beta_j \varepsilon^2_{j,t-1} + \gamma_j \sigma^2_{j,t-1},$$

where $\tilde{\varepsilon}_{j,t}$ follows the law of a Student's t-distribution with ν_j degrees of freedom, i.e. $\varepsilon \sim t_{\nu_j}(0,1)$. K_j is determined by optimizing the Schwarz information criterion (SIC). Corresponding p-values are stated in brackets.

The four time series pairs display very similar patterns. Correlation coefficients are severely dependent upon ϑ. In addition, as can be seen for high absolute equity return values, correlations become more erratic with higher absolute values of ϑ. This is mainly due to outliers distorting calculations. The structure of return exceedance correlations is typically asymmetric. Moving into

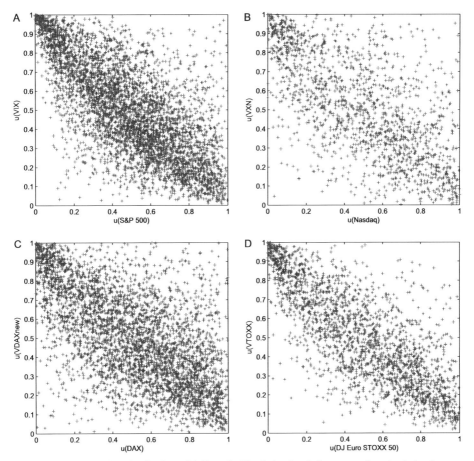

Figure 4. Empirical quantile distribution of daily volatility index level changes and equity index log-returns. This figure illustrates daily empirical quantile distributions of the marginal distribution's innovations mapped into the unit square. Each marginal time series j is modeled as an auto-regressive GARCH(1,1) process, specified as:

$$x_{j,t} = \alpha_j + \sum_{k=1}^{K_j} \phi_{j,k} x_{j,t-k} + \sigma_{j,t} \tilde{\varepsilon}_{j,t}$$

$$\sigma_{j,t}^2 = \omega_j + \beta_j \varepsilon_{j,t-1}^2 + \gamma_j \sigma_{j,t-1}^2,$$

where $\tilde{\varepsilon}_{j,t}$ follows a Student's t-distribution with v_j degrees of freedom. K_j is determined by the minimization of the Schwarz information criterion (SIC) for each time series j. Quantiles are calculated using the probability integral transform. The empirical quantile distributions for the S&P 500/VIX (a), the Nasdaq 100/VXN (b), DAX/VDAXnew (c), and DJ Euro STOXX 50/VSTOXX (d) time series combinations are illustrated.

the distribution tails, ρ_ϑ rises in a steeper manner for positive equity returns. This seems counterintuitive at first sight. The positive skewness of volatility index changes in combination with negative third moments of equity returns should lead to higher conditional variances and therefore to faster reductions of absolute correlation figures for negative values of ϑ. Yet, the behavior of correlation coefficients for negative equity returns can be explained by the existence of positive outliers in volatility changes. They lead to the calculation of distorted and very negative correlation coefficients. Regarding these aspects, one cannot gauge the magnitude of asymmetric dependence patterns by simply comparing empirical conditional correlations.

In order to circumvent these problems, we implement the copula-based test for dependence asymmetries outlined in the previous section. The estimated parameters of the marginal time series models introduced in Equation (4) are provided in Table 2.

Figure 4 illustrates the empirical joint distribution mapped into the unit square by inverting the residuals of Equation (4). The high concentration of concurrent extreme values is clearly observable for all four time series pairs. This is especially true for the upper-left tails.

Tail dependence, although a widespread concept, is an asymptotic quantity. Therefore, we calculate the empirical ratios

$$\frac{\text{Prob}(r_{\text{Equity Index}} \leq u, \Delta\text{Volatility Index} \geq 1 - u)}{u},$$

Table 3. Empirical descriptions of the dependence pattern between the time series of equity index log-returns and daily changes of implied volatility indices.

	Upper-left tail u			Lower-right tail $\bar{u}$		
	0.05	0.1	0.2	0.8	0.9	0.95
$u(r_{\text{S\&P500}})/u(\Delta\text{VIX})$	0.608 (131.25%)	0.577 (136.39%)	0.319 (34.69%)	0.451	0.244	0.138
$u(r_{\text{Nasdaq100}})/u(\Delta\text{VXN})$	0.236 (23.94%)	0.418 (48.09%)	0.566 (21.39%)	0.466	0.282	0.191
$u(r_{\text{DAX}})/u(\Delta\text{VDAXnew})$	0.322 (108.67%)	0.406 (131.30%)	0.486 (39.56%)	0.348	0.176	0.155
$u(r_{\text{STOXX50}})/u(\Delta\text{VSTOXX})$	0.622 (709.36%)	0.527 (139.86%)	0.620 (31.46%)	0.472	0.220	0.077

Note: This table outlines "empirical joint conditional quantile exceedance probabilities" for daily equity index log-return time series and daily implied volatility index level differences. They are defined as:

$$\frac{\text{Prob}(r_{\text{Equity Index}} \leq u, \Delta\text{Volatility Index} \geq 1 - u)}{u},$$

for $u = 0.05, 0.1$, and 0.2. Analogously,

$$\frac{\text{Prob}(r_{\text{Equity Index}} \geq \bar{u}, \Delta\text{Volatility Index} \leq 1 - \bar{u})}{1 - \bar{u}},$$

where $\bar{u} = 0.8, 0.9$, and 0.95. The values in brackets give the magnitude that upper-left tail probabilities outrange their corresponding lower-right tail counterparts. Values are calculated for the S&P 500/VIX, the Nasdaq 100/VXN, the DAX/VDAXnew, and the DJ Euro STOXX 50/VSTOXX time series pairs.

for $u = 0.05$, 0.1, and 0.2. For tackling the dependence structure in the lower-right tail, we analogously determine

$$\frac{\text{Prob}(r_{\text{Equity Index}} \geq \bar{u}, \Delta\text{Volatility Index} \leq 1 - \bar{u})}{1 - \bar{u}},$$

where $\bar{u} = 0.8$, 0.9, and 0.95. These can be interpreted as 'empirical joint conditional quantile exceedance probabilities'.[9] They are outlined in Table 3.

Empirical quantile exceedance probabilities of the upper-left tail are up to 7.1 times higher than their corresponding lower-right values. The magnitudes of the differences are stated in brackets. In order to gauge their significance, we fit the Student's t-copula and its skewed generalization. We then perform a likelihood ratio test between both dependence patterns as outlined in the previous section. Obtained results are presented in Table 4.

The high concentration of observations in the tails, which is also shown in Figure 4, translates into very low degrees of freedom values ranging between 3.06 and 5.59 for the Student's t-copula and between 6.30 and 7.24 for its asymmetric counterpart. ν is slightly lower for the Student's t-copula for all four time series pairs. This might be due to the fact that the dependence structure of the skewed t-distribution is able to capture the high concentration of observations in the upper-left tail by the skewness parameters rather than by lower degrees of freedom. γ is typically negative for equity return time series and positive for volatility index level changes. This results in high dependence values in the upper-left tails of the bivariate distributions. One exemption from this finding is the slightly positive value of 0.008 for the Nasdaq 100 time series. This finding might be attributed to its short sample period that contains only very few abrupt equity market downturns that are

Table 4. Copula parameters and information criteria.

	Student's t-Copula	Skewed t-Copula		Student's t-Copula	Skewed t-Copula
Parameters of S&P 500 returns and VIX level changes			Parameters of Nasdaq 100 returns and VXN level changes		
ν	5.59	6.82	ν	3.06	6.30
$\gamma_{r_{\text{S\&P500}}}$	–	-0.057	$\gamma_{r_{\text{Nasdaq100}}}$	–	0.008
$\gamma_{\Delta\text{VIX}}$	–	0.257	$\gamma_{\Delta\text{VXN}}$	–	0.195
LLH	-10322.52	$-10047.67^{\dagger}$	LLH	-4934.82	$-4282.98^{\dagger}$
AIC	4.62	4.49	AIC	5.91	5.13
BIC	4.64	4.52	BIC	5.96	5.19
Parameters of DAX returns and VDAXnew level changes			Parameters of DJ Euro STOXX 50 returns and VSTOXX level changes		
ν	5.05	6.54	ν	5.53	7.24
$\gamma_{r_{\text{DAX}}}$	–	-0.111	$\gamma_{r_{\text{STOXX50}}}$	–	-0.182
$\gamma_{\Delta\text{VDAX}}$	–	0.271	$\gamma_{\Delta\text{VSTOXX}}$	–	0.354
LLH	-10217.26	$-9835.88^{\dagger}$	LLH	-5283.04	$-5117.44^{\dagger}$
AIC	5.13	4.94	AIC	4.74	4.59
BIC	5.16	4.97	BIC	4.79	4.64

This table illustrates the parameters for the symmetric and the skewed t-copulae. ν specifies the degrees of freedom and γ is the vector of skewness parameters. LLH denotes the respective log-likelihood, AIC, and BIC the information criteria of Akaike and Bayesian. The values are calculated for the S&P 500/VIX, the Nasdaq 100/VXN, the DAX/VDAXnew, as well as the DJ Euro STOXX 50/VSTOXX time series pairs.
† indicates significance of a pseudo-likelihood ratio test between the ordinary t-copula and its skewed generalization at a level of one per cent.

accompanied by positive upward spikes in the corresponding volatility index VXN. (See also the time series plot in Figure 2.) Log-likelihood values are range between -10322.52 ($r_{S\&P500}/\Delta VIX$) and -4934.82 ($r_{Nasdaq100}/\Delta VXN$) for the symmetric setting and between -10047.67 ($r_{S\&P500}/\Delta VIX$) and -4282.98 ($r_{Nasdaq100}/\Delta VXN$) for its generalized framework. Pseudo-likelihood ratio tests can be rejected with a significance level of 1% for all four time series pairs. This is confirmed by the information criteria of Akaike and Schwarz. Both lead to the rejection of the Student's t-copula in favor of its skewed generalization for all four dependence structures.

We conclude that the dependence between equity index log-returns and implied volatility level changes is significantly higher in the case of market downturns.

4. Conclusion

We use the copula theory to test for asymmetric dependence structures between daily changes of the VIX, VXN, VDAXnew, and VSTOXX volatility index changes and their corresponding equity index returns. As a first contribution, we propose a likelihood ratio test that is able to control for both tail dependence and asymmetries in dependence structures. The idea is simple and easy to implement. Conditional on an ordinary auto-regressive GARCH (GARCH) model for the univariate marginal distributions, we fit a skewed t-copula as outlined in Demarta and McNeil (2005). As this dependence structure entails the ordinary t-copula as a special case, a simple likelihood ratio test serves to test for asymmetry in the dependence pattern of the joint distribution.

Applying our framework to empirical data, we find that the negative dependence between daily equity returns and level changes of implied volatility significantly increases during periods of equity market turmoil. To the best of our knowledge, this study is the first empirical implementation of the skewed t-copula to generate meta-skewed t-distributions. Our estimation is based on a slightly modified version of the EM algorithm by Demarta and McNeil (2005). Its application leads to significantly better empirical fits in the description of the dependence pattern between equity returns and implied volatility changes.

Acknowledgements

We thank the participants of the 'Conference on Copulae and Multi-Variate Probability Distributions in Finance' in Warwick, UK, and our anonymous referees for very helpful suggestions and comments.

Notes

1. See, e.g. Aas and Haff (2006).
2. See, e.g. Embrechts, McNeil, and Straumann (2002).
3. See, e.g. Koutmos and Booth (1995), Fortin and Kusmics (2002), and the references therein.
4. The likelihood is called 'pseudo' as it is conditioned on the time series models of the univariate marginal distributions. Genest, Ghoudi, and Rivest (1995) prove the consistency and asymptotic normality of the copula parameter estimators if the data sample is iid. Also see, among others, Demarta and McNeil (2005).
5. Values of the new VIX have been backfilled to 2 January 1990. As its calculation is only based on observable values, it can be determined in an unbiased manner. For its theoretic construction, see e.g. Carr and Madan (1998), Demeterfi et al. (1999), and Britten-Jones and Neuberger (2000).
6. Using a similar calculation method to the VIX, values of the VDAXnew have been backfilled to 2 January 1992.
7. See, e.g. Fleming, Ostdiek, and Whaley (1995), Moraux, Navatte, and Villa (1998), Whaley (2000), Blair, Poon, and Taylor (2001), Corrado and Miller (2005), as well as Simon (2003). This list is by no means exhaustive.
8. A different method would be to use changes in the logarithm of the closing level. This method leads to conclusions that are very similar to our results.
9. See, e.g. Demarta and McNeil (2005).

10. The variable X has the law of an inverse Gamma distribution $Ig(\alpha, \beta)$ if it follows the density function

$$f(x) = \frac{\beta^{\alpha} x^{-\alpha-1} e^{-\beta/x}}{\Gamma(\alpha)},$$

where $x > 0$, $\alpha > 0$, and $\beta > 0$.

11. In the case of the skewed t-copula, the EM algorithm by Demarta and McNeil (2005), ν was also determined by numerically solving

$$-\psi\left(\frac{\nu}{2}\right) + \ln\left(\frac{\nu}{2}\right) + 1 - \overline{\xi}^{[k]} - \overline{\vartheta}^{[k]} = 0.$$

This procedure requires the calculation of

$$\xi_t^{[k]} = \frac{1}{2} \ln\left(\frac{\rho_t^{[k]} + \nu^{[k]}}{\gamma^{[k]\prime} \Sigma^{[k]-1} \gamma^{[k]}}\right) + \frac{\partial K_{-(\nu+d)/2+\alpha}\left(\sqrt{(\rho_t^{[k]} + \nu_t^{[k]})(\gamma^{[k]\prime} \Sigma^{[k]-1} \gamma^{[k]})}\right)/\partial\alpha|_{\alpha=0}}{K_{(\nu+d)/2}\left(\sqrt{(\rho_t^{[k]} + \nu_t^{[k]})(\gamma^{[k]\prime} \Sigma^{[k]-1} \gamma^{[k]})}\right)}$$

and $\overline{\xi}_t^{[k]} = 1/T \sum_{t=1}^{T} \xi_t^{[k]}$, which depend upon the specification of $\partial\alpha$. In order to avoid this dependence, we decide to directly determine ν by a gradient method, although this requires more computational effort.

References

Aas, K., and I. Haff. 2006. The generalized hyperbolic skew student's t-distribution. *The Journal of Financial Econometrics* 4, no. 2: 275–309.

Ang, A., and G. Bekaert. 2002. International asset allocation with regime shifts. *The Review of Financial Studies* 15, no. 4: 1137–87.

Ang, A., and J. Chen. 2002. Asymmetric correlations of equity portfolios. *The Journal of Financial Economics* 63, no. 3: 443–494.

Barndorff-Nielsen, O., and N. Shephard. 2001. Normal modified stable processes. *Theory of Probability and Mathematical Statistics* 65, no. 1: 1–19.

Blair, B., S.-H. Poon, and S. Taylor. 2001. Forecasting S&P 100 volatility: the incremental information content of implied volatility and high-frequency index returns. *The Journal of Econometrics* 105, no. 1: 2–26.

Boyer, B., M. Gibson, and M. Loretan. 1999. Pitfalls in tests for changes in correlations. Board of Governors of the Federal Reserve System: International Finance Discussion Papers, Number 597.

Britten-Jones, M., and A. Neuberger. 2000. Option prices, implied price processes, and stochastic volatility. *The Journal of Finance* 55, no. 2: 839–66.

Carr, P., and D. Madan. 1998. Towards a theory of volatility trading. In Volatility: New estimation techniques for pricing derivatives, ed. R. Jarrow, chap. 29, 417–27. Risk Publications.

Corrado, C., and T. Miller. 2005. The forecast quality of CBOE implied volatility indexes. *The Journal of Futures Markets* 25, no. 4: 339–73.

Das, S., and R. Uppal. 2004. Systemic risk and international portfolio choice. *The Journal of Finance* 59, no. 6: 2809–34.

Demarta, S., and A. McNeil. 2005. The t copula and related copulas. *International Statistical Review* 73, no. 1: 111–29.

Demeterfi, K., E. Derman, M. Kamal, and J. Zou. 1999. A guide to volatility and variance swaps. *The Journal of Derivatives* 6, no. 4: 9–32.

Embrechts, P., A. McNeil, and D. Straumann. 2002. Correlation and dependence in risk management: Properties and pitfalls. In *Risk management: Value at risk and beyond*, 176–223. Cambridge: Cambridge Univ. Press.

Fleming, J., B. Ostdiek, and R. Whaley. 1995. Predicting stock market volatility: A new measure. *The Journal of Futures Markets* 15, 3: 265–302.

Forbes, K., and R. Rigobon. 2002. No contagion, only interdependence: measuring stock market comovements. *The Journal of Finance* 57, no. 5: 2223–61.

Fortin, I., and C. Kusmics. 2002. Tail-dependence in stock return pairs. *The International Journal of Intelligent Systems in Accounting, Finance & Management* 11, no. 2: 89–107.

Genest, C., K. Ghoudi, and L.-P. Rivest. 1995. A semiparametric estimation procedure of dependence parameters in multivariate families of distributions. *Biometrika* 82, no. 3: 543–52.

Hu, L. 2006. Dependence patterns across financial markets: A mixed copula approach. *Applied Financial Economics* 16, no. 10: 717–729.

Hu, W., and A. Kercheval. 2008. The skewed t distribution for portfolio credit risk. *Advances in econometrics* 22: 55–83.

Joe, H. 1997. *Multivariate models and dependence concepts*. London: Chapman & Hall.

Jondeau, E., and M. Rockinger. 2006. The Copula-GARCH model of conditional dependencies: An international stock market application. *The Journal of International Money and Finance* 25, no. 5: 827–853.

Jones, M., and M. Faddy. 2003. A skew extension of the t-distribution, with applications. *The Journal of the Royal Statistical Society: Series B* 65, no. 1: 1–329.

Koutmos, G., and G. Booth. 1995. Asymmetric volatility transmissions in international stock markets. *The Journal of International Money and Finance* 14, no. 6: 747–62.

Longin, F., and B. Solnik. 2001. Extreme correlation of international equity markets. *The Journal of Finance* 56, no. 2: 649–76.

McNeil, A., R. Frey, and P. Embrechts. 2005. *Quantitative risk management: Concepts, techniques and tools*, eds: D. Duffie and S. Schaefer. Princeton Univ. Press.

Mencía, J., and E. Sentana. 2004. Estimation and testing of dynamic models with generalized hyperbolic innovations. Working Paper, CEPR Discussion Paper No. 5177.

Moraux, F., P. Navatte, and C. Villa. 1998. The predictive power of the french market volatility index: A multi horizons study. *The European Finance Review* 2, no. 3: 303–20.

Nelsen, R. 1999. *An introduction to copulas*. Springer Series in Statistics. 2nd ed. New York.

Oakes, D. 1994. Multivariate survival distributions. *The Journal of Nonparametric Statistics* 3, no. 3&4: 343–54.

Patton, A. 2006. Modelling asymmetric exchange rate dependence. *International Economic Review* 47, 2: 527–56.

Prause, K. 1999. The generalized hyperbolic model: estimation, financial derivatives, and risk measures. PhD thesis, Mathematics Faculty, Univ. of Freiburg.

Shih, J., and T. Louis. 1995. Inferences on the association parameter in copula models for bivariate survival data. *Biometrics* 51, no. 4: 1384–99.

Simon, D. 2003. The NASDAQ volatility index during and after the bubble. *The Journal of Derivatives* 11, no. 2: 9–24.

Whaley, R. 1993. Derivatives on market volatility: Hedging tools long overdue. *The Journal of Derivatives* 1, no. 1: 71–84.

Whaley, R. 2000. The investor fear gauge. *The Journal of Portfolio Management* 26, no. 3: 12–17.

Appendix: The EM algorithm for the estimation of the skewed *t*-copula

This section describes the EM algorithm based upon Demarta and McNeil (2005), McNeil, Frey, and Embrechts (2005), and Hu and Kercheval (2008) we apply for the calibration of the skewed *t*-copula model. Our setting differs from the latter two references in two respects. First, the framework by McNeil, Frey, and Embrechts (2005) is specified to estimate a skewed *t*-distribution of **X**. Hu (2006)proposes to directly fit the distribution. In contrast, we explicitly determine the parameter values out of the empirical rank distribution $\hat{F}(\mathbf{u})$ in order to allow for 'meta-skewed *t*-distributions', whose marginals may differ in functional form. Second, in contrast to Demarta and McNeil (2005), the so-called E step of our algorithm comprises a numerical maximization of the conditional log-likelihood by altering ν in order to avoid dependence upon the numerical accuracy of derivative parameters.

Following Demarta and McNeil (2005), we denote $C_{\nu, P, \gamma}^{t}(\mathbf{U} \in [0, 1]^d)$ to be the copula of a *d*-dimensional skewed $t_{\nu, \mathbf{0}}^{d}, P, \gamma(\mathbf{X})$ distribution, with *P* being a correlation matrix. In general, the skewed *t*-distribution can be written as

$$\mathbf{X} = \mu + \gamma W + \sqrt{W}\mathbf{Z}, \tag{A1}$$

where $\gamma \in \mathbb{R}^d \neq \mathbf{0}$, $W \sim Ig(\nu/2, \nu/2)$, and independent $\mathbf{Z} \in \mathbb{R}^d \sim N(\mathbf{0}, \mathbf{\Sigma})$.[10] The resulting density function is specified by

$$f(\mathbf{x}) = c \frac{K_{(\nu+d)/2}\left(\sqrt{(\nu + (\mathbf{x} - \mu)'\mathbf{\Sigma}^{-1}(\mathbf{x} - \mu))\gamma'\mathbf{\Sigma}^{-1}\gamma}\right)\exp((\mathbf{x} - \mu)'\mathbf{\Sigma}^{-1}\gamma)}{\left(\sqrt{(\nu + (\mathbf{x} - \mu)'\mathbf{\Sigma}^{-1}(\mathbf{x} - \mu))\gamma'\mathbf{\Sigma}^{-1}\gamma}\right)^{-(\nu+d)/2}\left(1 + \frac{(\mathbf{x} - \mu)'\mathbf{\Sigma}^{-1}(\mathbf{x} - \mu)}{\nu}\right)^{(\nu+d)/d}},$$

with K_{λ} denoting the modified Bessel function of the third kind. *c* as the normalizing constant is defined as:

$$c = \frac{2^{(2-(\nu+d))/2}}{\Gamma(\nu/2)(\pi\nu)^{d/2}|\mathbf{\Sigma}|^{1/2}}.$$

Defining the vector $\theta = (\mu, \mathbf{\Sigma}, \gamma)$, the log-likelihood can be written as:

$$\ln \mathscr{L}(\mathbf{X}_1, \ldots, \mathbf{X}_T, \theta, \nu) = \sum_{t=1}^{T} \ln f_{\mathbf{X}}(\mathbf{X}_t, \theta, \nu).$$

The conditional independence between $\mathbf{X}_t$ and $W_1, \ldots, W_T$, $\forall t$, leads to

$$\ln \tilde{\mathscr{L}}(\theta, \mathbf{X}_1, \ldots, \mathbf{X}_T, W_1, \ldots, W_T) = \sum_{t=1}^{T} \ln f_{\mathbf{X}|W}(\mathbf{X}_t | W_t, \mu, \Sigma, \gamma) + \sum_{t=1}^{T} \ln h_W(W_t).$$

This enables us to maximize the two sums separately. The parameters μ, Σ, and γ are separated from the term controlled by ν. Yet, the distribution of W_t is latent. As such, in the first step of the EM algorithm, the 'E step', we maximize the expectation of the objective function given the observations $\mathbf{X}_1, \ldots, \mathbf{X}_T$ and the parameter estimates of algorithm step k, $\theta^{[k]}$

$$\max_{\nu} E(\ln \tilde{\mathscr{L}}(\nu, \mathbf{X}_1, \ldots, \mathbf{X}_T, W_1, \ldots, W_T | \mathbf{X}_1, \ldots, \mathbf{X}_T, \theta^{[k]}).$$

In the subsequent step, the 'M step', the objective function is maximized by altering the parameters θ.

Define $\mathbf{u}_1$ and $\mathbf{u}_2$ to be the marginal distributions of the bivariate copula C. The algorithm can be specified by the following subsequent steps:

- Set the iteration indicator $k = 1$. Specify the starting value of ν as $\nu^{[1]} = 30$. In order to determine the 'pseudo-sample' $\mathbf{X}$, we invert the univariate distributions $\mathbf{u}_1$ and $\mathbf{u}_2$ by the ordinary symmetric t-distribution $t(0, 1, \nu^{[1]})$. Set $\mu^{[1]} = \mathbf{0}$, $\Sigma^{[1]} = \text{Cov}(\mathbf{X})$, and $\gamma^{[1]}$ close to the zero vector to specify a distribution close to the symmetric Student's t specification.
- For convenience, define

$$\rho_t^{[k]} = (\mathbf{X}_t - \mu^{[k]})'(\Sigma^{[k]})^{-1}(\mathbf{X}_t - \mu^{[k]}).$$

For the maximization of the augmented likelihood, given W_t, $t = 1, \ldots, T$, we calculate the auxiliary variables

$$\vartheta_t^{[k]} = \left(\frac{\rho_t^{[k]} + \nu^{[k]}}{\gamma^{[k]\prime}\Sigma^{[k]-1}\gamma^{[k]}} \right)^{-1/2} \frac{K_{(\nu+d+2)/2}\left(\sqrt{(\rho_t^{[k]} + \nu^{[k]})(\gamma^{[k]\prime}\Sigma^{[k]-1}\gamma^{[k]})} \right)}{K_{(\nu+d)/2}\left(\sqrt{(\rho_t^{[k]} + \nu^{[k]})(\gamma^{[k]\prime}\Sigma^{[k]-1}\gamma^{[k]})} \right)},$$

and

$$\eta_t^{[k]} = \left(\frac{\rho_t^{[k]} + \nu^{[k]}}{\gamma^{[k]\prime}\Sigma^{[k]-1}\gamma^{[k]}} \right)^{1/2} \frac{K_{(\nu+d-2)/2}\left(\sqrt{(\rho_t^{[k]} + \nu^{[k]})(\gamma^{[k]\prime}\Sigma^{[k]-1}\gamma^{[k]})} \right)}{K_{(\nu+d)/2}\left(\sqrt{(\rho_t^{[k]} + \nu^{[k]})(\gamma^{[k]\prime}\Sigma^{[k]-1}\gamma^{[k]})} \right)}.$$

In case of the symmetric t-copula, we have instead $\theta_t^{[k]} = (\nu^{[k]} + d)/\rho_t^{[k]} + \nu^{[k]}$, $\eta_t^{[k]} = (\rho_t^{[k]} + \nu^{[k]})/\nu^{[k]} + d - 2$, and a further auxiliary variable $\xi_t^{[k]} = \ln((\rho_t^{[k]} + \nu^{[k]})/2) - \psi((d + \nu^{[k]})/2)$, where ψ denotes the digamma function.

- Defining $\overline{\vartheta}^{[k]} = 1/T \sum_{t=1}^{T} \vartheta_t^{[k]}$ and $\overline{\eta}^{[k]} = 1/T \sum_{t=1}^{T} \eta_t^{[k]}$, we can update the parameter estimations by

$$\gamma^{[k+1]} = \frac{\sum_{t=1}^{T} \vartheta_t^{[k]}(\overline{\mathbf{X}} - \mathbf{X}_t)}{T(\overline{\vartheta}^{[k]}\overline{\eta}^{[k]} - 1)},$$

$$\mu^{[k+1]} = \frac{1/T \sum_{t=1}^{T} \vartheta_t^{[k]}\mathbf{X}_t - \gamma^{[k+1]}}{\overline{\vartheta}^{[k]}},$$

and

$$\Sigma^{[k+1]} = \frac{1}{T} \sum_{t=1}^{T} \vartheta_t^{[k]}(\mathbf{X}_t - \mu^{[k+1]})(\mathbf{X}_t - \mu^{[k+1]})' - \overline{\eta}^{[k]}\gamma^{[k+1]}\gamma^{[k+1]\prime}$$

- In the subsequent 'M step', $\nu^{[k+1]}$ is determined by maximizing the log-likelihood for the skewed t-copula. In the symmetric case, we can numerically solve the equation

$$-\psi\left(\frac{\nu}{2}\right) + \ln\left(\frac{\nu}{2}\right) + 1 - \overline{\xi}^{[k]} - \overline{\theta}^{[k]} = 0,$$

where $\overline{\xi}^{[k]} = 1/T \sum_{t=1}^{T} \xi_t^{[k]}$.[11]
- Set the iteration counter $k = k + 1$ and repeat the entire procedure (omitting step 1) until the likelihood estimation converges up to a pre-specified level.

Dynamic copula quantile regressions and tail area dynamic dependence in Forex markets

Eric Bouyé and Mark Salmon

Financial Econometrics Research Centre, Warwick Business School, UK

We introduce a general approach to nonlinear quantile regression modelling based on the copula function
that defines the dependency structure between the variables of interest. Hence, we extend Koenker and
Bassett's (1978. Regression quantiles. *Econometrica*, 46, no. 1: 33–50.) original statement of the quantile
regression problem by determining a distribution for the dependent variable Y conditional on the regressors
X, and hence the specification of the quantile regression functions. The approach exploits the fact that
the joint distribution function can be split into two parts: the marginals and the dependence function (or
copula). We then deduce the form of the (invariably nonlinear) conditional quantile relationship implied by
the copula. This can be achieved with arbitrary distributions assumed for the marginals. Some properties
of the copula-based quantiles or c-quantiles are derived. Finally, we examine the conditional quantile
dependency in the foreign exchange market and compare our quantile approach with standard tail area
dependency measures.

1. Introduction

The problem of characterizing the conditional dependence between random variables at a given
quantile is an important practical issue in risk management and portfolio design. It is also one
which is difficult to address if the joint distribution of the variables involved is nonelliptic and
fat tailed as is standard with financial returns. Tail area dependency for instance may be quite
different to that implied by correlation and may signal where downside protection can be found
if two assets do not show positive causal dependency in their extreme quantiles. One goal of this
paper is to introduce a general approach to this problem through nonlinear quantile regression
modelling where the form of the quantile regression is implied by the copula linking the assets
involved.

Our starting point is the joint distribution for the variables which will almost certainly be non-
Gaussian. Working down, in a general to specific manner, this multivariate distribution can be
split into two parts – the marginal densities and the dependence function or copula that joins
these marginals together to give the joint distribution function. Since the copula function holds
all information on the different forms of dependency that exist between the assets, we can see that
the form of the conditional quantile relationship is implied by the copula function. We refer below
to this relationship as a *copula-quantile regression* (c-quantile) to distinguish it from a quantile

regression function which may have been assumed to be linear or estimated nonparametrically, as is common.

A second objective of this paper is to apply the c-quantile idea to assess the form and degree of conditional dependence between foreign exchange rates. Correlation analysis is implicitly based on an assumption of multivariate ellipticity and may give very misleading results if the assumption is incorrect, in particular multivariate Gaussianity implies asymptotic tail area independence unless the correlation is unity and a multivariate t-distribution symmetric tail dependence. An important issue in financial markets is to consider exactly how exchange rates are inter-related in different market conditions, and by using c-quantiles, we show how we can examine the entire conditional distribution at a range of quantile levels rather than just measure the correlation or the degree of limiting dependence which is captured by standard tail area dependency measures. Patton (2006) and Hartmann, Straetmans, and De Vries (2003) have considered the dependence between exchange rates using related but different techniques from those employed in this article. We also consider dynamic dependency both across and within exchange rates and show how the c-quantile method provides an approach different from that considered by Engle and Manganelli (2004) who *assumed* the form of the conditional autoregressive value-at-risk models which they proposed for risk management in their CAViAR framework. (See Bouyé, Gaussel and Salmon, 2001, for a more general approach to assessing dynamic dependence using copulae.) The form of our dynamic c-quantiles follows immediately from the determination of the joint distribution and the copula rather than by assumption. In this way, we are also able to examine the question of market efficiency at all quantiles including the tails of the distributions, instead of simply through a mean regression, by exploiting a natural test for *independence* that follows from the copula.

In the next section, we briefly review regression quantiles as proposed and developed by Koenker and Bassett (1978) and then the concept of copula is defined and the implications for the assessing the forms of dependence between two assets are presented. We then introduce the concept of a copula quantile curve, derive some properties of this c-quantile curve and provide some examples for particular copulae. In the next section, the copula quantile regression model is formally defined and we briefly discuss the estimation issue. Then the application to analysing c-quantile regressions and tail area dependence in foreign exchange markets is presented. A final section offers some conclusions.

2. Regression quantiles

Koenker and Bassett (1978) introduced linear quantile regression in the following way. Let $(y_1, \ldots, y_T)$ be a random sample on Y and $(\mathbf{x}_1, \ldots, \mathbf{x}_T)'$ a random k-vector sample on X.

DEFINITION 1 *The pth quantile regression is any solution to the following problem*:

$$\min_{\boldsymbol{\beta} \in \mathbb{R}^k} \left(\sum_{t \in \mathcal{T}_p} p|y_t - \mathbf{x}_t'\boldsymbol{\beta}| + \sum_{t \in \mathcal{T}_{1-p}} (1-p)|y_t - \mathbf{x}_t'\boldsymbol{\beta}| \right)$$

with $\mathcal{T}_p = \{t: y_t \geq \mathbf{x}_t'\boldsymbol{\beta}\}$ and $\mathcal{T}_{1-p}$ its complement. This can be alternatively expressed as:[1]

$$\min_{\boldsymbol{\beta} \in \mathbb{R}^k} \left(\sum_{t=1}^{T} (p - \mathbb{I}_{\{y_t \leq \mathbf{x}_t'\boldsymbol{\beta}\}})(y_t - \mathbf{x}_t'\boldsymbol{\beta}) \right). \tag{1}$$

Nonlinearity in quantile regression was developed by Powell (1986) using a censored model and the consistency of nonlinear quantile regression estimation has been investigated by White (1994), Engle and Manganelli (2004) and Kim and White (2003) among others. For a recent overview of quantile regression see Koenker (2005) or Koenker and Hallock (2001). As noted by Buchinsky (1998), quantile regression models have a number of useful properties: (i) with non-Gaussian error terms, quantile regression estimators may be more efficient than least-square estimators, (ii) the entire conditional distribution can be characterized, (iii) different relationships between the regressor and the dependent variable may arise at different quantiles. In this paper, we attempt to resolve one basic issue when using quantile regression, how to specify the functional form of the quantile regression. We achieve this by deriving a conditional distribution for Y given X from the copula which then implies the structural form of the quantile regression. For simplicity, our model is developed for the one regressor case, corresponding to a bivariate copula but it may, in principle, be extended to multiple regressors.

3. Copulae and dependence

We now derive some theoretical properties of copula quantile curves and start by briefly reviewing the definition of a copula function and Sklar's theorem, which ensures the uniqueness of the copula when the margins are continuous. Then, we discuss the concepts of positive quadrant dependence (PQD) and the left tail decreasing (LTD) property and consider how these two concepts are related. These definitions are then used to demonstrate that the concavity (respectively, convexity) of the copula in its first argument induces a positive (respectively, negative) dependence at each quantile level.

DEFINITION 2   *A bivariate copula is a function* $\mathbf{C}$: $[0, 1]^2 \to [0, 1]$ *such that*:

(1) $\forall (u, v) \in [0, 1]^2$,

$$\begin{cases} \mathbf{C}(u, 0) = \mathbf{C}(0, v) = 0 \\ \mathbf{C}(u, 1) = u \text{ and } \mathbf{C}(1, v) = v \end{cases} \tag{2}$$

(2) $\forall (u_1, v_1, u_2, v_2) \in [0, 1]^4$, $u_1 \le u_2$ and $v_1 \le v_2$,

$$\mathbf{C}(u_2, v_2) - \mathbf{C}(u_1, v_2) - \mathbf{C}(u_2, v_1) + \mathbf{C}(u_1, v_1) \ge 0. \tag{3}$$

THEOREM 2 (Sklar's theorem)   *Let X and Y be two random variables with joint distribution* $\mathbf{F}$. *Then, there exists a unique copula* $\mathbf{C}$ *satisfying*

$$\mathbf{F}(x, y) = \mathbf{C}(F_X(x), F_Y(y)) \tag{4}$$

if F_X and F_Y are continuous and represent the marginal distribution functions of X and Y, respectively.

DEFINITION 3 (Order)   *Let $(\mathbf{C}, \mathbf{D}) \in \mathcal{C}^2$ with $\mathcal{C}$ the set of copulae. One says that $\mathbf{C}$ is greater than $\mathbf{D}$ ($\mathbf{C} \succ \mathbf{D}$ or $\mathbf{D} \prec \mathbf{C}$) if*

$$\forall (u, v) \in [0, 1]^2, \quad \mathbf{C}(u, v) \ge \mathbf{D}(u, v).$$

THEOREM 3 (Fréchet bounds)   *Let* $\mathbf{C} \in \mathcal{C}$. *Then,*

$$\mathbf{C}^- \prec \mathbf{C} \prec \mathbf{C}^+$$

where $\mathbf{C}^-$ *and* $\mathbf{C}^+$ *are such that*

$$\mathbf{C}^-(u, v) = \max(u + v - 1, 0)$$
$$\mathbf{C}^+(u, v) = \min(u, v).$$

The concept of order for copulae is important as it allows us to rank the dependence between random variables. One interesting copula is the product copula $\mathbf{C}^\perp$ – which corresponds to independence – so that $\mathbf{C}^\perp(u, v) = uv$ (see Figure 1 below).

DEFINITION 4 (Lehman 1966)   *The pair* (X, Y) *is PQD* (**PQD**(X, Y)) *if*

$$\Pr\{X \le x, Y \le y\} \ge \Pr\{X \le x\} \Pr\{Y \le y\} \tag{5}$$

In terms of copulae, this definition can be restated $\mathbf{C}^\perp \prec \mathbf{C}$.

DEFINITION 5 (Esary and Proschan 1972)   *Y is LTD in X* (**LTD**$(Y \mid X)$) *if*

$$\forall y, \quad \Pr\{Y \le y \mid X \le x\} \text{ is a nonincreasing function of } x. \tag{6}$$

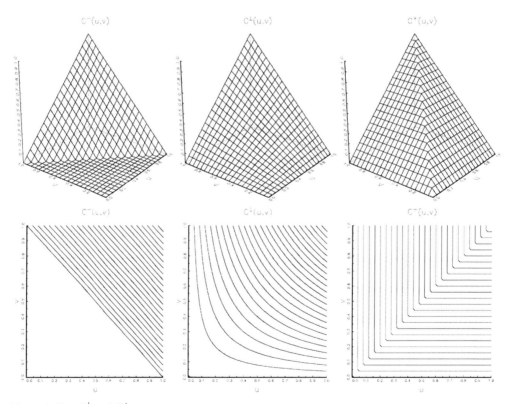

Figure 1. $\mathbf{C}^-$, $\mathbf{C}^\perp$ and $\mathbf{C}^+$.

This definition can be equivalently expressed using copulae as follows.

THEOREM 4 (Nelsen 1998)

$$\mathbf{LTD}(Y \mid X) \Longleftrightarrow \frac{\mathbf{C}(u, v)}{u} \text{ is nonincreasing in } u$$

$$\Longleftrightarrow \frac{\partial \mathbf{C}(u, v)}{\partial u} \leq \frac{\mathbf{C}(u, v)}{u}. \tag{7}$$

THEOREM 5 *Let $\mathbf{C} \in \mathcal{C}$. The following holds*

$$If \ \forall (u, v) \in [0, 1]^2, \quad \frac{\partial^2 \mathbf{C}(u, v)}{\partial u^2} \leq 0, \quad then \ \mathbf{C}^{\perp} \prec \mathbf{C} \tag{8}$$

$$If \ \forall (u, v) \in [0, 1]^2, \quad \frac{\partial^2 \mathbf{C}(u, v)}{\partial u^2} \geq 0, \quad then \ \mathbf{C} \prec \mathbf{C}^{\perp}. \tag{9}$$

Proof We refer to Nelsen (1998, pp. 151–60), for the proof. The first part is based on the fact that $\partial^2 \mathbf{C}(u, v)/\partial u^2 \leq 0 \Rightarrow \mathbf{LTD}(Y \mid X) \Rightarrow \mathbf{PQD}(X, Y)$. $\qquad\square$

This theorem tells us that if the copula function is concave in the marginal distribution F_X, then the random variables X and Y are positively related, i.e. their copula value is greater than that given by the independence copula $\mathbf{C}^{\perp}$. Conversely, convexity implies a negative relationship i.e. the copula linking X and Y lies below the independence copula $\mathbf{C}^{\perp}$. For simplicity, we still have not introduced the parameter(s) of the copula function, functions of which measure the degree and different forms of dependence between the variables; let us denote these parameters by $\delta \in \Delta$. Then, through the family of copula functions, we can distinguish three classes.

(1) Copulae that only exhibit negative dependence:

$$\forall \delta \in \Delta, \quad \forall (u, v) \in [0, 1]^2, \quad \text{then } \mathbf{C}(u, v; \delta) \prec \mathbf{C}^{\perp}(u, v).$$

(2) Copulae that only exhibit positive dependence:

$$\forall \delta \in \Delta, \quad \forall (u, v) \in [0, 1]^2, \quad \text{then } \mathbf{C}^{\perp}(u, v) \prec \mathbf{C}(u, v; \delta).$$

(3) Copulae that exhibit both negative and positive dependence depending on the parameter values:

$$\forall \delta \in \Delta^-, \quad \forall (u, v) \in [0, 1]^2, \quad \text{then } \mathbf{C}(u, v; \delta) \prec \mathbf{C}^{\perp}(u, v)$$

$$\forall \delta \in \Delta^+, \quad \forall (u, v) \in [0, 1]^2, \quad \text{then } \mathbf{C}^{\perp}(u, v) \prec \mathbf{C}(u, v; \delta).$$

In the next section, the concept of a quantile curve of Y conditional on X is defined and we derive several results that are directly deduced from the underlying copula properties outlined above.

4. Quantile curves

First, the pth c-quantile curve of y conditional on x or pth c-quantile curve is defined. Second, its main properties are exhibited. Third, the case of radially symmetric variables is studied. Finally, the quantile curves are developed for three special cases: the Kimeldorf and Sampson, Gaussian and Frank copulae.

4.1 *Definitions*

We restrict the study to *monotonic* copula for simplicity. Define the probability distribution of y conditional on x by $p(y|x; \delta)$, where

$$p(y|x; \delta) = \Pr\{Y \le y \mid X = x\}$$

$$= \mathbf{E}(\mathbb{I}_{\{Y \le y\}} \mid X = x)$$

$$= \lim_{\varepsilon \to 0} \Pr\{Y \le y \mid x \le X \le x + \varepsilon\}$$

$$= \lim_{\varepsilon \to 0} \frac{\mathbf{F}(x + \varepsilon, y; \delta) - \mathbf{F}(x, y; \delta)}{F_X(x + \varepsilon) - F_X(x)}$$

$$= \lim_{\varepsilon \to 0} \frac{\mathbf{C}[F_X(x + \varepsilon), F_Y(y); \delta] - \mathbf{C}[F_X(x), F_Y(y); \delta]}{F_X(x + \varepsilon) - F_X(x)}$$

$$p(y|x; \delta) = C_1[F_X(x), F_Y(y); \delta], \tag{10}$$

with $C_1(u, v; \delta) = \partial/\partial u\, C(u, v; \delta)$. Since the distribution functions F_X and F_Y are nondecreasing, $p(y|x; \delta)$ is nondecreasing in y. Using the same argument, $p(y|x; \delta)$ is nondecreasing in x if $C_{11}(u, v; \delta) \le 0$ and nonincreasing in x if $C_{11}(u, v; \delta) \ge 0$, where $C_{11}(u, v; \delta) = \partial^2 \mathbf{C}(u, v; \delta)/\partial u^2$.

DEFINITION 6 *For a parametric copula* $\mathbf{C}(\cdot, \cdot; \delta)$ *the pth copula quantile curve of y conditional on x is defined by the following implicit equation*

$$p = C_1[F_X(x), F_Y(y); \delta], \tag{11}$$

where $\delta \in \Delta$ *the set of parameters.*

Under some conditions,[2] Equation (11) can be expressed as follows in order to capture the relationship between X and Y:

$$y = \mathbf{q}(x, p; \delta), \tag{12}$$

where $\mathbf{q}(x, p; \delta) = F_Y^{|-1|}(D(F_X(x), p; \delta))$ with D the partial inverse in the second argument of C_1 and $F_Y^{|-1|}$ the pseudo-inverse of F_Y. Note that the relationship (12) can alternatively be written using uniform margins as:

$$v = \mathbf{r}(u, p; \delta), \tag{13}$$

with $u = F_X(x)$ and $v = F_Y(y)$.

4.2 *Properties*

Two properties are demonstrated. The first tells us that the quantile curve shifts up with the quantile level. The second indicates that the quantile curve has a positive (respectively, negative) slope if the copula function is concave (respectively, convex) in its first argument.

PROPERTY 1 *If* $0 < p_1 \le p_2 < 1$, *then* $\mathbf{q}(x, p_1; \delta) \le \mathbf{q}(x, p_2; \delta)$.

PROPERTY 2   *Let $x_1 \leq x_2$.*
If $\mathbf{C}(u, v)$ is concave in u then $\mathbf{q}(x_1, p; \delta) \leq \mathbf{q}(x_2, p; \delta)$
If $\mathbf{C}(u, v)$ is convex in u then $\mathbf{q}(x_1, p; \delta) \geq \mathbf{q}(x_2, p; \delta)$.

Proof   Given the implicit function theorem, y may be expressed as a function of x and p i.e.
$y = \mathbf{q}(x, p; \delta)$. Let us rewrite Equation (11) as $F(x, p, \mathbf{q}(x, p; \delta)) = 0$. Thus,

$$\frac{\partial F}{\partial x}(x, p, \mathbf{q}(x, p; \delta)) + \frac{\partial F}{\partial y}(x, p, \mathbf{q}(x, p; \delta))\frac{\partial \mathbf{q}}{\partial x}(x, p; \delta) = 0$$

$$\frac{\partial F}{\partial p}(x, p, \mathbf{q}(x, p; \delta)) + \frac{\partial F}{\partial y}(x, p, \mathbf{q}(x, p; \delta))\frac{\partial \mathbf{q}}{\partial p}(x, p; \delta) = 0.$$

Then,

$$\frac{\partial \mathbf{q}}{\partial x}(x, p; \delta) = -\frac{(\partial F/\partial x)(x, p, \mathbf{q}(x, p; \delta))}{(\partial F/\partial y)(x, p, \mathbf{q}(x, p; \delta))}$$

$$\frac{\partial \mathbf{q}}{\partial p}(x, p; \delta) = -\frac{(\partial F/\partial p)(x, p, \mathbf{q}(x, p; \delta))}{(\partial F/\partial x)(x, p, \mathbf{q}(x, p; \delta))}.$$

Just note that $F(x, p, y) = C_{1.}[F_X(x), F_Y(y); \delta] - p$, it follows that

$$\frac{\partial \mathbf{q}}{\partial x}(x, p; \delta) = -\frac{f_X(x)C_{2.}[F_X(x), F_Y(y); \delta]}{f_Y(y)C_{11}[F_X(x), F_Y(y); \delta]}$$

$$\frac{\partial \mathbf{q}}{\partial p}(x, p; \delta) = \frac{1}{f_Y(y)C_{11}[F_X(x), F_Y(y); \delta]}. \tag{14}$$

As $\forall (u, v) \in [0, 1]^2$, $C_{11}[u, v; \delta] \geq 0$, $f_X(x) \geq 0$ and $f_Y(y) \geq 0$, this completes the proof.   □

4.3 *Symmetric case*

An interesting case concerns the radial symmetry of X and Y. Indeed, in this case, a remarkable relationship exists between the pth quantile curve and the $(1 - p)$th quantile curve. First, the definition of radial symmetry is given. Then, a theorem is stated and a corollary that informs us about the slopes of the quantile curves is provided.

DEFINITION 7   *Two random variables X and Y are radially symmetric about (a, b) if*

$$\Pr\{X \leq x - a, Y \leq y - b\} = \Pr\{X \geq x + a, Y \geq y + b\}. \tag{15}$$

THEOREM 6 (Nelsen 1998)   *Let X and Y be, respectively, symmetric about a and b. They are radially symmetric about (a, b) iff their copula $\mathbf{C}$ satisfies*:

$$\mathbf{C}(u, v) = u + v - 1 + \mathbf{C}(1 - u, 1 - v). \tag{16}$$

COROLLARY 7   *If the copula $\mathbf{C}$ satisfies Equation (11), then*

$$C_{1.}(u, v; \delta) = 1 - C_{1.}(1 - u, 1 - v; \delta)$$

$$C_{2.}(u, v; \delta) = C_{2.}(1 - u, 1 - v; \delta)$$

$$C_{11}(u, v; \delta) = C_{11}(1 - u, 1 - v; \delta).$$

THEOREM 8 (Radial symmetry and copula quantile curves)   *If two random variables X and Y are radially symmetric about (a, b), then*

$$\mathbf{q}(a - x, p; \delta) + \mathbf{q}(a + x, 1 - p; \delta) = 2b. \tag{17}$$

Proof   From Equation (15),

$$\Pr\{Y \leq y - b \mid X \leq x - a\} = \Pr\{Y \geq y + b \mid X \geq x + a\}.$$

In terms of copula,

$$C_{1.}[F_X(a - x), F_Y(b - y); \delta] = 1 - C_{1.}[F_X(a + x), F_Y(b + y); \delta]$$
$$p(a - x, b - y) = 1 - p(a + x, b + y)$$

Then, for $p(a - x, b - y) = p$,

$$b - y = \mathbf{q}(a - x, p; \delta)$$
$$b + y = \mathbf{q}(a + x, 1 - p; \delta)$$

and the proof follows. $\square$

Note that a direct implication of this theorem is $\mathbf{q}(a, 1/2; \delta) = b$.

COROLLARY 9   *If two random variables X and Y are radially symmetric about (a, b), then*

$$\frac{\partial \mathbf{q}}{\partial x}(a - x, p; \delta) = \frac{\partial \mathbf{q}}{\partial x}(a + x, 1 - p; \delta). \tag{18}$$

4.4   *Examples*

We first describe a case for the Kimeldorf and Sampson copula where the copula quantiles can be derived analytically. We then describe how to develop c-quantiles for the general class of Archimedean copulae and two specific Archimedean copulae that we use in the empirical analysis below: the Joe–Clayton copula (BB7 in Joe 1997), which was used by Patton (2006), and BB3. We then study two copulae that allow both positive and negative slopes for the quantile curves, depending on the value of their dependence parameter. These are the Gaussian copula where the dependence pattern is measured by correlation but where the marginal distributions may be non-Gaussian. We then show that we have to be careful when selecting copula since some copulae, such as the Frank copula, may not allow us to adequately capture the full range of behaviour in the distribution of the dependent variable Y.

4.4.1   *Kimeldorf and Sampson copula*
Consider the copula given by

$$C(u, v) = (u^{-\theta} + v^{-\theta} - 1)^{-1/\theta} \text{ for } \theta > 0,$$

we then have

$$C_1(v|u) = \frac{\partial C(u, v)}{\partial u}$$

$$= -\frac{1}{\theta}(u^{-\theta} + v^{-\theta} - 1)^{-(1+\theta)/\theta}(-\theta u^{-(1+\theta)})$$

$$= (1 + u^{\theta}(v^{-\theta} - 1))^{-(1+\theta)/\theta}$$

solving $p = C_1(v|u)$ for v gives

$$C_1^{-1}(v|u) = v = (p^{(-\theta/1+\theta)} - 1)u^{-\theta} + 1)^{-1/\theta},$$

which provides us with the c-quantiles relating v and u for different values of p. Using the empirical distribution functions for $u = F_X(x)$ and $v = F_Y(y)$, we can find explicit expressions for the conditional c-quantiles for the variable Y conditional on X

$$y = F_Y^{-1}((p^{(-\theta/1+\theta)} - 1)F_X(x)^{-\theta} + 1)^{-1/\theta}).$$

4.4.2 Archimedean copulae
4.4.2.1 General case.
An Archimedean copula is defined as follows:

$$C(u, v) = \phi^{-1}[\phi(u) + \phi(v)] \tag{19}$$

with ϕ a continuous and strictly decreasing function from $[0, 1]$ to $[0, \infty]$ such that $\phi(1) = 0$. ϕ is often called the generator function. From $p = \partial/\partial u C(u, v)$, we obtain

$$p = \frac{\phi'(u)}{\phi'(C(u, v))}$$

$$p = \frac{\phi'_\delta(u)}{\phi'(\phi^{-1}[\phi(u) + \phi(v)])} \tag{20}$$

and the quantile regression curve for Archimedean copulae can in general be deduced as

$$v = \mathbf{r}(u, p; \delta)$$

$$v = \phi^{-1}\left[\phi\left(\phi'^{-1}\left(\frac{1}{p}\phi'(u)\right)\right) - \phi(u)\right].$$

Introducing $u = F_X(x)$ and $v = F_Y(y)$, the equation for the c-quantile above becomes

$$y = F_Y^{-1}\left(\phi^{-1}\left[\phi\left(\phi'^{-1}\left(\frac{1}{p}\phi'(F_X(x))\right)\right) - \phi(F_X(x))\right]\right).$$

4.4.3 Two specific Archimedean copulae
4.4.3.1 Joe–clayton (BB7).
For the copula defined by

$$C_{\delta,\theta}(u, v) = 1 - (1 - [(1 - (1 - u)^\theta)^{-\delta} + (1 - (1 - v)^\theta)^{-\delta} - 1]^{-1/\delta})^{1/\theta} \tag{21}$$

with $\theta \geq 1$ and $\delta > 0$, see Joe (1997, p. 153). This two-parameter copula is Archimedean as

$$C_{\delta,\theta}(u, v) = \phi_{\delta,\theta}^{-1}[\phi_{\delta,\theta}(u) + \phi_{\delta,\theta}(v)]$$

with

$$\phi_{\delta,\theta}(s) = [1 - (1 - s)^\theta]^{-\delta} - 1$$

$$\phi_{\delta,\theta}^{-1}(s) = 1 - [1 - (1 + s)^{-1/\delta}]^{1/\theta}$$

$$\phi_{\delta,\theta}'(s) = -[1 - (1 - s)^\theta]^{-\delta-1}\delta[-(1 - s)^\theta\theta/(-1 + s)] \tag{22}$$

It only allows positive dependence and we can see that

$$\lim_{\delta \to \infty} C_{\delta,\theta}(u, v) = C^+(u, v)$$

$$\lim_{\theta \to \infty} C_{\delta,\theta}(u, v) = C^+(u, v).$$

An important property is that each parameter, respectively, measures lower (δ) and upper (θ) tail dependence as we show below. Moreover this copula encompasses two copulae sub-families as for $\theta = 1$ one obtains the Kimeldorf and Sampson (1975) copula:

$$C_\delta(u, v) = (u^{-\delta} + v^{-\delta} - 1)^{-1/\delta},$$

and for $\delta \to 0$ the Joe (1993) copula:

$$C_\theta(u, v) = 1 - ((1 - u)^\theta + (1 - v)^\theta - (1 - u)^\theta(1 - v)^\theta)^{1/\theta}.$$

4.4.3.2 BB3. For the BB3 copula defined below (Joe 1997),

$$C_{\delta,\theta}(u, v) = \exp(1 - [\delta^{-1} \ln(\exp(\delta\tilde{u}^\theta) + \exp(\delta\tilde{v}^\theta) - 1)]^{1/\theta}) \tag{23}$$

with $\theta \geq 1$ and $\delta > 0$. This copula is archimedean as

$$C_{\delta,\theta}(u, v) = \phi_{\delta,\theta}^{-1}[\phi_{\delta,\theta}(u) + \phi_{\delta,\theta}(v)]$$

with

$$\phi_{\delta,\theta}^{-1}(s) = \exp(-[\delta^{-1} \ln(1 + s)]^{1/\theta}) \tag{24}$$

Again this copula allows us to model positive dependence and

$$\lim_{\delta \to \infty} C_{\delta,\theta}(u, v) = C^+(u, v)$$

$$\lim_{\theta \to \infty} C_{\delta,\theta}(u, v) = C^+(u, v).$$

The lower and upper tail area dependence measures are given by

$$\lambda_L = \begin{cases} 2^{-1/\delta} \text{ if } \theta = 1 \\ 1 \text{ if } \theta > 1 \end{cases} \tag{25}$$

$$\lambda_U = 2 - 2^{1/\theta}.$$

Again each parameter, respectively, measures lower (δ) and upper (θ) tail dependence.

4.4.4 Gaussian copula

The bivariate copula in this case is written as:

$$\mathbf{C}(u, v; \rho) = \Phi_2(\Phi^{[-1]}(u), \Phi^{[-1]}(v); \rho) \qquad (26)$$

with Φ_2 the bivariate Gaussian distribution and Φ the univariate distribution.

$$p = \Phi\left(\frac{\Phi^{[-1]}(v) - \rho\Phi^{[-1]}(u)}{\sqrt{1 - \rho^2}}\right)$$

or equivalently solving for v we find the pth c-quantile curve (see Figure 2) to be

$$v = \mathbf{r}(u, p; \rho) = \Phi\left(\rho\Phi^{[-1]}(u) + \sqrt{1 - \rho^2}\Phi^{[-1]}(p)\right).$$

The slope of the pth quantile curve is given by (Figure 2):

$$\frac{\partial\mathbf{r}(u, p; \rho)}{\partial u} = \rho\frac{\phi\left(\rho\Phi^{[-1]}(u)\sqrt{1 - \rho^2}\Phi^{[-1]}(p)\right)}{\phi(\Phi^{[-1]}(u))}.$$

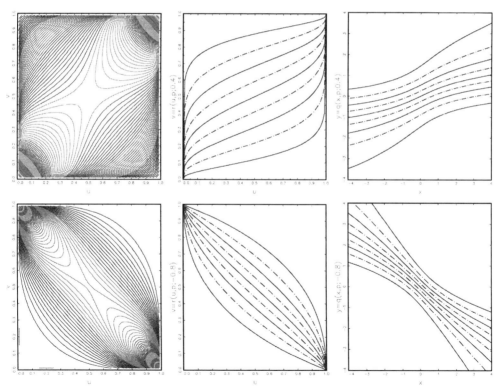

Figure 2. Gaussian copula densities, pth copula quantile curves (for $p = 0.1, 0.2, \ldots, 0.9$) for (u, v) and (x, y) under the hypothesis of Student's margins ($\nu = 3$) for $\rho = 0.4$ (upper plots) and $\rho = -0.8$ (lower plots).

A positive correlation is characterized by a positive slope and conversely for a negative correlation. Moreover,

$$\frac{\partial \mathbf{r}(u, p; \rho)}{\partial p} = \sqrt{1 - \rho^2} \frac{\phi\left(\rho \Phi^{[-1]}(u) + \sqrt{1 - \rho^2} \Phi^{[-1]}(p)\right)}{\phi(\Phi^{[-1]}(u))},$$

which is always positive. Then, the higher the p, the higher the quantile curve. The relationship between y and x for the pth quantile is:

$$y = F_Y^{[-1]}\left[\Phi\left(\rho\Phi^{[-1]}(F_X(x)) + \sqrt{1 - \rho^2}\Phi^{[-1]}(p)\right)\right]. \tag{27}$$

Let assume that X and Y are jointly bivariate Gaussian with $\mu_X = \mathbf{E}[X]$, $\mu_Y = \mathbf{E}[Y]$, $\sigma_X^2 = \text{Var}[X]$, $\sigma_Y^2 = \text{Var}[Y]$ and $\rho = \text{Corr}[X, Y]$. Then, given in Equation (27), the relationship becomes linear and we have

$$y = \mathbf{q}(x_t, p; \rho) = a + bx$$

with slope and intercept values determined by the quantile level;

$$a = \mu_Y + \sigma_Y\sqrt{1 - \rho^2}\Phi^{[-1]}(p) - \rho\frac{\sigma_Y}{\sigma_x}\mu_X$$

$$b = \rho\frac{\sigma_Y}{\sigma_x}$$

4.4.5 Frank copula
This copula is given by

$$\mathbf{C}(u, v; \delta) = -\frac{1}{\delta}\ln\left(1 + \frac{(e^{-\delta u} - 1)(e^{-\delta v} - 1)}{e^{-\delta} - 1}\right). \tag{28}$$

By computing its first derivative with respect to u, one obtains the pth copula quantile curve, $p = \mathbf{C}_{1.}(u, v; \delta)$ as

$$p = e^{-\delta u}((1 - e^{-\delta})(1 - e^{-\delta v})^{-1} - (1 - e^{-\delta u}))^{-1}$$

or equivalently,

$$v = -\frac{1}{\delta}\ln(1 - (1 - e^{-\delta})[1 + e^{-\delta u}(p^{-1} - 1)]^{-1}).$$

From the definition of the uniform distribution, one obtains the nonlinear relationship between x and y for the pth quantile as:

$$y = F_Y^{[-1]}\left[-\frac{1}{\delta}\ln(1 - (1 - e^{-\delta})[1 + e^{-\delta F_X(x)}(p^{-1} - 1)]^{-1})\right]. \tag{29}$$

We can see that the Frank copula might not always be a good choice as shown in Figure 3 since the full range of potential values for the variables may not be captured. So for $u \in [0, 1]$,

$$-\frac{1}{\delta}\ln(1 - (1 - e^{-\delta})p) \leq \mathbf{r}(u, p; \delta) \leq -\frac{1}{\delta}\ln\left(\frac{1 - e^{-\delta}}{1 + e^{-\delta}(p^{-1} - 1)}\right) \quad \text{for } \delta > 0$$

and

$$-\frac{1}{\delta}\ln(1 - (1 - e^{-\delta})p) \geq \mathbf{r}(u, p; \delta) \geq -\frac{1}{\delta}\ln\left(\frac{1 - e^{-\delta}}{1 + e^{-\delta}(p^{-1} - 1)}\right) \quad \text{for } \delta < 0.$$

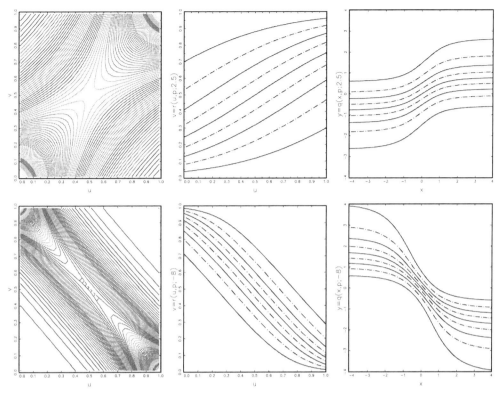

Figure 3. Frank copula densities, copula pth quantile curves (for $p = 0.1, 0.2, \ldots, 0.9$) for (u, v) and (x, y) under the hypothesis of Student's margins ($\nu = 3$) for $\delta = 2.5$ (upper plots) and $\delta = -8$ (lower plots).

5. Copula quantile regression and tail area dependency

Given the development above the concept of a copula quantile regression can be seen to be just a special case of nonlinear quantile regression. Let $(y_1, \ldots, y_T)$ be a random sample on Y and $(x_1, \ldots, x_T)$ a random k-vector sample on X.

DEFINITION 8 *The pth copula quantile regression* $\mathbf{q}(\mathbf{x}_t, p; \delta)$ *is a solution to the following problem*:

$$\min_{\delta} \left(\sum_{t \in \mathcal{T}_p} p|y_t - \mathbf{q}(\mathbf{x}_t, p; \delta)| + \sum_{t \in \mathcal{T}_{1-p}} (1 - p)|y_t - \mathbf{q}(\mathbf{x}_t, p; \delta).| \right) \qquad (30)$$

with $\mathcal{T}_p = \{t : y_t \geq \mathbf{q}(\mathbf{x}_t, p; \delta)\}$ *and* $\mathcal{T}_{1-p}$ *its complement. This can be expressed alternatively as*:

$$\min_{\delta} \left(\sum_{t=1}^{T} (p - \mathbb{I}_{\{y_t \leq \mathbf{q}(\mathbf{x}_t, p; \delta)\}})(y_t - \mathbf{q}(\mathbf{x}_t, p; \delta)) \right). \qquad (31)$$

This definition indicates that the estimate of the dependence parameter δ is provided by an L^1 norm estimator. This general problem has been investigated by Koenker and Park (1996) who proposed an algorithm for problems with response functions that are nonlinear in parameters and we refer to their paper for a detailed discussion of the development of an interior point algorithm to solve the estimation problem. The main idea is to solve the nonlinear L^1 problem by splitting it into a succession of linear L^1 problems.

It might be surprising that the probability level p appears in Equation (30) as an argument of the function $\mathbf{q}$ itself. This is simply because we have adopted a top-down strategy in our modelling by first specifying the joint distribution and then deriving the implied quantile function. By postulating given margins for X and Y and their copula, we derive a specific parametric functional for $\mathbf{q}(\mathbf{x}_t, p; \boldsymbol{\delta})$. In fact, the probability level is implicit in the original quantile regression definition of Koenker and Bassett (1978). In the applications below, we use nonparametric estimates of the empirical marginal distribution functions but estimate the parameters of the copula quantile parameters, $\boldsymbol{\delta}$, as described above. Conditions for the consistency of this semiparametric approach to the estimation of copula-based time-series models have been discussed in Chen and Fan (2006).

The c-quantile approach, developed above, enables us to examine the dependency between assets at any given quantile, including extreme quantiles and we can now compare this approach with the standard asymptotic tail area dependency measures. We may in fact not often be interested in dependency in the far extremes where highly infrequent but potentially disasterous joint loss may occur and we may be more interested in the more frequent dependency where large but not extreme loss can arise, and in this latter case, the c-quantile approach should provide a better measure of association between the assets.

5.1 Tail area dependency

Tail dependence measures, for both the upper tail, λ_U, and lower tail, λ_L, have been developed, and discussed, for instance in Joe (1997), Mari and Kotz (2001) and Coles, Heffernan and Tawn (1999). Upper tail independence is normally thought to be shown by $\lambda_U = 0$ and a value of $\lambda_U \in (0, 1]$ indicates the degree of upper tail dependence with lower tail dependence $\lambda_L \in (0, 1]$ similarly defined.

For two random variables, (X, Y) with marginal distributions $F_1(X)$ and $F_2(Y)$, λ_U and λ_L are linked to the asymptotic behaviour of the copula in the left and right tails. So for the lower tail index, we have

$$\lambda_L = \lim_{\alpha \searrow 0} \frac{C(\alpha, \alpha)}{\alpha} \tag{32}$$

$$= \lim_{\alpha \searrow 0} (\Pr\{F_2(Y) \leq \alpha | F_1(X) \leq \alpha\})$$

$$= \lim_{\alpha \searrow 0} (\Pr\{Y \leq F_2^{-1}(\alpha) | X \leq F_1^{-1}(\alpha)\}) \tag{33}$$

and

$$\lambda_U = \lim_{\alpha \nearrow 1} \Pr\{Y > F_2^{-1}(\alpha) | X > F_1^{-1}(\alpha)\}$$

$$= \lim_{\alpha \nearrow 1} \frac{\Pr\{Y > F_2^{-1}(\alpha), X > F_1^{-1}(\alpha)\}}{\Pr\{X > F_1^{-1}(\alpha)\}}$$

$$= \lim_{\alpha \nearrow 1} \frac{\bar{C}(\alpha, \alpha)}{1 - \alpha}$$

$$= \lim_{\alpha \nearrow 1} \frac{1 - 2\alpha + C(\alpha, \alpha)}{1 - \alpha} \tag{34}$$

Given the survival copula of two random variables with copula $C(\cdot, \cdot)$ is given by

$$\hat{C}(u, v) = u + v - 1 + C(1 - u, 1 - v),$$

and the joint survival function for two uniform random variables with distribution function given by $C(u, v)$ is given by

$$\bar{C}(u, v) = 1 - u - v + C(u, v) = \hat{C}(1 - u, 1 - v);$$

hence, it follows that

$$\lim_{\alpha \nearrow 1} \frac{\bar{C}(\alpha, \alpha)}{1 - \alpha} = \lim_{\alpha \nearrow 1} \frac{\hat{C}(1 - \alpha, 1 - \alpha)}{(1 - \alpha)} = \lim_{\alpha \searrow 0} \frac{\hat{C}(\alpha, \alpha)}{\alpha}. \tag{35}$$

Which implies that the coefficient of upper tail dependence of $C(\cdot, \cdot)$ is the coefficient of lower tail dependence of $\hat{C}(\cdot, \cdot)$.

A major difficulty with interpreting asymptotic tail area dependency, however, is that independence in the sense of *the factorization of the bivariate distribution* in the tails implies $\lambda_U = 0$ but $\lambda_U = 0$ does not imply factorization and hence independence. There may still be dependence in the tails even though there is asymptotic independence. An additional condition must be used to ensure factorization; Ledford and Tawn (1998), for instance, show that we also need to satisfy $\bar{\lambda} = 0$ as a necessary condition, where

$$\bar{\lambda} = \lim_{\alpha \nearrow 1} \frac{2 \log \Pr\{X > F_X^{-1}(\alpha)\}}{\log \Pr\{X > F_X^{-1}(\alpha), Y > F_Y^{-1}(\alpha)\}} - 1$$

$$= \lim_{\alpha \nearrow 1} \frac{2 \log(1 - \alpha)}{\log[1 - 2\alpha + C(\alpha, \alpha)]} - 1$$

$$= \lim_{\alpha \nearrow 1} \frac{2 \log(1 - \alpha)}{\log \bar{C}(\alpha, \alpha)} - 1$$

if $\bar{\lambda} > 0$ large values occur simultaneously more frequently than if they were independent and if $\bar{\lambda} < 0$ simultaneous large movements occur less frequently than under independence. $\bar{\lambda} = 1$ if and only if $\lambda_U > 0$ while it takes values in $[-1, 1)$ when $\lambda_U = 0$ which enables us to quantify the strength of dependence in the tail. Values of $\bar{\lambda} > 0, \bar{\lambda} = 0, \bar{\lambda} < 0$ loosely correspond to when the variables are positively associated in the extremes, exactly independent and negatively associated.

The two indices $(\lambda_U, \bar{\lambda})$ are then used to measure extreme upper tail dependence:

(1) $(\lambda_U > 0, \bar{\lambda} = 1)$ indicates asymptotic dependence and λ_U measures the degree of upper tail dependence or
(2) $(\lambda_U = 0, \bar{\lambda} < 1)$ indicates asymptotic independence and $\bar{\lambda}$ measures the strength of dependence in the tail.

5.1.1 Parametric and nonparametric estimation of tail dependency

The standard lower and upper tail dependence measures for Archimedean copulae are defined in general by

$$\lambda_{\text{L}} = \lim_{\alpha \to 1^-} \frac{1 - 2\alpha + \phi^{-1}(2\phi(\alpha))}{1 - \alpha}$$

$$\lambda_{\text{U}} = \lim_{\alpha \to 0^+} \frac{\phi^{-1}(2\phi(\alpha))}{\alpha}$$

(36)

and for the Joe–Clayton copula specifically are given by

$$\lambda_{\text{L}} = 2^{-1/\delta}$$

$$\lambda_{\text{U}} = 2 - 2^{1/\theta};$$

(37)

hence MLE estimates of the parameters of the copula provide direct parametric estimates of the tail area dependency measures and we shall employ these formula below.

Alternatively, we can use an empirical or nonparametric copula $C_n(1/n, j/n) = 1/n \sum_{i=1}^{n} \mathcal{I}(X_i \le X_{(i)}, Y_i \le Y_{(i)})$ to estimate tail area dependency given the order statistics $X_{(1)} \le X_{(2)} \le \cdots X_{(n)}$ and $Y_{(1)} \le Y_{(2)} \le \cdots Y_{(n)}$. Since we have

$$\lambda_{\text{L}} = \lim_{\alpha \searrow 0} \frac{C(\alpha, \alpha)}{\alpha},$$

which implies

$$C(\alpha, \alpha) = \lambda_{\text{L}}\alpha + o(\alpha)$$

(38)

for $0 \le \alpha \le 1$, where $o(\alpha)/\alpha \to 0$ as $\alpha \to 0$. A natural estimator of λ_{L} is given by the derivative which is approximated by the secant

$$\hat{\lambda}_{\text{L}}^1 = \left(\frac{k}{n}\right)^{-1} \hat{C}_n\left(\frac{k}{n}, \frac{k}{n}\right).$$

Alternatively a least squares estimator can be applied to Equation (38) to give a second estimator

$$\hat{\lambda}_{\text{L}}^2 = \left(\sum_{i=1}^{k}\left(\frac{i}{n}\right)^2\right)^{-1} \sum_{i=1}^{k}\left(\frac{i}{n}.\hat{C}_n\left(\frac{i}{n}, \frac{i}{n}\right)\right).$$

(39)

A third estimator is given by recognizing that the copula $C(u, v)$ can be approximated by the mixture of the comonotonicity and independence copulae, M and Π, giving

$$C(\alpha, \alpha) = \lambda_{\text{L}}\alpha + (1 - \lambda_{\text{L}})\alpha^2.$$

If we rewrite this as

$$C(\alpha, \alpha) - \alpha^2 = \lambda_{\text{L}}(\alpha - \alpha^2)$$

and again apply least squares to this expression, we get a third estimator

$$\hat{\lambda}_{\text{L}}^3 = \frac{\sum_{i=1}^{k}(\hat{C}_n(i/n, i/n) - (i/n)^2)(i/n - (i/n)^2)}{\sum_{i=1}^{k}(i/n - (i/n)^2)^2}.$$

As shown by Dobrić and Schmidt (2005), each of these are consistent estimators for λ_L provided k, the number of observations in the lower tail, is chosen so that $k \approx \sqrt{n}$. Our own experimentation with these estimators suggests that $\hat{\lambda}_L^2$ is the most reliable, with $\hat{\lambda}_L^3$ giving values that at times fall outside the feasible range $(0, 1)$. Dobrić and Schmidt provide some Monte Carlo evidence on the relative merits of each estimator depending on the sample size and the true degree of dependence. We use $\hat{\lambda}_L^2$ below to calculate both lower and upper tail dependence using the relationship in Equation (35).

6. Measuring dependence in FX markets

We now turn to apply the methods discussed above and to examine the dependency between three exchange rates, both in the extremes and at a range of quantiles describing the conditional distributions. We start by considering the static relationship between the dollar–yen, dollar–sterling and dollar–DM rates using 522 *weekly* returns from August 1992 to August 2002; the rates themselves are shown in the Figure 4. below. We then turn to consider the dynamic dependence of conditional quantiles both within and between these rates. All three exchange rates fail univariate normality tests with excess kurtosis and a positive skew except for the sterling–dollar rate which shows a negative skew over the sample period (see Figures 5, 6, 7 and Figures 14, 15, 16 for non parametric quantile regressions). For comparison purposes, we follow Patton (2006) and start by imposing a Gaussian copula to combine these non-Gaussian marginals and then examine the sensitivity of our conclusions by using the Joe–Clayton (BB7) copula. The Gaussian copula is examined first simply because multivariate Gaussianity is a standard assumption in practice and also because we know that the Gaussian Copula implies asymptotic independence and hence it provides a useful basis for a comparison between quantile dependence and the tail area dependence measures.

Figure 4. Exchange rates.

We compute the nonlinear quantile regression estimates of $\hat{\rho}(p)$ such that:

$$\hat{\rho}(p) = \arg\min\left(\sum_{t=1}^{T}\left(p - \mathbb{I}_{\{S_{1t} \leq \mathbf{q}(S_{2t}, p; \rho, \hat{\theta}_1, \hat{\theta}_2)\}}\right)\left(S_{1t} - \mathbf{q}\left(S_{2t}, p; \rho, \hat{\theta}_1, \hat{\theta}_2\right)\right)\right). \quad (40)$$

Assuming a Gaussian copula, the relationship between any two exchange rates S_1 and S_2 at the pth-quantile is[3]:

$$S_1 = \hat{F}_1^{|-1|}\left[\Phi(\hat{\rho}(p)\Phi^{|-1|}(\hat{F}_2(S_2)) + \sqrt{1 - \hat{\rho}^2(p)}\Phi^{|-1|}(p))\right], \quad (41)$$

with $\hat{F}_1$ and $\hat{F}_2$ the *empirical* marginal distribution functions for the two exchange rates. The estimates of the copula parameter (which in this case is just the correlation coefficient) at each quantile level $\hat{\rho}(p)$, expressed in percentage terms, are reported in Tables 1 and 2 together with their estimated standard deviations. The mean regression results are also reported for information. The lower the p, the higher the quantile regression curve.

The results in Tables 1 and 2 indicate significant (ie. nonzero) dependence using standard inference procedures at all quantile levels and for all exchange rates using the Gaussian copula.[4] There is a relatively low degree of association indicated between the yen:dollar and the sterling:dollar rates and a much higher association indicated at all quantile levels for the dollar:sterling and dollar:DM rates. A fairly symmetric degree of dependence is indicated as we range from the 5% quantile to the 95% quantile with relatively minor differences from the mean regression results. We find the same qualitative conclusions in these two cases when we reverse the causality in Table 2. What is striking, however, are the results for yen:dollar and DM:dollar, where we can see a clear asymmetric structure in the dependency between the lower quantiles and the upper quantiles with much stronger dependency being shown in the lower quantiles when the yen is the dependent variable (and vice versa in the upper quantiles when the DM is the dependent variable). Use of the mean or median regression in this case could give a substantially misleading idea of the

Table 1. c-Quantile regression estimates based on a Gaussian copula (with standard errors).

S_1 on S_2	USD/Y on USD/£	USD/Y on USD/DM	USD/£ on USD/DM
5%	14.2 (5.4)	37.7 (3.5)	49.1 (4.6)
10%	16.5 (4.7)	31.9 (4.2)	57.2 (4.0)
50%	20.2 (3.8)	32.9 (4.0)	72.0 (3.1)
90%	14.1 (5.5)	28.5 (4.7)	63.2 (3.6)
95%	13.2 (5.9)	23.3 (5.7)	55.8 (4.1)
Mean regression	18.3 (4.2)	32.0 (4.2)	65.2 (3.5)

Table 2. Reverse c-quantile regression estimates based on a Gaussian copula.

S_1 on S_2	USD/£ on USD/Y	USD/DM on USD/Y	USD/DM on USD/£
5%	14.4 (5.9)	21.4 (6.2)	51.2 (4.0)
10%	17.5 (4.9)	20.1 (6.6)	57.7 (3.6)
50%	20.5 (4.1)	33.4 (4.0)	64.3 (3.2)
90%	22.8 (3.7)	37.1 (3.6)	66.1 (3.1)
95%	16.9 (5.0)	34.3 (3.9)	51.2 (4.0)
Mean regression	19.2 (4.4)	32.0 (4.2)	62.1 (3.3)

relative joint risks. These results clearly show that there is still a fair degree of quantile dependence at both the upper and lower tails even though we know that the standard tail dependence measures would indicate independence since we are using the Gaussian copula. We have also found a fair degree of symmetry in the dependency between the rates using copula quantiles except in the case of yen:dollar and DM:dollar where we find asymmetry; results that are broadly in line with Patton (2006). Different information is provided by the quantile dependence measures at fairly extreme quantiles than that shown by the implied (asymptotic) tail area dependence measure.

We next compare these Gaussian copula results with those from using the Joe–Clayton copula[5] in Tables 3 (returns) and 4 (levels) where the stars in the following tables indicate significance at the 95% level from the value of one for θ (upper tail dependency) and zero for δ. (lower tail dependency). We can see the same indication of upper tail dependence in the yen:DM dollar rates in levels and sterling:DM dollar rates in the upper tail in returns but not in levels in contrast to the Gaussian copula results. Some lower tail dependence is found for the yen:sterling dollar rates and sterling:DM dollar rates in levels and more strongly in the sterling:DM in returns. Otherwise we find little or no dependence at all with $\hat{\theta}(p)$ being approximately 1 and $\hat{\delta}(p)$ not significantly different from 0 for most quantile levels. The obvious advantage from using the Joe–Clayton copula is that we can separate the dependence parameters θ and δ with their distinct interpretations from the correlation which describes the entire dependence structure with the Gaussian copula.

Next we compute the upper and lower tail indices for the returns of the three exchange rates using both the nonparametric estimator λ_L^2 discussed above and then the parametric estimates using these estimated copula parameters. The nonparametric estimates are shown in Table 5 and

Table 3. Joe–clayton c-quantile regression estimates: returns.

	r_t					
	USD/Y on USD/£		USD/Y on USD/DM		USD/£ on USD/DM	
p	$\hat{\theta}(p)$	$\hat{\delta}(p)$	$\hat{\theta}(p)$	$\hat{\delta}(p)$	$\hat{\theta}(p)$	$\hat{\delta}(p)$
5%	1.07	0.00	1.17*	0.00	1.42*	0.19*
10%	1.07	0.00	1.17*	0.00	1.39*	0.21*
50%	1.06	0.03	1.13	0.09	1.21*	0.37*
90%	1.05	0.08	1.10	0.21	1.07	0.53*
95%	1.04	0.09	1.09	0.23	1.06	0.55*

Table 4. Joe–Clayton c-quantile regression estimates: levels.

	S_t					
	USD/Y on USD/£		USD/Y on USD/DM		USD/£ on USD/DM	
p	$\hat{\theta}(p)$	$\hat{\delta}(p)$	$\hat{\theta}(p)$	$\hat{\delta}(p)$	$\hat{\theta}(p)$	$\hat{\delta}(p)$
5%	1.01	0.67*	1.39*	0.00	1.04	0.44*
10%	1.02	0.54*	1.39*	0.00	1.03	0.44*
50%	1.00	0.00	1.37*	0.00	1.00	0.35*
90%	1.00	0.00	1.25*	0.17	1.00	0.15
95%	1.00	0.00	1.24*	0.20	1.00	0.11

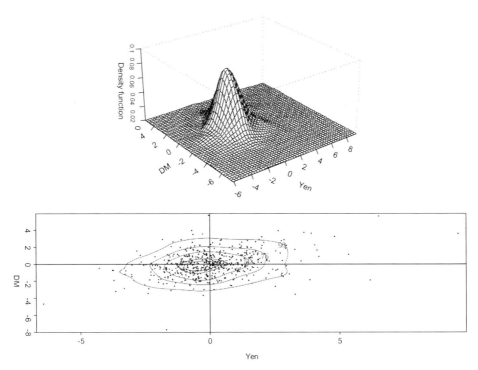

Figure 5. Empirical yen/DM bivariate return distribution.

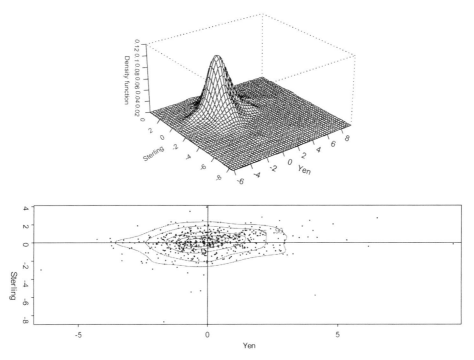

Figure 6. Empirical yen/sterling bivariate return distribution.

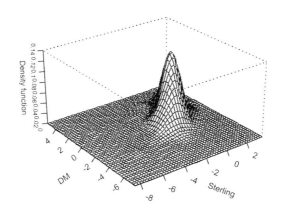

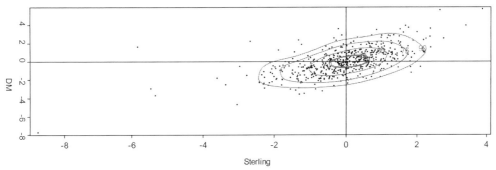

Figure 7. Empirical sterling/DM bivariate return distribution.

Table 5. Upper and lower tail index nonparametric estimates.

λ_L^2	λ_U^2		
	Yen	Sterling	DM
Yen	–	0.16	0.03
Sterling	0.09	–	0.32
DM	0.20	0.38	–

the parametric estimates in Table 6 using the relevant formulae for the Joe-Clayton copula (37), with the upper tail dependency parameters given above the main diagonal and the lower tail dependency given below.

These two sets of estimates differ in interesting ways; we can clearly see the moderate degree of both higher and lower tail dependence in both the nonparametric and parametric estimates for the DM:dollar and sterling:dollar rates but critically this is not strongly shown at the median parameter estimates. In fact, the upper tail dependency is shown only at the 5% quantile and not at all at the 95% quantile. Conversely, the lower tail dependence suggested by the nonparameteric estimate is only shown at the 95% quantile parameter estimates. The weak relationship between the yen and sterling dollar rates is shown effectively at all quantiles. The degree of both lower and upper nonparametric tail dependence between the yen and the DM rates is not found at

Table 6. Upper and lower tail dependencies using Joe–Clayton c-quantile regression parameter estimates: returns.

	r_t					
	USD/Y on USD/£		USD/Y on USD/DM		USD/£ on USD/DM	
p	λ_U	λ_L	λ_U	λ_L	λ_U	λ_L
5%	0.09	0.00	0.19*	0.00	0.37*	0.03*
10%	0.09	0.00	0.19*	0.00	0.35*	0.04*
50%	0.08	0.00	0.15	0.00	0.23*	0.15*
90%	0.06	0.00	0.12	0.04	0.09	0.27*
95%	0.05	0.00	0.11	0.05	0.08	0.28*

any quantile. It is, however, clear that we get substantially more information regarding the joint risk structure from carrying out this analysis using the c-quantile parameter estimates through being able to examine the dependence at all quantiles rather than simply through the mean. The question that is implicitly raised is whether we are really interested in asymptotic dependence or the dependence as shown by the quantile results at the particular level with which the risk manager may be concerned. Coles, Heffernan, and Tawn (1999) have also suggested that λ_U (and hence also λ_L) can be viewed as quantile-based by varying the level α in Equations (32) and (34) through the range [0, 1] as opposed to the normal limiting values at 0 and 1. It is not, however, enitrely clear if the interpretation of λ_U at a particular α corresponds to a quantile-based measure of *upper tail* dependence instead of simply a measure of quantile dependence. Carrying out their suggestion produces the results shown in Figures 8–13, where their χ and $\bar{\chi}$ statistics and 95% confidence intervals which correspond to our λ_U and $\bar{\lambda}$ statistics evaluated at each α value are shown.[6] The yen:sterling rates can be seen from these figures to be effectively independent except as we get close to the upper tail which contradicts our c-quantile results shown above. The yen:DM rates also appear to show weak dependence from these figures with somewhat more upper tail dependence as suggested by the quantile regression results above. The sterling:DM results show dependence that appears to decline as we get close to the upper tail and then explodes as we get to the tail; however, at this point, the confidence intervals are very wide. It would seem that the c-quantile approach is providing an alterantive and potentially more reliable view of tail area and moderate quantile dependence.

6.1 *Dynamic c-quantiles*

We next compute the nonlinear *dynamic* quantile regression estimates $(\hat{\delta}(p), \hat{\theta}(p))$ using the Joe–Clayton copula on returns so that we are examining the dependence between r_t and r_{t-1}:

$$\left(\hat{\delta}(p), \hat{\theta}(p)\right) = \arg\min \left(\sum_{t=1}^{T} \left(p - \mathbb{I}_{\{r_t \leq \mathbf{q}(r_{t-1}, p; \delta, \theta)\}} \right) (r_t - \mathbf{q}(r_{t-1}, p; \delta, \theta)) \right) \quad (42)$$

with

$$\mathbf{q}(r_{t-1}, p; \delta, \theta) = \hat{F}^{|-1|} \left[\phi_{\delta,\theta}^{-1} \left[\phi_{\delta,\theta} \left(\phi_{\delta,\theta'}^{-1} \left(\frac{1}{p} \phi_{\delta,\theta'}(\hat{F}(r_{t-1})) \right) \right) - \phi_{\delta,\theta}(\hat{F}(r_{t-1})) \right] \right] \quad (43)$$

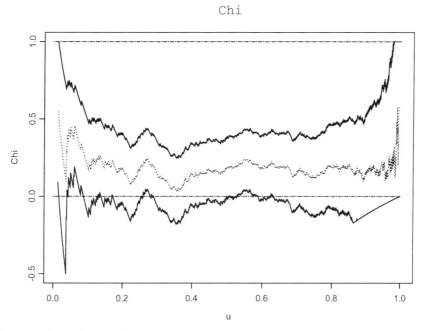

Figure 8. Yen:sterling estimates of λ for varying α.

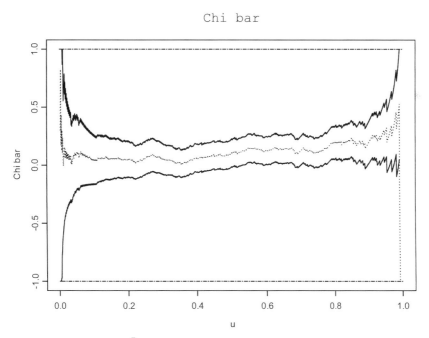

Figure 9. Yen:sterling estimates of $\bar{\lambda}$.

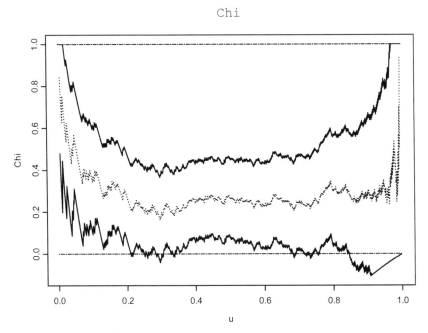

Figure 10. Yen:DM estimates of λ.

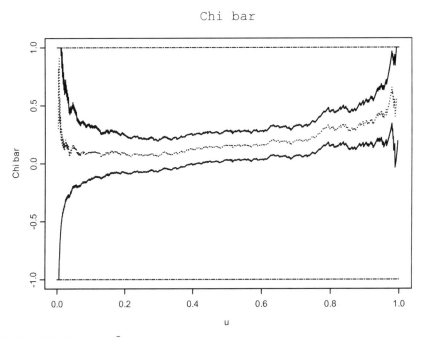

Figure 11. Yen:DM estimates of $\bar{\lambda}$.

Chi

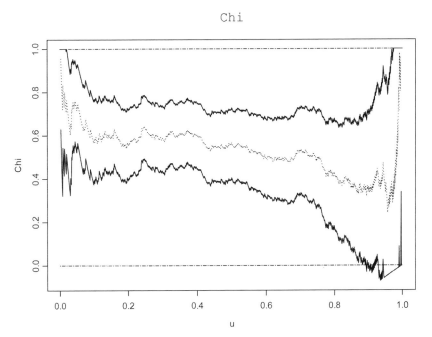

Figure 12. Sterling:DM estimates of λ.

Chi bar

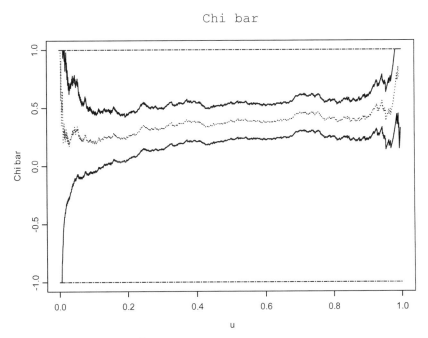

Figure 13. Sterling:DM estimates of $\bar{\lambda}$.

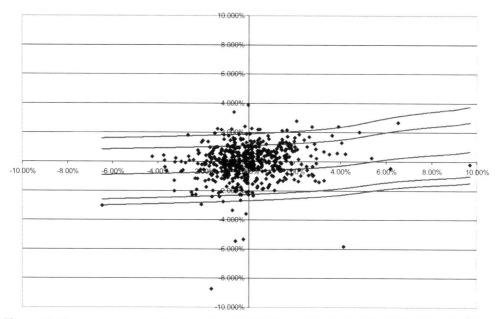

Figure 14. Non-parametric quantile regression of USD/Y on USD/£ for 5%, 10%, 50%, 90%, 95% probability levels.

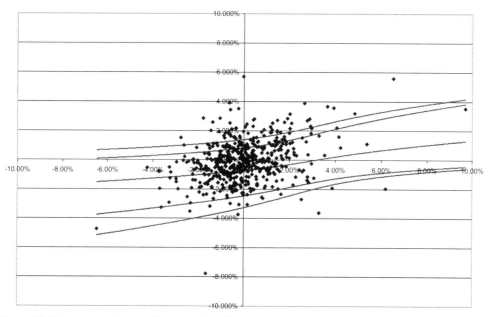

Figure 15. Non-parametric quantile regression of USD/Y on USD/DM for 5%, 10%, 50%, 90%, 95% probability levels.

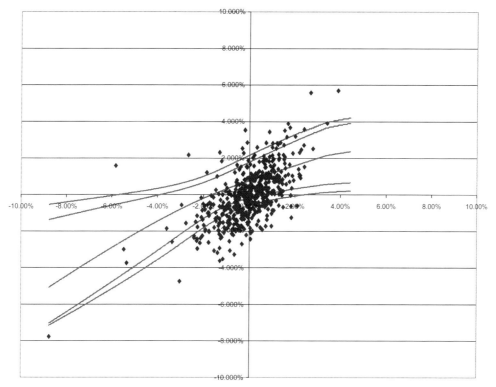

Figure 16. Non-parametric quantile regression of USD/£ on USD/DM for 5%, 10%, 50%, 90%, 95% probability levels.

Table 7. c-Quantile regression estimates of the relative return of the exchange rate $r_t = S_t/S_{t-1} - 1$ on r_{t-1}.

| | $r_{t-1}{:}r_t$ | | | | | |
| | USD/Y:USD/Y | | USD/£:USD/Y | | USD/DM:USD/Y | |
p	$\hat{\theta}(p)$	$\hat{\delta}(p)$	$\hat{\theta}(p)$	$\hat{\delta}(p)$	$\hat{\theta}(p)$	$\hat{\delta}(p)$
5%	1.00	0.00	1.00	0.00	1.00	0.00
10%	1.01	0.00	1.00	0.00	1.00	0.00
50%	1.03*	0.00	1.00	0.00	1.00	0.00
90%	1.05*	0.00	1.01	0.00	1.01	0.00
95%	1.05*	0.00	1.01	0.00	1.02	0.00

with $\phi_{\delta,\theta}$ the generator of the copula defined in Equation (24) and $\hat{F}$ the empirical distribution function of the exchange rate return r_t. The estimates are given in Tables 7–9 below.

These results show that there is no significant dynamic dependence, either between cross-rates or within rates, at *any* quantile level between the returns of the exchange rates in this weekly data. The Joe–Clayton parameter estimates indicate independence even in the relative extremes of the joint distribution. This result appears to suggest that Forex markets retain efficiency, in a very standard sense, even when the markets are in crisis and in either the upper or lower tail. These

Table 8. c-Quantile regression estimates of the relative return of the exchange rate $r_t = S_t/S_{t-1} - 1$ on r_{t-1}.

	$r_{t-1}:r_t$					
	USD/Y:USD/£		USD/£:USD/£		USD/DM:USD/£	
p	$\hat{\theta}(p)$	$\hat{\delta}(p)$	$\hat{\theta}(p)$	$\hat{\delta}(p)$	$\hat{\theta}(p)$	$\hat{\delta}(p)$
5%	1.02	0.00	1.00	0.08	1.00	0.06
10%	1.02	0.00	1.00	0.07	1.00	0.06
50%	1.02	0.00	1.00	0.01	1.00	0.04
90%	1.02	0.00	1.00	0.00	1.02	0.00
95%	1.02	0.00	1.00	0.00	1.03*	0.00

Table 9. c-Quantile regression estimates of the relative return of the exchange rate $r_t = S_t/S_{t-1} - 1$ on r_{t-1}.

	$r_{t-1}:r_t$					
	USD/Y:USD/DM		USD/£:USD/DM		USD/DM:USD/DM	
p	$\hat{\theta}(p)$	$\hat{\delta}(p)$	$\hat{\theta}(p)$	$\hat{\delta}(p)$	$\hat{\theta}(p)$	$\hat{\delta}(p)$
5%	1.00	0.02	1.00	0.08	1.00	0.06
10%	1.00	0.02	1.00	0.07	1.00	0.06
50%	1.00	0.02	1.00	0.04	1.00	0.04
90%	1.00	0.01	1.00	0.00	1.02	0.00
95%	1.00	0.01	1.00	0.00	1.02	0.00

Table 10. Tail area dependency Measures on lagged own returns.

Tail area dependency	λ_L	λ_U	$\bar{\lambda}_U$	$\bar{\lambda}_L$
Yen	0.017	0.186	0.061	−0.016
DM	0.0	0.011	−0.054	−0.114
Sterling	0.097	0.0	−0.0613	0.126

quantile results are confirmed, but not quite so clearly, as shown in Table 10, when we examine the asymptotic tail area dependency measures;

7. Conclusion

In this paper, we have developed and applied a new approach to measuring dependence through copula quantile regressions. The methodology rests on identifying the copula that captures the dependence structure between the series of interest and then deriving the implied conditional quantile regression specification. This enables us to examine the conditional dependence of one variable conditional on the other(s) at a range of quantile levels as opposed to the normal regression relationship, which only describes the form of dependence at the conditional expectation. In this way, we can explore causal dependencies at moderate risk levels that may be more relevant to risk managers than the normal approach given by examining standard asymptotic tail area dependency measures. We have developed several theoretical results describing the properties of c-quantiles and compared their performance with the standard tail area dependency measures.

Our empirical results using exchange rates are indicative of the structure that can be uncovered using copula-based quantile regressions. We found similar patterns of symmetric and asymmetric dependence as reported in Patton (2006) using different techniques. We also found when examining dynamic copula-quantile dependence that the independence shown between the returns of one exchange rate on its own lag applies at all quantiles and hence a much stronger 'efficiency' condition seems to apply, even into the tails of the distribution than implied by standard martingale efficiency conditions that involve the conditional expectation. We have also noted the computational difficulties that are likely to complicate the standard measures of (asymptotic) tail dependence.

Acknowledgements

First version January 2001, we would like to thank participants at the NSF/NBER Time Series Conference 2002 at Penn, the CIRANO Workshop in Financial Econometrics in Montreal, October 2002 and seminars at Nuffield College, Oxford, University of Melbourne, University of Western Australia, Australian National University, Cambridge University, Warwick University and the Bank of England for their comments on an earlier version of this paper; in particular Andrew Patton, Neil Shephard and Adrian Pagan.

Notes

1. Koenker and Bassett discuss properties of their estimator, especially through the following theorem:

THEOREM 1   *Let $\beta^\star(p, y, X) \in \mathcal{B}^\star(p, y, X)$. Then, the following properties hold*:

(1) $\beta^\star(p, \kappa y, X) = \begin{cases} \kappa\beta^\star(p, y, X) & for\, \kappa \in \mathbb{R}^+ \\ \kappa\beta^\star(1 - p, y, X) & for\, \kappa \in \mathbb{R}^- \end{cases}$,

(2) $\beta^\star(p, y + X\delta, X) = \beta^\star(p, y, X)\, for\, \delta \in \mathbb{R}^k$,

(3) $\beta^\star(p, y, X\Gamma) = \Gamma^{-1}\beta^\star(p, y, X)\, with\, \Gamma\, non\text{-}singular\, (k \times k)\, matrix.$

2. Note that C_1 has to be partially invertible in its second argument. If it is not analytically invertible, a numerical root-finding procedure can be used.
3. Again for simlicity, we start by examining the dependence between the level of the exchange rates while recognizing that on the basis of some statistical criteria exchange rate levels may appear to be nonstationary. However, it is in principle clear that exchange rates cannot follow a stochastic process with an infinite variance which can also take negative values.
4. It is natural that we find contemporaneous dependence between the exchange rates given the presence of triangular arbitrage relationships in the market.
5. The Joe–Clayton copula was preferred by the data in AIC comparisons with several alternative copulae including the Gaussian copula.
6. We are grateful to Jan Heffernan for making the SPLUS code for computing these figures publically available.

References

Bouyé, E., N. Gaussel and M. Salmon. 2001. Investigating dynamic dependence using copulae. FERC Working Paper, Warwick Business School.

Buchinsky M. 1998. Recent advances in quantile regression models: A practical guideline for empirical research. Journal of Human Resources 33, no. 1: 88–126.

Chen, X., and Y. Fan. 2006. Estimation of copula based semiparametric time series models. Journal of Econometrics 130: 307–35.

Coles, S.G., J.E. Heffernan and J.A. Tawn. 1999. Dependence measures for extreme value analysis. Extremes 2, 339–65.

Darsow, W.F., B. Nguyen, and E.T. Olsen. 1992. Copulas and Markov processes. *Illinois Journal of Mathematics* 36, no. 4: 600–42.

Dobrić, J., and F. Schmidt. 2005. Nonparametric estimation of the lower tail dependence λ_L in bivariate copulas. Journal of Applied Statistics 32: 387–407.

Engle, R.F. and S. Mangenelli. 2004. CAViaR: Conditional autoregressive value at risk by regression quantiles. *Journal of Business and Economic Statistics* 22, no. 4: 367–81.

Esary, J.D., and F. Proschan. 1972. Relationships among some concepts of bivariate dependence. *Annals of Mathematical Statistics* 43, no. 2: 651–55.

Hartmann, P., S. Straetmans and C.G. deVries. 2003. A global perspective on extreme currency linkages. In Asset price bubbles: The implications for monetary, regulatory and international policies, ed. W.C. Hunter, G.G. Kaufman, and M. Pomerleano, 361–82, Cambridge, MA: MIT Press.

Joe, H. 1997. *Multivariate models and dependence concepts.* Vol. 73, *Monographs on statistics and applied probability.* 73 London: Chapmann & Hall.

Kim T.-H., and H. White. 2003. Estimation, inference and specification testing for possibly misspecified quantile regression, *Advances in Econometrics* 17: 107–32.

Koenker R. 2005. *Quantile regression.* Vol. 38, *Econometric society monographs.* Cambridge University Press.

Koenker, R., and G. Bassett, Jr. 1978. Regression quantiles. *Econometrica* 46, no. 1: 33–50.

Koenker, R., and K. Hallock. 2001. Quantile regression, *Journal of Economic Perspectives* 15: 143–56.

Koenker, R., and B.J. Park. 1996. An interior point algorithm for nonlinear quantile regression. *Journal of Econometrics* 71: 265–83.

Lehmann, E.L. 1966. Some concepts of dependence. *Annals of Mathematical Statistics* 37, no. 5: 1137–53.

Mari, D.D. and S. Kotz. 2001. *Correlation and dependence.* London: Imperial College Press.

Nelsen, R.B. 1998. *An introduction to copulas.* Vol. 139, *Lectures notes in statistics.* New York: Springer Verlag.

Patton A. 2006. Modelling asymmetric exchange rate dependence. *International Economic Review* 47, no. 2: 527–56.

Powell, J. 1986. Censored regression quantiles. *Journal of Econometrics* 32: 143–55.

White, H. 1984. *Estimation, Inference and Specification Analysis.* Cambridge: Cambridge University Press.

Risk and return of reinsurance contracts under copula models

Martin Eling[a] and Denis Toplek[b]

[a]Institute of Insurance, University of Ulm, Helmholtzstr. 22, 89069 Ulm, Germany; [b]Institute of Insurance Economics, University of St Gallen, Kirchlistrasse 2, 9010 St Gallen, Switzerland

The aim of this article is to study the influence of nonlinear dependencies on the payoff of reinsurance contracts and the resulting effects on a non-life insurer's risk and return profile. To achieve this, we integrate several copula models and reinsurance contracts in a dynamic financial analysis framework and conduct numerical tests within a simulation study. Depending on the reinsurance contract and the copula concept employed, we find large differences in risk assessment for the ruin probability and for the expected policyholder deficit. This has important implications for management decisions, as well as for regulators and rating agencies that use these risk measures for deriving capital standards and ratings.

1. Introduction

A risk management instrument that insurance companies use as protection against large losses is reinsurance contracts, in which the insurer cedes parts of its claim distribution tails to a reinsurance company. Both for the primary insurer and for the reinsurer it is crucial to incorporate extreme events and nonlinear dependencies in evaluating classical reinsurance contracts as well as alternative risk transfer (ART) contracts. One such innovative contract type is double trigger reinsurance contracts (see, e.g. Gründl and Schmeiser 2002), in which the potential coverage depends on both underwriting and financial risk, i.e. the insurer will be compensated only if the claims are high *and* the capital market is down. This contract design incorporates manifold dependencies between assets, between liabilities, and between assets and liabilities, all of which are crucial when evaluating such contracts and thus must be taken into account.

The aim of this article is to provide such an evaluation both for selected classical and innovative types of reinsurance contracts from the perspective of a primary insurer. For this purpose, we use dynamic financial analysis (DFA) and the copula concept. DFA is a financial modeling approach that projects financial results under a variety of possible scenarios, showing how outcomes might be affected by changing internal and external conditions (see Casualty Actuarial Society 2006). DFA has become an important tool for decision making and an essential part of enterprise risk management, particularly within the field of non-life insurance and reinsurance. In our context DFA is very useful, since it takes a holistic view on the companies' assets and liabilities and allows the integration of various dependencies. The resulting integrated analysis at the level of the whole company adds value to an isolated view on the risk and return of reinsurance contracts.

Although the use of simulation in risk management began much earlier, practitioners started using these techniques intensively in the late 1990s. DFA emerged in the mid-1990s when the Casualty Actuarial Society (2006) introduced simulation models for property–casualty insurers. Several surveys and applications of DFA have been published in academic journals. Lowe and Stanard (1997) and Kaufmann, Gadmer and Klett (2001) both provide an introduction to DFA by presenting a model framework and an application of their model. Blum et al. (2001) investigate the impact of foreign exchange risks on reinsurance decisions within a DFA framework. D'Arcy and Gorvett (2004) apply DFA to search for an optimal growth rate in the property–casualty insurance business.

The second branch of literature on which our article builds is the copulas concept. Copulas and the problem of mapping nonlinear dependencies in an insurance context is widely discussed in the actuarial literature as well as in the finance literature (see, e.g. Rank 2006). Wang (1998) contains a broad survey on the use of copulas in insurance company risk management, presenting models and algorithms for the aggregation of correlated risk portfolios. Frees and Valdez (1998) also provide an introduction to the use of copulas in risk measurement by describing several families of copulas, their basic properties, and their relationships to measures of dependence. Oakes (1982, 1989), Hougaard, Harvald and Holm (1992), and Carriere (1994) analyze dependency structures in survival models for the estimation of life tables. Tibiletti (1995) provides an application of copulas in the context of insurance demand and Wang (1996) and Frees, Carriere and Valdez (1996) apply copulas in the context of insurance pricing. Klugman and Parsa (1999) as well as Dias (2004) develop appropriate models to analyze finance and insurance data by fitting copulas to empirical data.

Combining these two branches of literature, Eling and Toplek (2007) integrate nonlinear dependencies in a DFA framework using the copulas concept and evaluate their effects on the insurer's risk and return distribution within a simulation study. However, they do not evaluate reinsurance contracts under different copulas. Another related paper is Blum, Dias and Embrechts (2002), which discusses the use of copulas to handle the measurement of dependence in ART products. They provide an example using Danish fire data and evaluate risk and return of different ART contracts. However, these authors concentrate on ART, not on classical reinsurance. Furthermore, their focus is on risk and return of ART contracts and not on a holistic company model, which is provided using DFA.

Our aim is to contribute to this literature by evaluating the risk and return profile of an insurance company after integrating different reinsurance contracts under several copulas models. For this purpose, we use an extended version of the DFA model presented by Eling and Toplek (2007). The focus of this article is on cross-sectional dependence in the lines of business and asset classes and between assets and liabilities modeled with copulas. Furthermore, the model takes temporal dependence into consideration for premiums. This temporal dependence is modeled with classical autoregressive processes. We consider three common reinsurance contract designs, i.e. a stop loss contract, an excess-of-loss contract, and a double trigger contract. Because we cannot determine which copula provides the best description of 'true' events, we compare different forms of copulas (i.e. elliptical (Gaussian and t) and Archimedean copulas (Clayton, Gumbel, and Frank)) and evaluate the possible impact in a stress-testing sense. All contract parameters have been calibrated to result in the same risk and return profile in a setting without nonlinear dependencies. This allows us to identify the pure impact of different copulas on the reinsurance contracts.

Our main findings are as follows. First, depending on the copula concept employed, we find different recommendations for management for each reinsurance contract under consideration, which emphasizes the importance of considering nonlinear dependencies in management decisions. Second, we find that the reinsurance contracts are especially useful in reducing ruin probability, but not in reducing the expected policyholder deficit (EPD), a finding of particular relevance for policyholders, as these have to bear the loss in case of insolvency. Third, we find large differences in risk assessment for different copulas and reinsurance contracts, a result that is of importance for regulators and rating agencies that use these measures as a foundation of capital assessment and ratings. All these results indicate that taking nonlinear dependencies into account is crucial for proper risk assessment and decision making in enterprise risk management.

The rest of the article is organized as follows. In Section 2, we present a DFA framework containing the essential elements of a non-life insurance company and describe how we integrated the copulas and reinsurance contracts in the DFA framework. A DFA simulation study to examine the effects of the copulas on risk and return is presented in Section 3. Section 4 concludes.

2.   Integration of copulas and reinsurance in DFA

2.1   *Dynamic financial analysis*

Our DFA model framework builds upon the models presented in Eling, Parnitzke and Schmeiser (2006) and Eling and Toplek (2007). We extend their framework with a modified claims process consisting of different lines of business. Catastrophe losses in each line of business are modeled using a Poisson distribution for the claim number and a Pareto distribution for the claim size. We denote EC_t as the equity capital of the insurance company at the end of time period t ($t \in 1, \ldots, T$) and E_t as the company's earnings in t. The development of the equity capital over time can thus be written as:

$$EC_t = EC_{t-1} + E_t. \tag{1}$$

The earnings E_t are given by the investment result I_t and the underwriting result U_t. Taxes are paid contingent on positive earnings (tr denotes the tax rate):

$$E_t = I_t + U_t - \max(\text{tr} \cdot (I_t + U_t), 0). \tag{2}$$

On the asset side, we consider the returns of high-risk investments (e.g. stocks, given by r_{1t}) and the returns of low-risk investments (e.g. bonds, given by r_{2t}). We calculate the company's portfolio return r_{pt} by weighting the returns with the portion of high-risk investments α_{t-1} and $1\text{-}\alpha_{t-1}$:

$$r_{pt} = \alpha_{t-1} \cdot r_{1t} + (1 - \alpha_{t-1})r_{2t}. \tag{3}$$

The company's investment results can be calculated by multiplying the portfolio return with the funds available for investment:

$$I_t = r_{pt} \cdot (EC_{t-1} + P_{t-1} - Ex_{t-1}^P). \tag{4}$$

The other major portion of an insurer's income is generated by the underwriting business. The underwriting result is calculated as premiums P_{t-1} (due at the beginning of the year) minus claims C_t (due by the end of the year) minus upfront costs Ex_{t-1}^P minus claim settlement costs Ex_t^C:

$$U_t = P_{t-1} - C_t - Ex_{t-1}^P - Ex_t^C. \tag{5}$$

There are two factors that determine the premium level in our model: The first one is the underwriting cycle, a cyclical pattern of premium rate level observed in insurance markets. As done in

Cummins and Outreville (1987), we model the underwriting cycle using an autoregressive process of order two (with a_0, a_1, and a_2 for lags 0, 1, and 2). The current rate level Π_t depends on the premium levels of the two previous periods and a random error term ε_t:

$$\Pi_t = a_0 + a_1 \Pi_{t-1} + a_2 \Pi_{t-2} + \varepsilon_t. \tag{6}$$

The second one (cr) is a consumer response factor that represents a link between the premium written and the company's safety level (see Wakker, Thaler, and Tversky 1997). We determine the safety level by considering the equity capital at the end of the previous period. The premium income in our model is given as:

$$P_{t-1} = \mathrm{cr}_{t-1}^{\mathrm{EC}_{t-1}} \cdot \Pi_{t-1} \cdot \beta_{t-1} \cdot \mathrm{MV}. \tag{7}$$

The parameter β_{t-1} denote the company's portion of the relevant market in t. The underwriting market accessible to the insurer (MV) is obtained with $\beta = 1$.

The claims C consist of non-catastrophe losses and catastrophe losses ($C = C_{\mathrm{ncat}} + C_{\mathrm{cat}}$). We model an insurer with several lines of business, only two of which are exposed to catastrophe claims C_{cat}. We use homeowner and householder insurance as examples of these two lines. The catastrophe losses in the two lines of business are modeled using a compound Poisson process with a Poisson distribution for the claim number n and a Pareto distribution for the claim size x (see Klugman, Panjer and Wilmot 2004). The non-catastrophe losses C_{ncat} are log-normally distributed and could arise from the above-mentioned two lines of business, but could also be generated from other lines of business that are not exposed to catastrophe losses (e.g. third-party liability car insurance or credit insurance).

Two types of costs are integrated in the model: upfront costs (Ex_{t-1}^P) and claim settlement costs (Ex_t^C). The upfront costs depend linearly on the level of written market volume (modeled with the factor γ), and nonlinearly on the change in written market volume (modeled with the factor η, e.g. because of increased advertising and promotion efforts). The upfront costs Ex_{t-1}^P are thus calculated as:

$$\mathrm{Ex}_{t-1}^P = \gamma \cdot \beta_{t-1} \cdot \mathrm{MV} + \eta \cdot ((\beta_{t-1} - \beta_{t-2}) \cdot \mathrm{MV})^2. \tag{8}$$

Claim settlement costs are calculated as a portion δ of the claims ($\mathrm{Ex}_t^C = \delta C_t$). For the sake of clarity, a table showing all model parameters is presented in Table 1.

2.2 *Integration of copulas*

The dependencies between different risk categories, i.e. between different asset classes (high-risk vs. low-risk investments), different kinds of liabilities (homeowner's vs. householder's insurance), and between assets and liabilities can be modeled by producing correlated random numbers. For the modeling of dependence structures of heavy-tailed and skewed risks, literature proposes that solely considering linear correlation is not appropriate (see, e.g. Embrechts, McNeil and Straumann 2002). Therefore, we utilize Kendall's rank correlations in our analysis, which do not depend on the marginal distributions (see, e.g. McNeil, Frey, and Embrechts 2005) and consider several types of tail dependence.

There are different definitions of tail dependence measures in the literature that can lead to different indications of asymptotic dependence and independence. To account for these differences, we consider two definitions. The first one can be called 'strong tail dependence' (see Charpentier

Table 1. Base parameter configuration.

Parameter	Symbol	Initial value at $t = 0$
Time period in years	T	5
Equity capital at the end of period t	EC_t	€75 million
Tax rate	tr	0.25
Portion invested in high-risk investments in period t	α_{t-1}	0.40
Normally distributed high-risk investment return in period t	r_{1t}	
Mean return	$E(r_{1t})$	0.10
Standard deviation of return	$\sigma(r_{1t})$	0.20
Normally distributed low-risk investment return in period t	r_{2t}	
Mean return	$E(r_{2t})$	0.05
Standard deviation of return	$\sigma(r_{2t})$	0.05
Risk-free return	r_f	0.03
Underwriting market volume	MV	€1000 million
Company's underwriting market share in period t	β_{t-1}	0.20
Premium rate level in period t	Π_t	1
Autoregressive process parameter for lag 0	a_0	1.191
Autoregressive process parameter for lag 1	a_1	0.879
Autoregressive process parameter for lag 2	a_2	−0.406
Consumer response function	$cr_{t-1}^{EC_{t-1}}$	1
Upfront expenses linearly depending on the written market volume	γ	0.05
Upfront expenses nonlinearly depending on the change in written market volume	η	0.001
Log-normal non-catastrophe claims as portion underwriting market share	C_{ncat}	
Mean claims	$E(C_{ncat})$	€153 million
Standard deviation of claims	$\sigma(C_{ncat})$	€4.59 million
Claim settlement costs as portion of claims	δ	0.05
Pareto catastrophe claims	C_{cat}	
Mean claims householder's (homeowner's) insurance	$E(C_{cat})$	€7.5 (2.5) million
Standard deviation of claims	$\sigma(C_{cat})$	€8.1 (2.7) million
Kendall's rank correlation between high-risk and low-risk investments	$\rho_{\tau 1}$	0.2
Kendall's rank correlation between householder and homeowner catastrophe losses	$\rho_{\tau 2}$	0.1
Kendall's rank correlation between assets and liabilities	$\rho_{\tau 3}$	−0.1
Excess of loss (attachment point/plafond/premium per year)		€26/140/2.51 million
Stop loss (attachment point/plafond/premium per year)		€215/280/2.18 million
Double trigger (attachment point/plafond/premium per year)		€15/160/2.90 million

2006) and is defined in Joe (1997, 33):

$$\lambda_L = \lim_{u \to 0+} \Pr(U_1 \leq u | U_2 \leq u) = \lim_{u \to 0} \frac{\Pr(U_2 \leq u, U_1 \leq u)}{\Pr(U_2 \leq u)},$$

where λ_L is the lower tail dependence parameter for two standard uniform random variables U_1, U_2 with joint distribution function $C(U_1, U_2)$. Analogously, upper tail dependence can be defined. An alternative way to define a tail dependence measure is provided by Ledford and

Tawn (1996):

$$\bar{\lambda}_{\mathrm{L}} = \lim_{u \to 0+} \frac{\log \Pr(U_2 \leq u)}{\log \Pr(U_2 \leq u, U_1 \leq u)},$$

where $\bar{\lambda}_{\mathrm{L}}$ is the coefficient of lower tail dependence. The definition by Ledford and Tawn (1996) can in some cases indicate dependence, whereas Joe's (1997) measure shows asymptotic independence and can thus also be called weak tail dependence (see Charpentier 2006); we will look at these differences in more detail later in our analysis.

We model dependencies by applying the copula concept, which separates the description of the dependence structure from the marginal distributions. Since our analysis focuses on ruin, lower tail dependence is the central aspect of the copulas considered. Lower tail dependent copulas will produce jointly low asset returns and high losses and thus reproduce the negative correlations between assets and liabilities. The high losses result from plugging the uniformly distributed random numbers generated with the lower tail dependent copula into the survival functions of the marginal distributions for the two lines of business.

We follow Eling and Toplek (2007) and examine the influence of different copulas using the Gauss copula, the t copula, and three non-exchangeable four-dimensional constructions based on distinct Archimedean copulas (Gumbel copula, Clayton copula, Frank copula). Our approach differs from that presented in Eling and Toplek (2007), in that we model dependencies between individual claim sizes and claim frequencies in different lines of business instead of different kinds of aggregate claim amounts.

The Gauss and the t copulas are the most widespread dependence concepts and have been considered broadly in risk management literature (see, e.g. McNeil, Frey, and Embrechts 2005). The Gauss copula is contained in the multivariate normal distribution and is asymptotically independent in both tails (see, e.g. McNeil, Frey, and Embrechts (2005, 211), using Joe's (1997) definition of tail dependence). However, as mentioned (e.g. in Juri and Wüthrich 2003), the Gauss copula does have weak dependence in the tails if tail dependence is measured according to Ledford and Tawn (1996):

$$C_P^{\mathrm{Gauss}}(\mathbf{u}) = \mathbf{\Phi}_P(\Phi^{-1}(u_1), \Phi^{-1}(u_2), \Phi^{-1}(u_3), \Phi^{-1}(u_4)). \tag{9}$$

Φ represents the standard univariate normal density function and $\mathbf{\Phi}_P$ stands for the joint density function of a four-dimensional Gaussian vector $\mathbf{u}$ with correlation matrix P. Another copula that arises from a multivariate distribution is the t copula which is included in the multivariate Student's t-distribution. In contrast to the Gauss copula, the t copula exhibits upper as well as lower tail dependence according to Joe's (1997) definition (see, e.g. McNeil, Frey, and Embrechts 2005, 211):

$$C_{\nu,P}^t(\mathbf{u}) = \mathbf{t}_{\nu,P}(t_\nu^{-1}(u_1), t_\nu^{-1}(u_2), t_\nu^{-1}(u_3), t_\nu^{-1}(u_4)), \tag{10}$$

where t_ν is the density function of a standard univariate t-distribution with degrees of freedom ν and $\mathbf{t}_\nu$ is the joint density function of a four-dimensional vector with correlation matrix P and degrees of freedom ν.

Following McNeil, Frey and Embrechts (2005), we calibrate the Gauss and the t copula using the relationship between Kendall's rank correlation ρ_τ and the off-diagonal elements ρ_{ij} of the correlation matrix P. The element ρ_{ij} represents the correlation between the two random variables X_i and X_j:

$$\rho_\tau(X_i, X_j) = (2/\pi) \arcsin \rho_{ij}. \tag{11}$$

Additionally, we implement three Archimedean copulas that can be easily constructed by the use of generator functions (see Nelsen 2006). We apply three different copulas to consider different

Table 2. Generator functions for Archimedean copulas.

| Copula | Lower tail dependence | | Generator $\phi(u)$ | Kendall's tau ρ_τ |
	Joe (1997)	Ledford and Tawn (1996)		
C_θ^{Gumbel}	No	No	$(-\ln u)^\theta$	$1 - 1/\theta$
$C_\theta^{\text{Clayton}}$	Yes	Yes	$\frac{1}{\theta}(u^{-\theta} - 1)$	$\theta/(\theta + 2)$
C_θ^{Frank}	No	Yes	$-\ln\left(\dfrac{e^{-\theta u} - 1}{e^{-\theta} - 1}\right)$	$1 - 4\theta^{-1}\left(1 - \theta^{-1}\int_0^\theta u/(\exp(t) - 1)\,dt\right)$

types of lower tail dependence according to Joe's (1997) definition (see, e.g. McNeil, Frey, and Embrechts 2005, 222). The Gumbel copula exhibits dependence only in the upper tail, the Clayton copula has only lower tail dependence, and the Frank copula contains no tail dependence in the sense of Joe (1997). However, the Frank copula has tail dependence in both tails if tail dependence is measured using the definition of Ledford and Tawn (1996). We include the Frank copula since it is less tail dependent than the Gauss copula (see, e.g. Charpentier 2003). The generator functions $\phi(u)$ for the three Archimedean copulas are given in Table 2. θ denotes the respective copula parameter for each of the copulas. The functional relationship between Kendall's rank correlation ρ_τ and the copula parameter θ can be used to calibrate Archimedean copulas to data. For the copulas applied in our model, these relationships are summarized in the last column of Table 2. For the Clayton copula, for example, Kendall's tau ρ_τ equals $\theta/(\theta + 2)$. The parameter value θ can be obtained for any given value of ρ_τ by inverting this relationship.

The correlation between high-risk and low-risk investments will be modeled by the generator function ϕ_1 and its corresponding parameter θ_1, the correlation between individual claim amounts and claim frequencies arising from losses in the two lines of business (householder's and homeowner's insurance) exposed to catastrophes will be modeled by ϕ_2 with parameter θ_2, and ϕ_3 where θ_3 is used to correlate assets and liabilities. The copula parameter values θ_1, θ_2, and θ_3 are calibrated based on the correlations $\rho_{\tau 1}$ (high-risk and low-risk investments), $\rho_{\tau 2}$ (losses in householder's and homeowner's insurance), and $\rho_{\tau 3}$ (assets and liabilities).

The family of multivariate Archimedean copulas includes both exchangeable and non-exchangeable copula constructions. In this article, we apply non-exchangeable constructions since exchangeable structures impose restrictive conditions on the dependence structure in a multivariate context (e.g. exchangeable copulas result in the same correlation within assets as between assets and liabilities). We select a four-dimensional non-exchangeable construction as described in McNeil, Frey and Embrechts (2005), consisting of three strict Archimedean generators with completely monotonic inverses and composite functions $\phi_3 \circ \phi_1^{-1}$ and $\phi_3 \circ \phi_2^{-1}$:

$$C(u_1, u_2, u_3, u_4) = \phi_3^{-1}(\phi_3 \circ \underbrace{\phi_1^{-1}(\phi_1(u_1) + \phi_1(u_2))}_{\text{high-risk and low-risk investments}} + \phi_3 \circ \underbrace{\phi_2^{-1}(\phi_2(u_3) + \phi_2(u_4))}_{\text{homeowner and householder}}). \quad (12)$$

We apply this four-dimensional non-exchangeable structure to construct two exchangeable groups. The first group consists of high-risk and low-risk investments and the second group consists of catastrophe losses from homeowner's and householder's insurance. Thus, we are able to calibrate the copulas according to different correlations for assets and liabilities. The requirement of complete monotonicity results in higher correlations for copulas on a lower level of the hierarchical

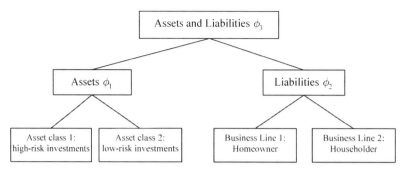

Figure 1. Dependence structure of non-exchangeable constructions based on Archimedean copulas.

structure. The level of correlation at higher hierarchical levels is thus limited (see Joe 1997, 89–91). In our application, the correlation between assets and liabilities must thus be smaller than the minimum of correlations of high-risk and low-risk investments and the correlations of catastrophe losses from homeowner and householder insurance.

We focus on the same copula for all three generating functions in the construction scheme (Equation (12)) to analyze the pure effects of different types of tail dependence (although the generators of the copulas shown in Figure 1 could be combined in the four-dimensional construction). Thus, the generators ϕ_1, ϕ_2, and ϕ_3 differ only in their respective parameter values, which are calibrated using Kendall's rank correlation ρ_τ.

Following Embrechts, Lindskog and McNeil (2001), we generate random deviates from the Archimedean copulas by applying the inverse transform method to the conditional distributions with numerical root-finding techniques. Savu and Trede (2006) apply this algorithm in a financial market context. Berg and Aas (2007) compare the non-exchangeable Archimedean model with a pair-copula construction, examine estimation as well as simulation techniques, and test the goodness of fit with two data sets. Non-exchangeable constructions based on Archimedean copulas usually result in large expressions and are computationally demanding. We therefore limit ourselves to the basic description in Table 2 and refer to Appendix 1 for the full mathematical expressions.

Non-exchangeable constructions based on Archimedean copulas following the scheme of Equation (12) introduce a hierarchy in the dependence structure that can be represented by a tree diagram (Figure 1). While Blum, Dias and Embrechts (2002) consider bivariate data in their model, our problem requires an approach that can account for four hierarchically dependent dimensions.

We model losses in homeowner and householder insurance by generating a claim frequency in each line of business from a Poisson distribution with mean λ using the generated correlated random numbers. In the next step, we generate individual claim amounts for the given number of claims by bootstrapping from the generated correlated random numbers (see Efron and Tibshirani 1993).

2.3 *Integration of reinsurance*

We consider three types of reinsurance contracts widely used in practice. The first is an excess-of-loss contract, the second is a stop loss contract, and the third one is a double trigger contract.

Excess-of-loss (XL) contracts can be found in property and casualty insurance, particularly in catastrophe-exposed lines of business that experience strong variations in loss ratios due to fluctuations in claim size (see Cummins, Lalonde, and Phillips 2004). Under this type of contract, the ceding insurer pays the reinsurance premium P_{XL} at the beginning of each year. In return, he is indemnified for that portion of each loss x_i in excess of a given attachment point A_{XL}. Usually, the reinsurer's payment is limited to a certain maximum amount M_{XL} (also called the limit). The payment from the reinsurer at the end of each year (S_{XL}) can thus be calculated by (n denotes the annual number of claims):

$$S_{XL} = \sum_{i=1}^{n} \min(\max(0, x_i - A_{XL}), M_{XL}). \tag{13}$$

Stop loss (SL) reinsurance is common for businesses that exhibit substantial variation in loss ratios due to fluctuations in loss frequency, e.g. hailstorm and windstorm insurance (see Denuit and Vermandele 1998). Under these contracts, coverage is linked to primary insurer's gross premium income, with deductible A_{SL} and limit M_{SL} expressed as a claims ratio. The contract delimits the claim amount for the full contract period (usually 1 year) and does not refer to a single claim. At the beginning of each year the insurer pays the reinsurance premium P_{SL}. The payment from the reinsurer at the end of each year (S_{SL}) is given by

$$S_{SL} = \min\left(\max\left(0, \left(\sum_{i=1}^{n} x_i\right) \bigg/ P_{t-1} - A_{SL}\right), M_{SL}\right) \cdot P_{t-1}. \tag{14}$$

Double trigger reinsurance is a relatively new type of contract from the area of ART (see Gründl and Schmeiser 2002). The potential coverage from this type of contract depends on both underwriting and financial risk. For example, the primary insurer is compensated only if the claims are high *and* the capital market is down. At the beginning of each year the insurer pays the reinsurance premium P_{DT}. Therefore, he receives the following payment from the reinsurer (S_{DT}) at the end of each year:

$$S_{DT} = 1_{[r_p<Y]} \cdot \sum_{i=1}^{n} \min(\max(0, x_i - A_{DT}), M_{DT}) = 1_{[r_p<Y]} \cdot S_{XL}. \tag{15}$$

Double trigger reinsurance contracts are a combination of a long put option ($1_{[r_p<Y]}$, with r_p as the companies portfolio return and Y as the trigger return level) and an excess-of-loss reinsurance contract (with deductible A_{DT} and limit M_{DT}). They serve as protection against worst cases, i.e. negative outcomes both on the capital market and the underwriting business. It is also possible to use a stop loss contract instead of the excess-of-loss contract when designing the double trigger reinsurance. In any case, such a contract incorporates manifold dependencies between the assets, between the liabilities, and between assets and liabilities, all of which must be taken into account when evaluating such contracts.

2.4 *Measurement of risk, return, and performance*

As done in Eling, Parnitzke and Schmeiser (2006) and Eling and Toplek (2007) we measure risk, return, and performance of the reinsurance strategies considering seven financial ratios. We measure return using the expected gain per annum, which is the expected gain divided by the number of years. Denoting the expected gain from time 0 to time T as $E(\text{EC}_T) - \text{EC}_0$, the expected gain $E(G)$ is given by $(E(\text{EC}_T) - \text{EC}_0)/T$.

Three risk measures are analyzed: the standard deviation, the probability of ruin, and the EPD. The standard deviation of the gain per annum $\sigma(G) = \sigma(\text{EC}_T)/T$ is a measure of total risk, because it takes into account both positive and negative deviations from the expected value. In the field of insurance, risk is often measured using downside risk measures such as the ruin probability (RP) or the EPD. These measures, which are also known as lower partial moments of order 0 and 1 (see Price, Price, and Nantell 1985), only take negative deviations from a certain threshold, e.g. the expected value, into account. The ruin probability can be written as $\text{RP} = \text{Pr}(\hat{\tau} \leq T)$, with $\hat{\tau} = \inf\{t > 0; \text{EC}_t < 0\}$ with $t = 1, 2, \ldots, T$ describing the first occurrence of ruin (i.e. a negative equity capital).

While the ruin probability does not provide any information regarding the severity of insolvency (see Butsic 1994; Barth 2000) or the time value of money (see Powers 1995; Gerber and Shiu 1998), the EPD takes exactly these features into account:

$$\text{EPD} = \sum_{t=1}^{T} E[\max(-\text{EC}_t, 0)] \cdot (1 + r_{\text{f}})^{-t},$$

where r_{f} stands for the risk-free rate of return.

We consider the Sharpe ratio and its two modified versions as performance measures. The Sharpe ratio gives the relationship between the risk premium (mean excess return above the risk-free interest rate) and the standard deviation of returns ($\text{SR}_\sigma = (E(\text{EC}_T) - \text{EC}_0 \cdot (1 + r_{\text{f}})^T)/\sigma(\text{EC}_T)$; see Sharpe 1966). In the numerator, the risk-free return is subtracted from the expected value of the equity capital in T. Using the standard deviation as measure of risk, the Sharpe ratio SR_σ also considers positive deviations of the returns in relation to the expected value. However, since risk is often calculated by downside measures, we also use the ruin probability and the EPD in the denominator of the Sharpe ratio. The Sharpe ratio based on ruin probability is denoted by $\text{SR}_{\text{RP}} = (E(\text{EC}_T) - \text{EC}_0 \cdot (1 + r_{\text{f}})^T)/\text{RP}$. The Sharpe ratio based on EPD is given by $\text{SR}_{\text{EPD}} = (E(\text{EC}_T) - \text{EC}_0 \cdot (1 + r_{\text{f}})^T)/\text{EPD}$.

3. Measuring the influence of copulas on reinsurance

3.1 Model specifications

In the following simulation study, we consider a typical German non-life insurance company by using corresponding data and solvency rules. The data come from the regulatory annual statements filed with the German Federal Financial Supervisory Authority BaFin (see BaFin 2005). However, we do not model a *specific* company in the market; instead, we consider a *typical* company using industry-wide averages and stylized numbers, e.g. those for market volume.

The time horizon T is 5 years. The market volume MV (i.e. $\beta = 1$) of the underwriting market accessible to the insurance company is €1000 million. In $t = 0$, the insurer has a share of $\beta_0 = 0.2$ in the insurance market, so that the premium income for the insurer at a premium rate level equal to 1 in the underwriting cycle is €200 million. We apply the empirical findings of Cummins and Outreville (1987) and parameterize the underwriting cycle (see Equation (6)) according to the German all-lines underwriting profit ratios. These parameters of the autoregressive process are $a_0 = 1.191$, $a_1 = 0.879$, and $a_2 = -0.406$, which leads to an underwriting cycle length of 7.76 years ($2\pi / \arccos(a_1/2\sqrt{-a_2})$). The costs for the premiums written are $\text{Ex}_{t-1}^P = 0.05 \cdot \beta_{t-1} \cdot \text{MV} + 0.001 \cdot ((\beta_{t-1} - \beta_{t-2}) \cdot \text{MV})^2$. The tax rate tr is 0.25.

Asset returns are normally distributed. The continuous rate of return of the high- (low-) risk investment has a mean of 10% (5%) and a standard deviation of 20% (5%). German non-life insurance companies typically invest approximately 40% of their wealth in high-risk investments; the remaining 60% is invested in low-risk investments (see BaFin 2005, Table 510). We thus fix $\alpha_0 = 0.40$. The risk-free return r_f is 3%.

For the underwriting business, non-catastrophe losses are log-normally distributed, with a mean loss ratio of 76.5% and a standard deviation of 2.3% (see BaFin 2005, Table 541). The catastrophe claims are modeled using a Poisson distribution for the claim frequencies with a mean parameter of 1.2 and a Pareto distribution for the individual claim sizes having a mean of €7.5 million for homeowner insurance (€2.5 million for householder insurance) and a standard deviation of €8.1 million for homeowner insurance (€2.7 million for householder insurance). This corresponds to an additional 5% average loss ratio from catastrophe losses. The claim settlement costs are 5% of the claims ($\text{Ex}_t^C = 0.05 \cdot C_t$; see BaFin 2005, Table 541).

The consumer response parameter cr is 1 (0.95) if the equity capital at the end of the last period is above (below) the company's safety level. The company's safety level is determined by the minimum capital required (MCR), which is based on the Solvency I rules currently used in Germany. The Solvency I minimum capital is calculated as:

$$\text{MCR}_t = \max \begin{pmatrix} 0.18 \cdot (\min(P_{t-1}; \text{€50 million})) + 0.16 \cdot (\max(P_{t-1} - \text{€50 million}; 0)); \\ 0.26 \cdot (\min(C_t; \text{€35 million})) + 0.23 \cdot (\max(C_t - \text{€35 million}; 0)) \end{pmatrix}$$
(16)

(see § 53c of the German Insurance Supervision Act (VAG)). Following these rules, we calculate a minimum capital requirement of €38.54 million in $t = 1$ ($\max(0.18 \cdot \text{€50 million} + 0.16 \cdot \text{€150 million}; 0.26 \cdot \text{€35 million} + 0.23 \cdot \text{€128 million})$; note that premiums are €200 million and claims are 81.5% of €200 million). To comply with these rules, the insurance company is capitalized with €75 million in $t = 0$. This corresponds to an equity to premium ratio of 37.5%, which is a typical value for German non-life insurance companies (see BaFin 2005, Table 520).

We use random numbers with the following correlation structure. Kendall's rank correlation between high-risk and low-risk investments is 0.2. The Kendall's rank correlation between homeowner catastrophe losses and householder catastrophe losses is 0.1, and that between assets and liabilities is −0.1 (to generate the negative dependence between assets and liabilities, we apply the uniform random variates generated with the hierarchical Archimedean copulas to the survival functions of the marginal distributions for the liabilities; for the t copula, we use five degrees of freedom). There is no clear empirical evidence concerning these correlation values (see Lambert and Hofflander 1966; Haugen 1971; Kahane and Nye 1975; Li and Huang 1996); for that reason, we will present results for alternative parameter settings within robustness tests.

For the sake of comparability, all parameters of the reinsurance contracts are selected so that each reinsurance contract leads to the same expected gain and ruin probability in a setting without correlations (i.e. we assume independence between the assets, the liabilities, and assets and liabilities). This approach allows us to identify the effect of the distinct forms of dependence considered (i.e. the Gauss, t, Gumbel, Clayton, and Frank copulas) on the different contracts. From the perspective of ruin probability and expected gain and in an analysis without copulas, the insurance company would be indifferent concerning these contracts. We will find that this changes, if copulas are taken into account.

We evaluate three reinsurance contracts. The first is an excess-of-loss contract with an attachment point (A_{XL}) of €26 million, a maximum (M_{XL}) of €114 million, and a premium (P_{XL}) of €2.51 million at the beginning of each year. In the second case, the insurer signs a stop loss reinsurance contract with an attachment point (A_{SL}) of €215 million, a maximum (M_{SL}) of €65 million, and a premium (P_{SL}) of €2.18 million. The third is a double trigger contract. Under this contract, the attachment point (A_{DT}) is €15 million, the maximum (M_{DT}) is €145 million, and the premium (P_{DT}) is €2.90 million at the beginning of each year. Furthermore, we are operating under the assumption that the companies investment portfolio return (r_p) must be lower than $Y = 5\%$ in order to obtain a payment from the reinsurer. Considering the specifications of the three contracts these seem to be quite different. However, all three were calibrated to lead to identical ruin probability and expected gain in a case without correlations, which serves as a starting point for the evaluation of the different dependencies in the presented model.

All model parameters, their meanings, and their initial values are summarized in Table 1.

3.2 *Simulation results*

In Table 3, we present simulation results for six different dependence structures. All results have been calculated on the basis of a Monte Carlo simulation with 500,000 iterations (for details on Monte Carlo simulation, see, e.g. Glassermann 2004).

We first analyze the simulation results without reinsurance (Table 3). In the case without correlations (column 2), we find an expected gain of €33.43 million per annum with a standard deviation of €14.61 million. The ruin probability is 0.32%, which is below the requirements of many regulatory authorities. For example, the Solvency II framework planned for the European Union requires a ruin probability below 0.50% (see European Commission 2005). Considering the different copulas (columns 3–7), we find only minor effects on the mean returns, but a much greater impact on the risk measures. The effect on risk depends on the form of nonlinear dependency. When comparing the copulas with each other, we see that those with weak or no lower tail dependence (the Gumbel and Frank copulas) provide a relatively low ruin probability, whereas these values are much higher with lower tail dependent copulas (the t and Clayton copulas, according to Joe's (1997) definition). Note that the ruin probability for all copulas is above the standard regulatory requirements (e.g. 0.50% in Solvency II).

With the excess-of-loss reinsurance contract (Table 3), the expected gain per annum is reduced by €1.45 million to €31.98 million in the case without correlations (column 2). The ruin probability is reduced to 0.07%, which is less than a quarter of the value without reinsurance. The reinsurance contract thus reduces the ruin probability enough to qualify the firm for an investment grade rating. Considering the different copulas (columns 3–7), we find that risk is not reduced to the same degree. For example, with the Clayton copula, the ruin probability is only reduced by 55% and still amounts to 0.85%. The EPD only declines by 42% (compared with 89% in column 2, the case without copulas). These results, of course, also lead to much lower values for the performance measures, especially for those based on ruin probability and EPD. For example, SR_{RP} is 210.75 in the case without correlations, but only 17.12 with the Clayton copula. In general, large differences in risk assessment and performance measurement are found when considering different nonlinear dependencies.

The results for the stop loss contract are shown in Table 3. We again find an expected gain of €31.98 million and a ruin probability of 0.07% (column 2). As mentioned, the three reinsurance contracts are calibrated so as to have the same expected gain and ruin probability in the case without correlations, which allows us to identify the pure impact of copulas on the reinsurance contracts. And, indeed, we find large differences in risk assessment between the reinsurance contracts. For example, with the t copula, the ruin probability (0.65%; Stop loss, column 4) is 14% higher than the ruin probability of the excess-of-loss contract (0.57%; column 4). The EPD of the stop loss

Table 3. Results for the input parameters given in Table 1.

Dependence structure	Independence	Gauss	T	Gumbel	Clayton	Frank
Lower tail dependence						
Joe (1997)	No	No	Yes	No	Yes	No
Ledford and Tawn (1996)	No	Yes	Yes	No	Yes	Yes
No reinsurance						
$E(G)$ in million €	33.43	32.90	32.86	33.06	32.62	33.03
$\sigma(G)$ in million €	14.61	17.28	17.37	17.00	18.18	16.92
RP (%)	0.32	0.99	1.34	0.74	1.91	0.72
EPD in million €	0.06	0.19	0.32	0.23	0.99	0.17
SR_σ	2.12	1.77	1.75	1.80	1.66	1.81
SR_{RP}	48.29	15.35	11.39	20.86	7.93	21.18
SR_{EPD}	2.73	0.81	0.47	0.67	0.15	0.89
Excess of loss						
$E(G)$ in million €	31.98	31.65	31.64	31.74	31.54	31.71
$\sigma(G)$ in million €	13.93	16.34	16.39	16.18	16.95	16.10
RP (%)	0.07	0.36	0.57	0.28	0.85	0.26
EPD in million €	0.01	0.04	0.08	0.08	0.57	0.05
SR_σ	2.12	1.79	1.79	1.81	1.72	1.82
SR_{RP}	210.75	40.56	25.76	52.03	17.12	55.44
SR_{EPD}	22.85	3.42	1.87	1.89	0.26	3.02
Stop loss						
$E(G)$ in million €	31.98	31.59	31.58	31.70	31.45	31.66
$\sigma(G)$ in million €	14.06	16.54	16.59	16.35	17.20	16.27
RP (%)	0.07	0.40	0.65	0.29	0.95	0.28
EPD in million €	0.01	0.05	0.09	0.10	0.62	0.06
SR_σ	2.10	1.77	1.76	1.79	1.69	1.80
SR_{RP}	210.75	36.25	22.58	50.42	15.36	51.68
SR_{EPD}	20.14	3.12	1.62	1.41	0.23	2.34
Double trigger						
$E(G)$ in million €	31.98	32.11	32.09	32.07	32.12	32.10
$\sigma(G)$ in million €	13.57	15.64	15.57	15.61	16.06	15.48
RP (%)	0.07	0.14	0.21	0.15	0.36	0.13
EPD in million €	0.01	0.02	0.03	0.08	0.50	0.05
SR_σ	2.18	1.90	1.91	1.90	1.85	1.92
SR_{RP}	210.75	108.79	71.55	98.80	41.00	118.47
SR_{EPD}	11.88	8.38	5.59	1.78	0.30	3.30

Note: $E(G)$, expected gain per annum, $\sigma(G)$, standard deviation of the gain per annum; RP, ruin probability; EPD, expected policyholder deficit; SR_σ, Sharpe ratio based on standard deviation; SR_{RP}, Sharpe ratio based on ruin probability; SR_{EPD}, Sharpe ratio based on EPD.

is 34% above the EPD of the excess of loss in case of the Gumbel copula (0.10 vs. 0.08, column 5). Thus, in our simulation, the stop loss contract is less efficient in reducing risk and less useful in dealing with nonlinear dependencies than is the excess-of-loss contract, as it always results in higher risk as well as a lower return. The reason behind the superiority of the excess of loss is that the type of contract is designed to cover single, large losses, whereas the stop loss covers the whole loss amount incurred during a certain time period. Compared with the situation without correlations, the introduction of nonlinear dependencies results in a higher number of large losses, so that from the insurers point of view the excess-of-loss contract design appears more appropriate for handling these situations than the stop loss contract.

If risk reduction is management's primary goal, the double trigger (Table 3) is the most efficient reinsurance contract as it generally has the lowest values for ruin probability and EPD. This is because the double trigger contract is especially designed to cover worst-case situations, which become more frequent under nonlinear dependencies. But, again, there are large differences in risk assessment between the ruin probability and the EPD. While the ruin probability is much lower than that of the other reinsurance contracts, the EPD is not reduced to a corresponding degree. For example, with the Clayton copula, the ruin probability is 62% lower than that of the stop loss contract (0.36% vs. 0.95%, column 6), but the EPD is only 19% lower (0.50 vs. 0.62). Also of interest is that the double trigger contract provides the best performance numbers of all the reinsurance contracts – with one exception: the excess-of-loss contract provides the highest performance when considering the Gumbel copulas and the Sharpe ratio based on EPD (1.89 vs. 1.78 with the double trigger; note that the EPD of the excess-of-loss contract is 0.0775 vs. 0.0804 with the double trigger).

Thus depending on the copula concept employed, we find that different recommendations are appropriate concerning reinsurance contracts, making it appear essential to integrate nonlinear dependencies in the analysis. Furthermore, we find that even though reinsurance contracts are especially useful in reducing ruin probability, they cannot reduce EPD to the same extent. This is an especially important finding for policyholders and regulators because the EPD is more important for policyholders than it is for shareholders (see Bingham 2000), given that policyholders have to bear the amount of loss, while shareholders (in case of limited liability) have a limited downside risk. The large differences in risk assessment for different copulas and reinsurance contracts is another important result, as regulators and rating agencies use measures such as the ruin probability and the EPD as a foundation for capital assessment and ratings.

3.3 Robustness of findings

We check the robustness of our findings by varying the level of equity capital and the correlation settings. The results can be considered robust if the basic relations between the analyzed reinsurance contracts are independent of the given input parameter setting.

In the first step, we vary the level of equity capital in $t = 0$, which determines the company's safety level, leaving everything else constant. In Section 3.2, the level of equity capital was set at €75 million. To discover the impact of different levels of equity capital, we vary the equity capital in $t = 0$ from €50 to €100 million in €5 million intervals. The results are shown in Figure 2, where the ruin probability and the EPD are displayed as a function of equity capital. Due to the huge amount of data, we cannot present the results for all copulas. We thus concentrate on the Gauss and Clayton copulas; the results for the other copulas are presented in Figures 3–6.

As the level of equity capital increases, the ruin probability and the EPD decrease because the company's safety level is improved. The ruin probability is greatly reduced with the Gauss copula as well as with the Clayton copula, but the EPD is not reduced to a similar degree. In fact, there is a substantial residual risk with the EPD in case of the Clayton copula. Therefore, it seems that copulas are of relevance not only for low-capitalized companies, but also for well-capitalized companies. Furthermore, there is a lower bound for the EPD with the Clayton copula. The EPD of the reinsurance contracts is always above 0.45 and can hardly be reduced by increasing the equity capital level. Similar lower bounds can be found for other types of copulas, especially for

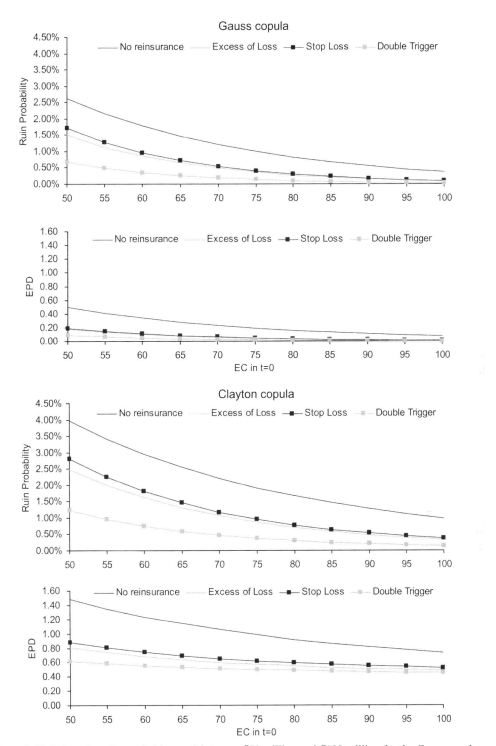

Figure 2. Variation of equity capital in $t = 0$ between €50 million and €100 million for the Gauss copulas (upper part) and the Clayton copula (lower part).

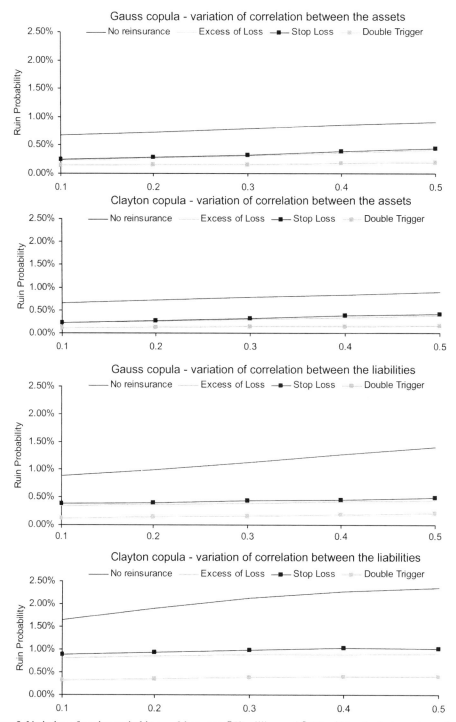

Figure 3. Variation of equity capital in $t = 0$ between €50 million and €100 million for independence (upper part) and the t copula (lower part).

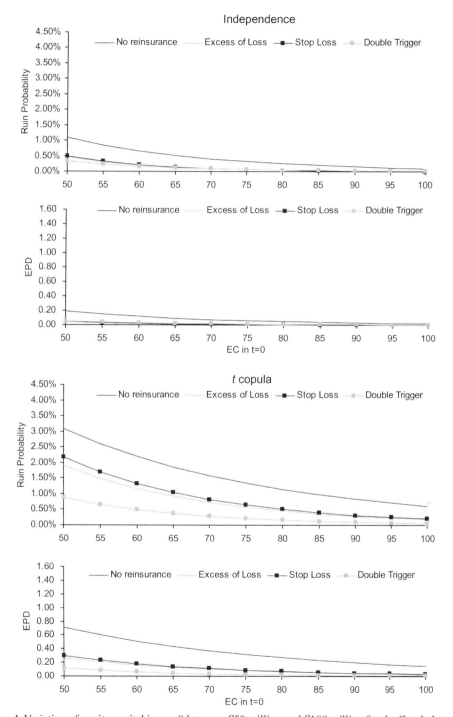

Figure 4. Variation of equity capital in $t = 0$ between €50 million and €100 million for the Gumbel copulas (upper part) and the Frank copula (lower part).

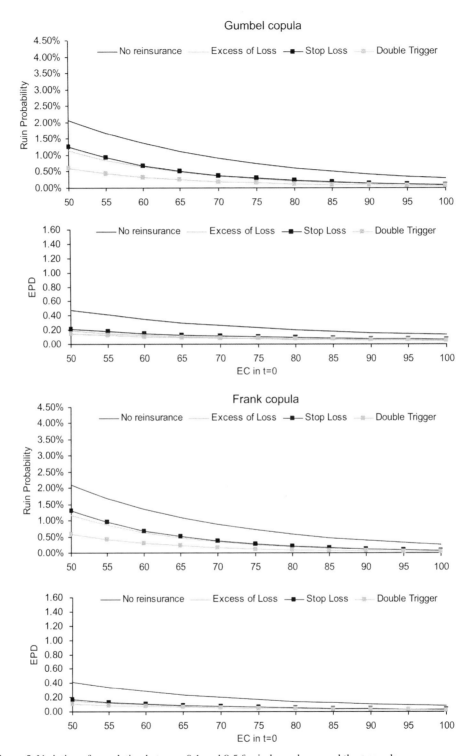

Figure 5. Variation of correlation between 0.1 and 0.5 for independence and the *t* copula.

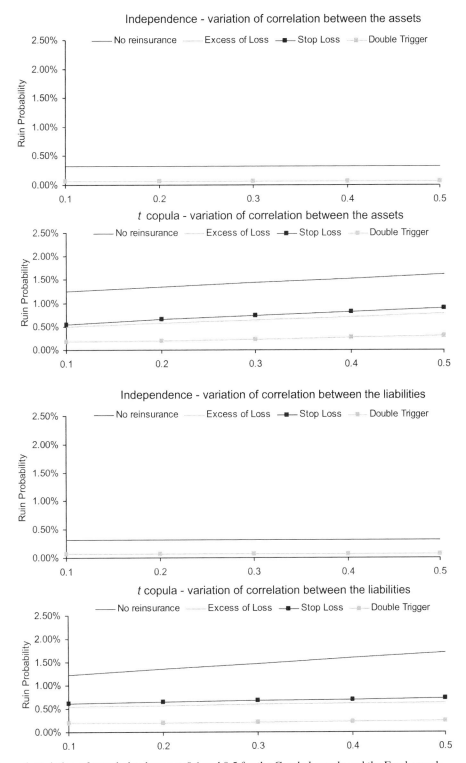

Figure 6. Variation of correlation between 0.1 and 0.5 for the Gumbel copula and the Frank copula.

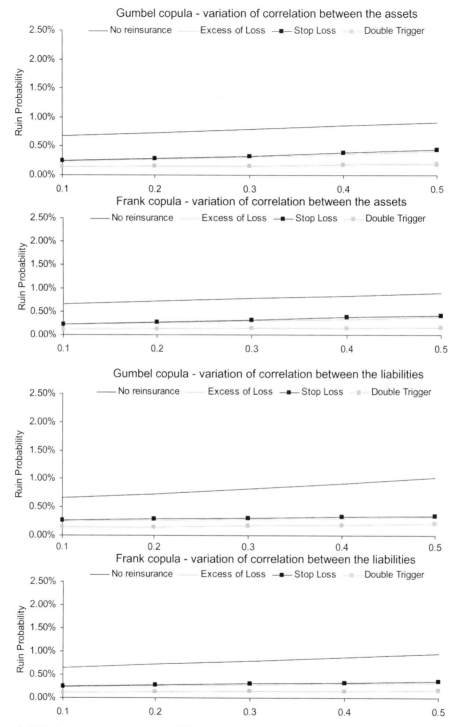

Figure 7. Variation of correlation between 0.1 and 0.5.

the Gumbel copula (Figures 3–6). This result is, again, especially relevant for policyholders and regulators, as policyholders have to carry the loss in case of insolvency.

In the second step, we vary the correlations in our simulation study. In the basic model, these are relatively low. Kendall's rank correlation between high-risk and low-risk investments is 0.2, between catastrophe losses in householder's and homeowner's insurance 0.1, and between assets and liabilities −0.1. To discover the impact of different correlation assumptions, we vary the correlation between the high-risk and low-risk investments from 0.1 to 0.5 in 0.1 intervals (upper part of Figure 7) and between catastrophe losses in householder's and homeowner's insurance also from 0.1 to 0.5 in 0.1 intervals (lower part of Figure 7). The correlation between assets and liabilities remains fixed at −0.1. The resulting ruin probability for the different reinsurance contracts is presented in Figure 7. Again, we concentrate on the Gauss and Clayton copulas; the results for the other copulas can be found in Figures 3–6.

We find that ruin probability increases with an increasing correlation between the assets under both the Gauss and the Clayton copula. This occurs because the higher the correlation, the higher the likelihood that negative outcomes are generated for both types of assets (i.e. low returns with the high-risk and the low-risk investments). Without reinsurance, the increase in ruin probability grows even larger when the correlation between the liabilities is varied. The reason for this is that with the given parametrization, the underwriting business is less profitable than the insurer's investments in the capital market. However, under the three reinsurance contracts, ruin probability increases only slightly with increasing correlation between the liabilities. Comparing the copulas, we find that the basic relations remain unchanged and thus the main results of the last section appear to be very robust.

4. Conclusion

The aim of this article is to extend previous literature by analyzing the influence of nonlinear dependencies on the payoff of reinsurance contracts and the resulting effects on a non-life insurer's risk and return profile. We therefore integrate different copula models (i.e. Gaussian, t, Clayton, Gumbel, and Frank) in a DFA framework and conduct numerous tests within a simulation study. Our approach is to keep constant the risk and return for three different reinsurance contracts (stop loss, excess-of-loss, double trigger) in a setting without dependencies and then to identify the impact of different copulas on the contracts.

There are three main conclusions, each with important implications for insurance company stakeholders.

1. Depending on the copula concept employed, management will prefer different types of reinsurance contracts. In our simulation, the double trigger is the most efficient contract (from a risk reduction perspective) in many cases, but there are situations when the excess-of-loss contract more efficiently deals with nonlinear dependencies. This result shows that it is important to take nonlinear dependencies into consideration when analyzing reinsurance contracts as they might lead to different management decisions. Ceteris paribus, the heavier and the more dependent the tails, the better is the double trigger reinsurance contract. Heaviness and tail dependence should thus be important considerations in pricing reinsurance contracts.
2. The reinsurance contracts we looked at are especially useful in reducing ruin probability but not as good at reducing the EPD when nonlinear dependencies are analyzed. This is an important result, especially for policyholders, who have to bear the amount of loss, and for regulators, who have to monitor insurer solvency in order to protect policyholders. Another important

finding in this context is that there is a lower bound for the EPD with some kinds of non-linear dependence. It thus appears that there remains a substantial residual risk that becomes apparent only when nonlinear dependencies are taken into consideration. This finding emphasizes the importance of nonlinear dependencies when analyzing reinsurance contracts for well-capitalized companies.

3. We find large differences in risk assessment under different copulas. For identical reinsurance contracts, the ruin probability and the EPD may differ widely depending on the copula concept employed. This finding is especially important for regulators and rating agencies that use these risk measures as a foundation for capital assessment and ratings. It thus seems important to analyze nonlinear dependencies in combination with reinsurance in the regulatory framework and in rating assessments, e.g. in stress testing and scenario analysis.

Considering the variety of our results it might seem difficult to derive practical implications from all the numbers presented. The purpose of this article is to evaluate the effect of reinsurance contracts under different forms of copulas and to study their effects on the risk and return of non-life insurers in a stress-testing sense. However, due to the impossibility of calibrating certain model elements, we cannot state which copula best fits actual data. Even so, our results are useful for many practical purposes. To date most insurers, reinsurers, rating agencies, and regulators do not take nonlinear dependencies into account (see, e.g. Embrechts, McNeil, and Straumann 2002). Thus one of the main contributions of this article is to show that this lack of consideration could have serious consequences for risk management.

Furthermore, our model provides a flexible way of integrating a variety of copulas, making it possible for insurers to get an idea of what could happen under different scenarios. Thus a second contribution of this article is to show how to incorporate nonlinear dependencies in risk management. In this context an interesting aspect is that European regulators strongly encourage insurers to develop internal risk models, e.g. for the calculation of the target capital under the new European Union's regulatory framework Solvency II (see Schmeiser 2004). These internal risk models are usually dynamic cash-flow-based models like the one presented in this article. Our model could thus be used to incorporate nonlinear dependencies into the regulatory framework. Considering our results, perhaps the most promising way to do this will be to incorporate dependence structures based on the Clayton copula, which would be a worst-case scenario.

As mentioned, due to the rare occurrence of extreme events, there is a lack of data and, consequently, very few empirical studies that focus on the dependence structure between different liabilities and between assets and liabilities. An important contribution for future research would thus be to further explore the empirical dependence structure, especially between different liabilities and between assets and liabilities. Results from such a study would be very helpful not only in calibrating the DFA model, but also in providing further empirical insights into the nature of extreme events.

The presented model framework can be used in the analysis of other research questions in different fields of risk management and corporate finance. An example in the field of risk management might be to consider different distributional assumptions for the assets as well as for the liabilities and to analyze their effects on insurer risk and return. In the field of corporate finance one could evaluate different tax systems and their impact on an insurer's financial situation by modifying the tax parameters integrated in the model. Furthermore, the model dynamics might be used to analyze time-varying dependence structures, e.g. between assets, which is empirically observable (see Dias and Embrechts 2007), between liabilities, or between assets and liabilities.

Acknowledgements

The authors are grateful to Charles D. Cowan, Nadine Gatzert, Michael Luhnen, Andrea Macarina, Thomas Parnitzke, Hato Schmeiser, and the participants of the European Journal of Finance and Warwick Business School Conference on Copulae and Multivariate Probability Distributions in Finance for valuable suggestions and comments.

References

BaFin. 2005. Jahresbericht 2004, Statistik der Bundesanstalt für Finanzdienstleistungsaufsicht – Erstversicherungsunternehmen, Bundesanstalt für Finanzdienstleistungsaufsicht. www.bafin.de.

Barth, M.M. 2000. A comparison of risk-based capital standards under the expected policy-holder deficit and the probability of ruin approaches. *Journal of Risk and Insurance* 67, no. 3: 397–414.

Berg, D., and K. Aas. 2007. Models for construction of multivariate dependence. Working Paper, Norwegian Computing Center, Oslo.

Bingham, R.E. 2000. Risk and return: Underwriting, investment, and leverage. In *Proceedings of the casualty actuarial society* 87, 31–78 Arlington.

Blum, P., M. Dacorogna, P. Embrechts, T. Neghaiwi, and H. Niggli. 2001. Using DFA for modeling the impact of foreign exchange risks on reinsurance decisions. *Casualty Actuarial Society Forum* 49–93. http://www.casact.org/pubs/forum/01sforum/01sf049.pdf/

Blum, P., A. Dias, and P. Embrechts. 2002. The ART of dependence modeling: The latest advances in correlation analysis. In *Alternative risk strategies*, ed. M. Lane. London: Risk Books.

Butsic, R.P. 1994. Solvency measurement for property-liability risk-based capital applications. *Journal of Risk and Insurance* 61, no. 4: 656–90.

Carriere, J. 1994. Dependent decrement theory. *Transactions of the Society of Actuaries* 46: 45–74.

Casualty Actuarial Society. 2006. *Dynamic Risk Modeling Handbook* (prepared by the CAS Dynamic Risk Modeling Working Party), Arlington.

Charpentier, A. 2003. Tail distribution and dependence measures. In *Proceedings XXXIV International ASTIN Colloquium.* Brussels: ASTIN Colloquium International Actuarial Association.

Charpentier, A. 2006. Dependence structures and limiting results, with applications in finance and insurance. PhD thesis, Leuven.

Cummins, J.D., and J.F. Outreville. 1987. An international analysis of underwriting cycles in property-liability insurance. *Journal of Risk and Insurance* 54, no. 2: 246–62.

Cummins, J.D., D. Lalonde, and R.D. Phillips. 2004. The basis risk of catastrophic-loss index securities. *Journal of Financial Economics* 71, no. 1: 77–111.

D'Arcy, S.P., and R. Gorvett. 2004. The use of dynamic financial analysis to determine whether an optimal growth rate exists for a property-liability insurer. *Journal of Risk and Insurance* 71, no. 4: 583–615.

Denuit, M., and C. Vermandele. 1998. Optimal reinsurance and stop-loss order. *Insurance: Mathematics and Economics* 22, no. 3: 229–33.

Dias, A. 2004. Copula inference for finance and insurance. PhD thesis, Zurich.

Dias, A., and P. Embrechts. 2007. Testing for structural changes in exchange rates dependence beyond linear correlation. Working Paper, Warwick Business School, Coventry.

Efron, B., and R.J. Tibshirani. 1993. *An Introduction to the Bootstrap*. Vol. 57 of *Monographs on statistics and applied probability*. Boca Raton, FL: Chapman & Hall/CRC.

Eling, M., and D. Toplek. 2007. *Modeling and management of nonlinear dependencies – copulas in dynamic financial analysis*. Working Paper, University of St Gallen, St Gallen.

Eling, M., T. Parnitzke, and H. Schmeiser. 2006. Management strategies and dynamic financial analysis. *Variance* 2, no. 1: 54–66.

Embrechts, P., P. Lindskog, and A. McNeil. 2001. Modeling dependence with copulas and applications to risk management. In *Handbook of heavy tailed distributions in finance*, ed. S.T. Rachev, 329–84. Amsterdam: Elsevier.

Embrechts, P., A. McNeil, and D. Straumann. 2002. Correlation and dependence in risk management: Properties and pitfalls. In *Risk management: Value at risk and beyond*, ed. M.A.H. Dempster, 176–223. Cambridge: Cambridge University Press.

European Commission. 2005. Policy issues for Solvency II – Possible amendments to the framework for consultation. Markt/2505/05, Brussels: European Commission.

Frees, E., J. Carriere, and E. Valdez. 1996. Annuity valuation with dependent mortality. *Journal of Risk and Insurance* 63, no. 2: 229–61.

Frees, E.W., and E.A. Valdez. 1998. Understanding relationships using copulas. *North American Actuarial Journal* 2, no. 1: 1–25.

Gerber, H.U., and E.S. Shiu. 1998. On the time value of ruin. *North American Actuarial Journal* 2, no. 1: 48–72.

Glassermann, P. 2004. *Monte Carlo methods in financial engineering*. New York: Springer.

Gründl, H., and H. Schmeiser. 2002. Pricing double-trigger reinsurance contracts: Financial versus actuarial approach. *Journal of Risk and Insurance* 69, no. 4: 449–68.

Haugen, R.A. 1971. Insurer risk under alternative investment and financing strategies. *Journal of Risk and Insurance* 38, no. 1: 71–80.

Hougaard, P., B. Harvald, and N.V. Holm. 1992. Measuring the similarities between the lifetimes of adult Danish twins born between 1881–1930. *Journal of the American Statistical Association* 87: 17–24.

Joe, H. 1997. *Multivariate models and dependence concepts*. London: Chapman & Hall.

Juri, A., and M.V. Wüthrich. 2003. Tail dependence from a distributional point of view. *Extremes* 6, no. 3: 213–46.

Kahane, Y., and D. Nye. 1975. A portfolio approach to the property-liability insurance industry. *Journal of Risk and Insurance* 42, no. 7: 579–98.

Kaufmann, R., A. Gadmer, and R. Klett. 2001. Introduction to dynamic financial analysis. *ASTIN Bulletin* 31, no. 1: 213–49.

Klugman, S.A., H.H. Panjer, and G.E. Wilmot. 2004. *Loss models: From data to decisions*. 2nd ed. Hoboken, NJ: John Wiley & Sons.

Klugman, S.A., and R. Parsa. 1999. Fitting bivariate loss distributions with copulas. *Insurance: Mathematics and Economics* 24, no. 1: 139–48 (initially presented at the Casualty Actuarial Society Ratemaking Seminar in 1995).

Lambert, E.W., and A.E. Hofflander. 1966. Impact of new multiple line underwriting on investment portfolios of property-liability insurers. *Journal of Risk and Insurance* 33, no. 2: 209–23.

Ledford, A.W., and J.A. Tawn. 1996. Statistics for near independence in multivariate extreme values. *Biometrika* 83, no. 1: 169–87.

Li, S.X., and Z. Huang. 1996. Determination of the portfolio selection for a property-liability insurance company. *European Journal of Operational Research* 88, no. 2: 257–68.

Lowe, S.P., and J.N. Stanard. 1997. An integrated dynamic financial analysis and decision support system for a property catastrophe reinsurer. *ASTIN Bulletin* 27, no. 2: 339–71.

McNeil, A., R. Frey, and P. Embrechts. 2005. *Quantitative risk management: Concepts, techniques and tools*. Princeton, NJ: Princeton Univ. Press.

Nelsen, R.B. 2006. *An introduction to copulas*. 2nd ed. New York: Springer.

Oakes, D. 1982. A model for association in bivariate survival data. *Journal of the Royal Statistical Society B* 44: 414–22.

Oakes, D. 1989. Bivariate survival models induced by frailties. *Journal of the American Statistical Association* 84: 487–93.

Powers, M.R. 1995. A theory of risk, return and solvency. *Insurance: Mathematics and Economics* 17, no. 2: 101–18.

Price, K, B. Price, and T.J. Nantell. 1985. Variance and lower partial moment measures of systematic risk: Some analytical and empirical results. *Journal of Finance* 37, no. 3: 843–55.

Rank, J. 2006. *Copulas: From theory to application in finance*. London: Risk Book.

Savu, C., and M. Trede. 2006. Hierarchical Archimedean copulas. Working Paper, University of Münster, Münster.

Schmeiser, H. 2004. New risk-based capital standards in the EU: A proposal based on empirical data. *Risk Management and Insurance Review* 7, no. 1: 41–52.

Sharpe, W.F. 1966. Mutual fund performance. *Journal of Business* 39, no. 1: 119–38.

Tibiletti, L. 1995. Beneficial changes in random variables via copulas: An application to insurance. *Geneva Papers on Risk and Insurance – Theory* 20: 191–202.

Wakker, P.P., R.H. Thaler, and A. Tversky. 1997. Probabilistic insurance. *Journal of Risk and Uncertainty* 15, no. 1: 7–28.

Wang, S. 1996. Premium calculation by transforming the layer premium density. *ASTIN Bulletin* 26: 71–92.

Wang, S. 1998. Aggregation of correlated risk portfolios: Models and algorithms. *Proceedings of the Casualty Actuarial Society* 85, 848–939.

Appendix 1: Full mathematical expressions for the non-exchangeable constructions based on Archimedean copulas

Gumbel copula:

$$C^{\text{Gumbel}}(u_1, u_2, u_3, u_4) = \exp(-|(-\ln(\exp(-|(-\ln u_1)^{\theta_1} + (-\ln u_2)^{\theta_1}|^{1/\theta_1}))^{\theta_3})$$

$$+ (-\ln(\exp(-|(-\ln u_3)^{\theta_2} + (-\ln u_4)^{\theta_2}|^{1/\theta_2}))^{\theta_3})|^{1/\theta_3}) \tag{A1}$$

Clayton copula:

$$C^{\text{Clayton}}(u_1, u_2, u_3, u_4) = ([(u_1^{-\theta_1} + u_2^{-\theta_1} - 1)^{-1/\theta_1}]^{-\theta_3} + [(u_3^{-\theta_2} + u_4^{-\theta_2} - 1)^{1/\theta_2}]^{-\theta_3} - 1)^{-1/\theta_3} \quad \text{(A2)}$$

Frank copula:

$$C^{\text{Frank}}(u_1, u_2, u_3, u_4)$$

$$= -\frac{\ln[((([(((\exp(-\theta_1 u_1) - 1)(\exp(-\theta_1 u_2) - 1))/(\exp(-\theta_1) - 1)) + 1]^{\theta_3/\theta_1} - 1)}{\theta_3} \\ \cdot \frac{([(((\exp(-\theta_2 u_3) - 1)(\exp(-\theta_2 u_4) - 1))/(\exp(-\theta_2) - 1)) + 1]^{\theta_3/\theta_2} - 1))/(\exp(-\theta_3) - 1)) + 1]}{\theta_3} \quad \text{(A3)}$$

Pricing bivariate option under GARCH-GH model with dynamic copula: application for Chinese market

Dominique Guégan and Jing Zang

PSE, MSE-CES, University Paris 1 Panthéon-Sorbonne, 106 Bd de l' hôpital, 75013, Paris, France

This paper develops the method for pricing bivariate contingent claims under general autoregressive conditionally heteroskedastic (GARCH) process. In order to provide a general framework being able to accommodate skewness, leptokurtosis, fat tails as well as the time-varying volatility that are often found in financial data, generalized hyperbolic (GH) distribution is used for innovations. As the association between the underlying assets may vary over time, the dynamic copula approach is considered. Therefore, the proposed method proves to play an important role in pricing bivariate option. The approach is illustrated for Chinese market with one type of better-of-two markets claims: call option on the better performer of Shanghai Stock Composite Index and Shenzhen Stock Composite Index. Results show that the option prices obtained by the GARCH-GH model with time-varying copula differ substantially from the prices implied by the GARCH-Gaussian dynamic copula model. Moreover, the empirical work displays the advantage of the suggested method.

1. Introduction

Following the great work of Black and Scholes (1973) and Merton (1973), the option pricing literature has been developed a lot. Over the years, various generalizations of the Brownian motion framework due to Black and Scholes (1973) have been used to model multivariate option prices. Examples include Margrabe (1978), Stulz (1982), Johnson (1987), Reiner (1992), and Shimko (1994). In all these papers, correlation was used to measure the dependence between assets. However, Embrechts, McNeil, and Strausmann (2002) and Forbes and Rigobon (2002) have pointed out that correlation may cause some confusion and misunderstanding. Indeed, it is a financial stylized fact that correlations observed under ordinary market differ substantially from correlations observed in hectic periods.

On the other hand, to take into account the heteroskedasticity of asset returns, a lot of models have been put forward, such as the constant-elasticity-of-variance model of Cox (1975), the jump-diffusion model in Merton (1976), the compound-option model in Geske (1979) and the displaced-diffusion model in Rubinstein (1983). Opposed to the aforementioned models, a bivariate diffusion model for pricing option on assets with stochastic volatilities was introduced by Hull and White (1987). Unfortunately, the bivariate diffusion option model requires the conditions stronger than no arbitrage and it faces the difficulty in empirical study that the variance rate is unobservable.

Through an equilibrium argument, Duan (1995) showed that options can be priced when the dynamics for the price of the underlying asset follows a GARCH process. This GARCH option pricing model has so far experimented some empirical successes in Heynen, Kemna, and Vorst (1994), Duan (1996) and Heston and Nandi (2000). In order to extend the risk neutralization developed in Rubinstein (1976) and Brennan (1979), Duan (1999) developed the GARCH option pricing model by providing a relatively easy transformation to risk-neutral distributions.

Now the distribution of the error term in GARCH process attracts a lot of attention. In Engle (1982), the normal distribution is used but alternative distributions such as the t distribution or the GED distribution have been considered to capture the excess kurtosis and fat tails. Unfortunately, as explained in Duan (1999), using t distribution to model continuously compounded asset returns is inappropriate, since the moment generating function of t distribution with any finite degree of freedom does not exist, and because of the symmetry of the GED distribution, a more flexible appropriate distribution is called for.

In Jensen and Lunde (2001), Stentoft (2006) and Christoffersen, Heston, and Jacobs (2006), it was found that the normal inverse Gaussian (NIG) models, the special case of generalized hyperbolic (GH) distribution, are able to outperform some of the most praised GARCH models when considering daily US stock return data. In particular, a big gain is found in modelling the skewness of equity returns as in Eberlein and Keller (1995) and Eberlein and Prause (2002). It is concluded that allowing conditional skewness leads to more accurate predictions of conditional variance and excess return. Moreover, GH distribution has the moment generating function, which gains an advantage over the t distribution.

As multivariate options are regarded as excellent tool for hedging the risk in today's finance, a more appropriate measure for dependence structure is required; here, we concentrate on the copula. Copulas are functions that join or 'couple' multivariate distribution functions to their one-dimensional marginal distribution functions (Joe 1997, Nelsen 1999). It has been known since the work of Sklar (1959) that any multivariate continuous distribution function can be uniquely factored into its marginals and a copula. In a word, copula has proved to be an interesting tool to take into account all the dependence structure and even to capture the nonlinear dependence of the data set.

Copulas have also been introduced to price bivariate options as shown in Rosenberg (1999), Cherubini and Luciano (2002). In these papers, all the appropriate preliminary copulas are supposed to remain static during the considered time period. However, most of the data sets often cover a reasonably long time period and economic factors induce changes in dependence structure. Thus the basic properties of financial products change in different periods (the stable period and the crisis period). Therefore, to price the bivariate option in a robust way, a dynamic copula approach should be adopted.

In the present paper, a new dynamic approach to price the bivariate option under GARCH-GH process using time-varying copula is proposed. By fitting two GARCH-GH models on two underlying assets, the return innovations are obtained. Observing that the dependence structure for the two series of innovations changes over time, we analyse the changes in copulas through moving windows. Then a series of copulas are selected on different subsamples according to AIC criterion (Akaike, 1974). Through this method, the changes of the copula can be observed and the change trend appears more and more clearly. Conditioning on the result of the moving window process, the dynamic copula with time-varying parameter is expressed similarly as in Dias and Embrechts (2003), Jondeau and Rockinger (2004), Granger, Teräsvirta, and Patton (2006), Patton (2006), Van den Goorbergh, Genest, and Werker (2005) and Guégan and Zhang (2009), for instance.

An innovating feature of the present paper is investigating the dynamic evolution of the copula's parameter as a time-varying function of predetermined variables, which gives a considerably dynamic expression to the changes of the copula and makes the changes of parameters more tractable.

In the empirical study, call option on the better performer based on two important Chinese equity index returns (Shanghai Stock Composite Index and Shenzhen Stock Composite Index) is used to illustrate the innovative method described previously. The Student t copula is the best-fitting copula and a time-varying parameter is considered. We provide the option prices implied by GARCH-NIG model with a time-varying copula and these prices are compared with those obtained by GARCH-Gaussian model. It can be observed that the prices implied by the GARCH-Gaussian are generally underestimated.

The remainder of this paper is organized as follows. In Section 2, the basic framework of option pricing is recalled and the notations are introduced. Section 3 introduces the time-varying copula for pricing bivariate options using marginals GH distributions. In Section 4, empirical study is described and results are provided. Section 5 concludes. In the appendix we provide the expression of Gaussian and Student t copulas.

2. Preliminaries and related works

We specify the framework for option pricing that we choose, then we introduce the model with which we work and the innovation distribution that we use.

2.1 *Option valuation*

This paper concentrates on an European option on the better performer of two assets, but the technique is sufficiently general to be applied for other alternative multivariate options as well. The call option on the better performer belongs to one type of better-of-two markets and can be referred to as call-on-max option. The payoff of a unit amount call-on-max option is

$$\max\{\max(S_1(T), S_2(T)) - K, 0\},$$

where S_i is the price at maturity T of the ith asset ($i = 1, 2$) and K is the strike price. In the following, $R_{i,t}$ is used to denote the return on ith index ($i = 1, 2$) from time $t - 1$ to time t, and the corresponding log-return is denoted as $r_{i,t} = \log(R_{i,t})$.

The fair value of the option is determined by taking the discounted expected value of the option's payoff under the risk-neutral distribution. As the call-on-max is typically traded over the counter, price data are not available. Therefore, valuation models cannot be tested empirically. However, comparing models with different assumptions can be implemented.

The approach of Black and Scholes (1973) for option pricing assumes the efficiency of the financial market and all the pricing theory developed after their seminal work lies on the existence of the risk-neutral measure. This measure verifies the martingale property for the theory of contingent claim pricing. Recently, some works have proposed new approaches for pricing, based on historical measure. These new works are really interesting because they are close to the reality (Barone-Adesi, Engle, and Mancini 2004). Nevertheless, the present work keeps a historical approach for pricing options using the risk-neutral environment.

2.2 GH distributions

In order to take into account specific stylized fact of the assets (skewness and kurtosis mainly), we will work with the GH distribution that we present briefly now. We refer to Eberlein and Keller (1995) for more details.

The one-dimensional GH distribution admits the following density function

$$f_{GH}(x; \lambda, \alpha, \beta, \delta, \mu) = \kappa(\lambda, \alpha, \beta, \delta)\tau^{(\lambda-1/2)} K_{\lambda-1/2}(\alpha\tau) \exp(\beta(x - \mu)), \qquad (1)$$

where K_λ is the modified Bessel function of the third kind and

$$\kappa(\lambda, \alpha, \beta, \delta) = \frac{(\alpha^2 - \beta^2)^{\lambda/2}}{\sqrt{2\pi}\alpha^{\lambda-1/2}\delta^\lambda K_\lambda(\delta\sqrt{\alpha^2 - \beta^2})},$$

$$\tau = \sqrt{\delta^2 + (x - \mu)^2},$$

and $x \in \mathbb{R}$.

The parameters λ, α, β, δ, and $\mu \in \mathbb{R}$ are interpreted as follows: $\mu \in \mathbb{R}$ is the location parameter and $\delta > 0$ is the scale parameter. The parameter $0 \leq |\beta| < \alpha$ describes the skewness and $\alpha > 0$ gives the kurtosis. Particularly, if $\beta = 0$, the distribution is symmetric, and if $\alpha \to \infty$, the Gaussian distribution is obtained in the limit. The parameter $\lambda \in \mathbb{R}$ characterizes certain subclasses of the distribution and considerably influences the size of the probability mass contained in the tails of the distribution. If the random variable x is characterized by a GH distribution, we denote it $x \sim GH(\lambda, \alpha, \beta, \delta, \mu)$.

Generally we will use in applications the parameters $\bar{\alpha} = \alpha\delta$ and $\bar{\beta} = \beta\delta$ corresponding to the scale and location invariant parameters. Then, the density function of the GH distribution expressed in terms of the invariant parameters becomes:

$$f_{GH}(x; \lambda, \bar{\alpha}, \bar{\beta}, \delta, \mu) = \kappa(\lambda, \bar{\alpha}, \bar{\beta}, \delta)\chi^{(\lambda-1/2)} K_{\lambda-1/2}(\bar{\alpha}\chi) \exp\left(\bar{\beta}\left(\frac{x - \mu}{\delta}\right)\right), \qquad (2)$$

where

$$\kappa(\lambda, \bar{\alpha}, \bar{\beta}, \delta) = \frac{(\bar{\alpha}^2 - \bar{\beta}^2)^{\lambda/2}}{\sqrt{2\pi}\bar{\alpha}^{\lambda-1/2}\delta^\lambda K_\lambda(\sqrt{\bar{\alpha}^2 - \bar{\beta}^2})},$$

$$\chi = \sqrt{1 + \left(\frac{x - \mu}{\delta}\right)^2},$$

and $x \in \mathbb{R}$. In that case, $GH(\lambda, \bar{\alpha}, \bar{\beta}, \delta, \mu)$ is a location-scale distribution family, and we have

$$x \sim GH(\lambda, \bar{\alpha}, \bar{\beta}, \delta, \mu) \Leftrightarrow \frac{x - \mu}{\delta} \sim GH(\lambda, \bar{\alpha}, \bar{\beta}, 1, 0). \qquad (3)$$

A special case of the GH distribution is the Normal Inverse Gaussian (NIG) distribution obtained by assuming that $\lambda = -1/2$ in Equation (1). The density function of the NIG distribution expressed in terms of the invariant parameters $\bar{\alpha} = \delta\alpha$ and $\bar{\beta} = \delta\beta$ is equal to:

$$f_{NIG}(x; \bar{\alpha}, \bar{\beta}, \delta, \mu) = \frac{\bar{\alpha}}{\pi\delta} \exp\left[\sqrt{\bar{\alpha}^2 - \bar{\beta}^2} + \bar{\beta}\left(\frac{x - \mu}{\delta}\right)\right] \frac{K_1\left(\bar{\alpha}\sqrt{1 + ((x - \mu)/\delta)^2}\right)}{\sqrt{1 + ((x - \mu)/\delta)}}, \qquad (4)$$

where $x, \mu \in \mathbb{R}$, $\delta > 0$ and $0 < |\bar{\beta}| < \bar{\alpha}$. If the random variable x has a NIG distribution, we denote it as $x \sim \text{NIG}(\bar{\alpha}, \bar{\beta}, \delta, \mu)$. In the next application, we will use this particular case of the GH distribution.

2.3 GARCH process transformation

Here we are interested in pricing options, thus we need to derive the joint risk-neutral return process from the objective bivariate distribution. Instead of deriving the bivariate risk-neutral distribution directly, we propose to transform each of the marginal process separately.

First of all, we assume that the one-period log-return for every index, under probability measure P, follows a GARCH process, that is, for $i = 1, 2$:

$$r_{i,t} = r + \lambda \sqrt{h_{i,t}} - \frac{1}{2}h_{i,t} + \varepsilon_{i,t},$$

where $\varepsilon_{i,t}$ has mean zero and conditional variance h_t under the historical measure P; r is the constant one-period risk-free rate of return and λ the constant unit risk premium (note that under conditional lognormality, one plus the conditionally expected rate of return equals $exp(r + \lambda \sqrt{h_{i,t}})$. It just suggests that λ can be interpreted as the unit risk premium). We further assume that $\varepsilon_{i,t}$ follows a GARCH(p,q) process of Bollerslev (1986) under measure P. Thus formally, we have:

$$\varepsilon_{i,t}|\varphi_{i,t-1} \sim D(0, h_{i,t}) \quad \text{under measure P},$$

where $D(\cdot)$ can be the Gaussian law or any more general distribution function F_D, with zero mean and variance $h_{i,t}$ and $\varphi_{i,t-1}$ is the information set of all information up to and including time $t - 1$. Then,

$$h_{i,t} = \alpha_{i,0} + \sum_{j=1}^{q}\alpha_{i,j}\varepsilon_{i,t-j}^2 + \sum_{j=1}^{p}\beta_{i,j}h_{i,t-j}.$$

Some parameter restrictions are $p \geq 0, q \geq 0$; $\alpha_{i,0} > 0$; $\alpha_{i,j} \geq 0 (j = 1, \ldots, q)$; $\beta_j \geq 0$ $(j = 1, \ldots, p)$ and $\sum_{j=1}^{q}\alpha_{i,j} + \sum_{j=1}^{p}\beta_j < 1$ to ensure covariance stationarity of the GARCH (p, q) process.

In order to develop the GARCH option pricing model and finally obtain the risk-neutral price, we follow the methodology of Duan (1999), assuming that $(\varepsilon_t)_t$ follows an NIG distribution that takes into account the skewness and the leptokurticity observed inside the distribution function of the real data sets. We recall the definition of the LRNVR principe introduced in Duan (1995) and provide the model under Q. We say that a pricing measure Q satisfies the locally risk-neutral valuation relationship (LRNVR) if the measure Q is absolutely continuous with respect to the measure P, and then r_{it} conditionally to $\varphi_{i,t-1}$ is distributed lognormally (under Q) with:

$$E^Q[R_{it}|\varphi_{i,t-1}] = e^r,$$

and

$$\text{var}^Q[r_{i,t}|\varphi_{i,t-1}] = \text{var}^P[r_{i,t}|\varphi_{i,t-1}],$$

almost surely with respect to measure P.

In the previous definition, the conditional variance under the two measures are required to be equal. This is necessary to estimate the conditional variance under P. This property and the fact that the conditional mean can be replaced by the risk-free rate yield a well-specified model that does not locally depend on preferences. This latter fact is proved in Duan (1995). Here we will reduce all preference consideration to the unit risk premium. Since Q is absolutely continuous with respect to P, the almost sure relationship under P also holds true under Q. Note that in this study we restrict to constant interest rate assumption even if stochastic interest rates can be considered, but then the resulting model is more complicated. It is not the purpose of this paper which focus mainly on the bivariate pricing and the use of dynamical copula.

The strategy developed by Duan (1999) to get a generalized version of the GARCH option pricing model is based on a transformation that is capable of converting the fat-tailed and/or skewed random variables into normally distributed ones. We follow the same idea inside this paper for the transformation of each asset which is an approximately extension of the result obtained in Gaussian case, for a GARCH - GH model. Thus, assuming that the GLRNVR principle is verified, the assets returns processes that follow a GARCH model under measure P can be characterized approximately by a simple risk-neutral dynamic GARCH model under measure Q defined such that:

$$r_{i,t} = r + \lambda \sqrt{h_{i,t}} - \frac{1}{2} h_{i,t} + \eta_{i,t}, \tag{5}$$

where

$$\eta_{i,t} = F_D^{-1}[\Phi(Z_{i,t} - \lambda)],$$

where $Z_{i,t}$, conditional on $\varphi_{i,t-1}$, is a Q-standard normal random variable and $\Phi(\cdot)$ denotes the standard normal distribution function, and

$$h_{i,t} = \alpha_{i,0} + \sum_{j=1}^{q} \alpha_{i,j}(\eta_{i,t} - \lambda \sqrt{h_{i,t-j}})^2 + \sum_{j=1}^{p} \beta_{i,j} h_{i,t-j}. \tag{6}$$

The previous relationships imply that the log-return $r_{i,t}$ follows a process close to a GARCH (p, q) under the risk-neutral measure. We use this approximation that provides a relatively easy transformation to generalize local risk-neutral distributions that is skewed and leptokurtic. According to this expression, the terminal asset price can be derived

$$S_{i,T} = S_{i,t} \exp\left[(T - t)r - \frac{1}{2} \sum_{s=t+1}^{T} h_{i,ts} + \sum_{s=t+1}^{T} \eta_{i,s} \right]. \tag{7}$$

Considering the importance of the martingale property for the theory of contingent claim pricing, it is necessary to note that the discount asset price process $e^{-r_t T} S_{i,T}$ is a Q-martingale. Therefore, under the GARCH specification, the call-on-max option, with exercise price K at maturity T, has the time t value given by

$$COM_t = e^{-\sum_{s=t+1}^{T} r_s} E^Q[\max\{\max(S_{1,T}, S_{2,T}) - K, 0\}]. \tag{8}$$

This equation provides the fair value for call-on-max option.

Now we are interested to get the multivariate distribution for this bivariate option. Since the dynamic of $r_{i,t}$ with respect of the measure Q is completely characterized by Equation (5), the valuation problem reduces to the task of computing the expectation in Equation (7). To get it, we can use Monte Carlo simulation to generate many sample paths in accordance with the previous system and take the discounted average of the contract payoff to yield the price for the derivative claim in question. The algorithm is provided in Section 4.3.

In this part, we consider a classical GARCH modelling for the underlying assets, but clearly it is possible to extend this approach to asymmetric GARCH processes, such as the EGARCH model [Nelson, 1991), the GJR model (Glosten, Jagannathan, and Runkle 1993) and the A-PARCH model (Ding, Granger, and Engle 1993), for instance.

The previous exercise mainly developed in Duan (1995) under Gaussian distribution has been extended to other GARCH model, with specific kernel pricings, with other distribution functions such as the mixing Gaussian distribution, Gourieroux and Monfort (2007), the NIG distribution, Gerber and Siu (1994), the GH distributions, Christoffersen, Heston, and Jacobs (2006). The work of Duan (1999), on which this exercise is based, appears as a particular case of these previous cited works that assume an exponential affine parametrization for the stochastic discount factor. Now, the general result obtained recently by Chorro, Guégan and Ielpo (2008a) applied on GARCH-GH model confirms the interest of the empirical approach developed here. Indeed, the authors, following a lot of works in the literature, show that if the returns are governed by any GARCH-GH model under the historical measure and if we consider an exponential affine parametrization for the stochastic discount factor, then the model remains stable under Q. The explicit form of the distribution is then available (Christoffersen, Heston, and Jacobs 2006, Elliot and Madan 1998, Gerber and Shiu 1994, Heston and Nandi 2000, Gourieroux and Monfort 2007, Chorro, Guégan and Ielpo 2008b).

3. Bivariate option pricing with dynamic copula

In the proposed scheme for valuating the bivariate option, the objective bivariate distribution of the log-returns $(r_{1,t}, r_{2,t})$ is specified conditionally on $\varphi_{t-1} = \sigma((r_{1,s}, r_{2,s}) : s \leq t - 1)$, the information set of all information up to and including time $t - 1$. In order to derive the joint risk-neutral log-return process from this objective bivariate conditional distribution in a convenient transformation way, it is proposed to transform each of the marginal process and then to determine the copula.

The objective marginals are specified by the model with GARCH-GH process introduced as in Equation (6) with the consideration that the distribution D is a GH distribution.

In order to work in a bivariate framework, we use the previous results for each asset and we conjecture that the objective and local risk-neutral conditional copulas remain the same. Indeed, the transformation to go through the historical to the risk-neutral measure has been done on each return. We assume that the bivariate dependency does not change whatever the measure we use: the historical one or the risk neutral one. The changes already appear in expression (6). Here we are mainly interested to fit the best copula making time-varying in the estimation procedure.

In order to price the option on the underlying assets $(r_{1,t}, r_{2,t})$ in a bivariate framework, we measure the dependence structure among these assets using copulas. The bivariate copula permits to take into account the dependence structure of these assets through their margins. Details are given in the appendix.

Since most of the data sets often cover a reasonably long time period, the economic factors induce some changes in the dependence structure. Therefore, a dynamic copula approach is adopted. After determining the change type of the copula as introduced in Dias and Embrechts (2003), Guégan and Zhang (2009) and Guégan and Caillault (2009), the corresponding dynamic copula approach is applied in a similar way as in Patton (2006). Compared with the method in Van den Goorbergh, Genest, and Werker (2005), our dynamic copula method does not depend on the specified regression of Kendall's tau on initial volatilities.

Here we use a different modelling for the copula's parameter $\theta_t = (\theta_{1,t}, \theta_{2,t}, \ldots, \theta_{m,t})$, such that

$$\theta_{l,t} = \theta_0 + \sum_{i=1}^{g} \eta_i \prod_{j=1}^{2} \varepsilon_{j,t-i} + \sum_{k=1}^{s} \zeta_k \theta_{l,t-k} \tag{9}$$

for $l = 1, 2, \ldots, m$ and $\eta_i, i = 1, 2, \ldots, g$, $\zeta_k, k = 1, 2, \ldots, s$ are scalar model parameters and $(\varepsilon_{1,t}, \varepsilon_{2,t})$ are standardized innovations.

To estimate the parameters in Equation (9), the maximum-likelihood method is needed. Recalling that the standardized innovations are assumed to be distributed conditionally as the GH distribution (GH), the bivariate conditional distribution function is such that

$$F(\varepsilon_{1,t}, \varepsilon_{2,t}; \theta_t) = C(\mathrm{GH}_1(\varepsilon_{1,t}), \mathrm{GH}_2(\varepsilon_{2,t}); \theta_t),$$

where C is the copula function, GH_i $(i = 1, 2)$ is the GH distribution function. The corresponding conditional density function is then

$$f(\varepsilon_{1,t}, \varepsilon_{2,t}; \theta_t) = c(\mathrm{GH}_1(\varepsilon_{1,t}), \mathrm{GH}_2(\varepsilon_{2,t}); \theta_t) \prod_{i=1}^{2} gh_i(\varepsilon_{i,t}),$$

where the copula density c is given by

$$c(u_1, u_2; \theta) = \frac{\partial^2 C(u_1, u_2; \theta)}{\partial u_1 \partial u_2},$$

with $(u_1, u_2) \in [0, 1]^2$ and gh_i $i = 1, 2$ represents the GH distribution density. The conditional log-likelihood function can be finally evaluated as

$$\sum_{t=b+1}^{n} \left(\log c(\mathrm{GH}_1(\varepsilon_{1,t}), \mathrm{GH}_2(\varepsilon_{2,t}); \theta_t) + \sum_{i=1}^{2} \log gh_i(\varepsilon_{i,t}) \right) \tag{10}$$

where $b = \max(p, r)$. Numerical maximization of Equation (10) gives the maximum-likelihood estimates of the model. However, the optimization of the likelihood function with several parameters is numerically difficult and time consuming. It is more tractable to estimate first the marginal model parameters and then the dependence model parameters using the estimates from the first step. In order to do so, the two marginal likelihood functions

$$\sum_{t=p+1}^{n} \log gh_i(\varepsilon_{i,t}) \quad \text{for } i = 1, 2, \ldots, d,$$

are independently maximized. Assuming that the marginal parameters estimates are obtained and plugged in Equation (10), the final function to maximize becomes

$$\sum_{t=b+1}^{n} (\log c(\mathrm{GH}_1(\varepsilon_{1,t}), \mathrm{GH}_2(\varepsilon_{2,t}); \theta_t)). \tag{11}$$

From this dependence estimates, $\hat{\theta}_t$ are obtained and the model is fitted. For one-parameter copulas, the time-varying parameter function can be presented directly for this parameter alone; but for multi-parameter copulas, the complexity of estimating parameters results in the choice of the one most important parameter, letting the others static.

4. Empirical work

4.1 *Models for each data set*

For the empirical work, the valuation scheme for the bivariate option under GARCH-GH model with dynamic copula outlined in Section 3 is applied to call-on-max option on the Shanghai Stock Composite Index and the Shenzhen Stock Composite Index. The sample contains 1857 daily observations from 4 January 2000 to 29 May 2007. The log-returns of Shanghai Stock Composite Index and Shenzhen Stock Composite Index are shown in Figure 1, it is noted that the outliers typically occur simultaneously and almost in the same direction.

In this empirical work, we restrict the GH distribution to the NIG distribution which gives a better fit to our data set. The NIG fitting results are shown in Figure 2 and Table 1. The fitted NIG distributions are asymmetric. But simulation provides skewness parameter $\bar{\beta}$ close to 0 and location parameter μ nearly equal to 0; thus, in order to make the GARCH-NIG fitting more tractable, an assigned symmetric NIG distribution with 0 location is refitted and the results are shown in Figures 3 and 4 and Table 2.

The parameter estimates for the GARCH (1,1) with symmetric NIG innovation models for the underlying assets log-returns are listed in Table 3, and in order to compare, the results for GARCH-Gaussian model are also provided. From the AIC and BIC values of the two types of model, GARCH-NIG models appear better for both Shanghai Stock Composite Index and Shenzhen Stock Composite Index.

4.2 *Dynamic copula method*

Here, we consider the bivariate vector composed of the two assets. Several kinds of copulas are considered to describe the dependence structure between these assets on the whole period,

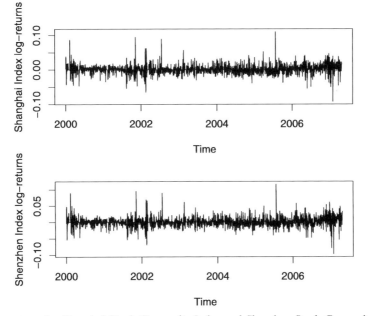

Figure 1. Log-returns for Shanghai Stock Composite Index and Shenzhen Stock Composite Index from 4 January 2000 to 29 May 2007.

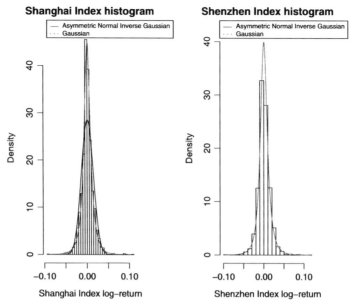

Figure 2. Asymmetric NIG fitting for log-returns of Shanghai Stock Composite Index and Shenzhen Stock Composite Index.

Table 1. Estimates of asymmetric NIG fitting parameters for marginal log-returns.

Parameter	Shanghai Index	Shenzhen Index
$\bar{\alpha}$	4.460e−01 (4.407e−03)	5.364e−01 (6.396e−03)
$\bar{\beta}$	1.607e−04 (2.256e−07)	8.440e−04 (2.981e−07)
μ	4.428e−04 (1.160e−07)	−1.171e−04 (1.719e−07)
σ	1.409e−02 (2.067e−07)	1.510e−02 (2.116e−07)
AIC	−10972.56	−10649.73
BIC	−10950.46	−10627.62

$\sigma = \delta\bar{\alpha}/\sqrt{\bar{\alpha}^2 - \bar{\beta}^2}$ is reparameterized as a dispersion parameter that can be seen as the volatility. Figures in brackets are standard errors.

including Gaussian, Frank, Gumbel, Clayton, and Student t copulas (Joe, 1997). All the copulas mentioned above are fitted to the support set of the standardized innovation pairs from GARCH-NIG and GARCH-Gaussian models respectively. The fitting results are listed in Table 4. AIC criterion is used to choose the best-fitting copula. From the models fitted to the standardized innovations for Shanghai and Shenzhen stock composite indexes, the one which has the smallest AIC value is the Student t copula both for GARCH-NIG and GARCH-Gaussian models. Therefore, Student t copula is considered as the best-fitting copula in the case of static dependence for both models.

Using moving window allows to observe the change trend in a direct way, and makes the dynamics specification more reasonable corresponding to the real setting. Therefore, the whole sample is divided into subsamples separated by the moving window. Sixteen windows each consisting of 300 observations are moved by 100 observations. Along with the moving of the window, a series

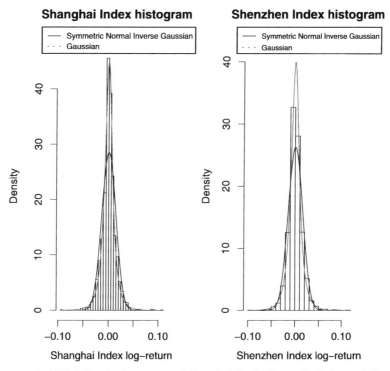

Figure 3. Symmetric NIG fitting for log-returns of Shanghai Stock Composite Index and Shenzhen Stock Composite Index.

of best-fitting copulas on different subsamples are decided by AIC criterion. The results for the best-fitting copulas on all subsamples for GARCH-NIG and GARCH-Gaussian model are shown in Table 5. The results listed in Table 5 show that on almost all subsamples, the Student t copula turns out to be the best-fitting copula for the GARCH-NIG model. So it is rather reasonable to assume that for the GARCH-NIG model, the copula family remains static as the Student t, while the parameter changes along the time. As far as the GARCH-Gaussian model is concerned, the copula changes a lot. For the second, third and fifth windows, although the Gaussian copula seems as the best fitting, the Student t copula offers the very close AIC value (with the difference not bigger than 2). And for the 7–11th windows, the Frank copula provides the best fitting, and the Student t copula is the second best fitting. Thus, we still assume that the copula family is static as the Student t but the parameters vary. In addition, it can be observed that the correlation does not change a lot for both GARCH-NIG and GARCH-Gaussian models while the degree of freedom varies obviously for both of the two models. Therefore, it seems reasonable to assume that the degree of freedom varies along time while the correlation remains static.

The time-varying function for the degree of freedom of the Student t copula is put forward as:

$$v_t = l^{-1}(s_0 + s_1\varepsilon_{1,t-1}\varepsilon_{2,t-1} + s_1 l(v_{t-1})),\tag{12}$$

where s_0, s_1, s_2 are real parameters and $l(\cdot)$ is a function defined by

$$l(v) = \log\left(\frac{1}{v-2}\right),$$

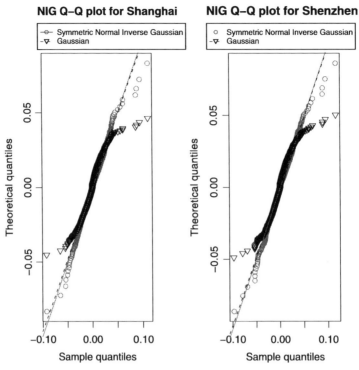

Figure 4. Q–Q plots of symmetric NIG fitting for log-returns of Shanghai Stock Composite Index and Shenzhen Stock Composite Index.

Table 2. Estimates of symmetric NIG fitting parameters for marginal log-returns.

Marginal	Shanghai Index	Shenzhen Index
$\bar{\alpha}$	4.536e−01 (4.539e−03)	5.275e−01 (6.117e−03)
$\bar{\beta}$	0.000	0.000
μ	0.000	0.000
σ	1.409e−02 (2.044e−07)	1.516e−02 (2.146e−07)
AIC	−10971.40	−10649.37
BIC	−10960.34	−10638.32

Figures in brackets are standard errors.

to ensure that the degree of freedom is not smaller than 2. The corresponding estimate results for the dynamic copula parameter described in Equation (13) are listed in Table 6.

4.3 *Pricing bivariate option*

Standard normal random variables can then be generated from this conditional Student t copula with a time-varying parameter, and according to two NIG margin distributions, log-return innovations can be sampled to compute the price of the option. Considering that the initial asset prices need to be close for the option to make sense, it is assumed here that they are normalized to unity.

Table 3. Estimates of GARCH-NIG and GARCH-Gaussian parameters for marginal log-returns.

	Shanghai Index	Shenzhen Index
GARCH-NIG		
m	6.065e−04 (1.952e−04)	7.260e−04 (2.300e−04)
$\bar{\alpha}$	8.103e−01 (2.807e−03)	7.959e−01 (5.837e−03)
α_0	3.597e−05 (2.032e−01)	3.532e−05 (1.989e−01)
α_1	2.758e−01 (3.865e−01)	3.015e−01 (5.477e−01)
β_1	5.651e−01 (2.988e−01)	5.558e−01 (7.747e−01)
AIC	−11037.14	−10708.29
BIC	−11009.51	−10680.66
GARCH-Gaussian		
m	3.833e−04 (2.419e−04)	3.761e−04 (2.882e−04)
α_0	5.136e−06 (7.682e−07)	5.529e−06 (9.011e−07)
α_1	8.115e−02 (4.726e−03)	8.721e−02 (5.496e−03)
β_1	8.966e−01 (5.034e−03)	8.950e−01 (5.249e−03)
AIC	−10793.11	−10518.3
BIC	−10771	−10496.2

Figures in brackets are standard errors.

Table 4. Copula fitting results.

Copula	Parameter	AIC value
GARCH-NIG		
Gaussian	9.191e−01 (4.205e−02)	−3517.934
Gumbel	3.732 (7.285e−02)	−3460.264
Clayton	3.905 (1.051e−01)	−2915.304
Frank	14.070 (3.242e−01)	−3255.558
Student t	9.221e−01 (3.914e−02); 3.675 (2.119)	−3683.532
GARCH-Gaussian		
Gaussian	9.314e−01 (4.402e−02)	−3757.412
Gumbel	3.971 (7.845e−02)	−3528.21
Clayton	4.081 (1.114e−01)	−2728.87
Frank	16.593 (3.611e−01)	−3591.436
Student t	9.349e−01 (5.095e−02); 5.807 (1.601)	−3797.926

Figures in brackets are standard errors and for Student t copula, the first parameter is the correlation, the second parameter is the degree of freedom.

Different maturities can be considered, and 1-month maturity (20 trading days) is displayed here just devoting itself to illustrating the approach. Moreover, the strike price is set at levels between 0.5 and 2.7. The risk-free rate is assumed to be 6% per annum, and λ is considered as 5%. Using the proposed dynamic copula method with time-varying parameter, the option prices are represented in Figure 5. Compared with the option prices implied by the GARCH-Gaussian dynamic model in Figure 6, it can be observed that the GARCH-Gaussian model generally underestimates the price.

Table 5. Dynamic copula analysis using moving window.

i^{th}	GARCH-NIG		GARCH-Gaussian	
	Co	Parameter	Co	Parameter
1	t	9.109e−1(1.032e−1); 2.444(1.302)	Ga	9.308e−1(1.034e−1)
2	t	9.064e−1(9.990e−2); 3.084(9.590e−1)	Ga	9.247e−1(1.036e−1)
3	t	9.308e−1(9.505e−2); 5.594(9.384e−1)	Ga	9.381e−1(1.103e−1)
4	t	9.451e−1(1.157e−1) 3.903(1.017)	t	9.539e−1(6.831e−2) 14.784(2.675)
5	t	9.602e−1(2.804e−1); 7.919(4.215)	Ga	9.646e−1(1.437e−1)
6	t	9.697e−1(1.142e−1) 6.826(3.352)	t	9.730e−1(1.164e−1) 15.262(5.337)
7	t	9.654e−1(1.442e−1); 8.098(3.385)	Fr	25.157(1.293)
8	t	9.598e−1(9.931e−2); 6.005(2.104)	Fr	22.866(1.193)
9	t	9.444e−1(2.117e−1); 7.087(3.630)	Fr	18.971(1.003)
10	t	9.385e−1(1.594e−1); 7.675(2.000)	Fr	18.115(9.655e−1)
11	t	9.419e−1(1.612e−1); 9.947(1.352)	Fr	18.914(1.000)
12	Gu	4.450(2.167e−1)	Gu	4.800(2.347e−1)
13	t	9.228e−1(1.533e−1); 5.682(2.388)	Ga	9.371e−1(1.143e−1)
14	t	8.831e−1(2.594e−1); 3.574(10.030)	Ga	9.062e−1(9.686e−2)
15	t	8.727e−1(7.247e−2) 3.300(8.206)	t	9.009e−1(1.092e−1) 5.012(3.371e−1)
16	t	8.493e−1(1.030e−1) 4.937(2.129)	t	8.765e−1(1.043e−1) 10.513(1.601)

Figures in brackets are standard errors. "Co" represents "Copula type", the short notes "t", "Gu", "Ga" and "Fr" represent respectively "Student t", "Gumbel", "Gaussian" and "Frank" copulas. And for the Student t copula, the first parameter is the correlation, the second parameter is the degree of freedom.

Table 6. Parameter estimates for dynamic Student t copula with time-varying parameter.

	GARCH-NIG	GARCH-Gaussian
p	9.176e−01 (2.361e−02)	9.267e−01 (2.483e−02)
s_0	4.384e−01 (1.497)	1.065 (5.452e−03)
s_1	−6.055e−02 (7.407e−01)	1.676e−01 (1.190e−03)
s_2	−9.414e−01 (4.165e−01)	−6.971e−01 (3.289e−02)

Figures in brackets are standard errors and p represent the correlation estimate.

The above pricing can be numerically assessed by repeating the following empirical Monte Carlo simulation steps.

(1) Identify two observable two-dimensional sufficient statistics at time t, i.e. $(r_{i,t}, h_{i,t})$ for $i = 1, 2$.

(2) Using the estimated results of the dynamic copula from the physical model, for each $i = 1, 2$, generate N standard Normal random numbers $Z_{i,T+1}^j$, $j = 1, \ldots, N$ in order to make an empirical adjustment. We first compute the discounted sample average of simulated asset price for time $t + 1$, and then multiply each of the N simulated asset prices by the ratio of the initial asset price over the discounted average. This adjustment ensures that the simulated sample has an empirical martingale property.

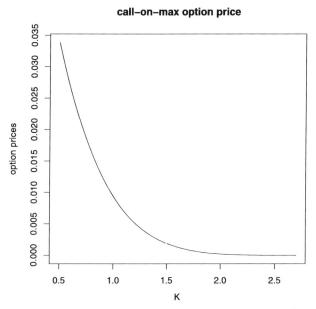

Figure 5. One-month maturity call-on-max option prices as a function of the strike using the method of dynamic Student t copula with time-varying parameter.

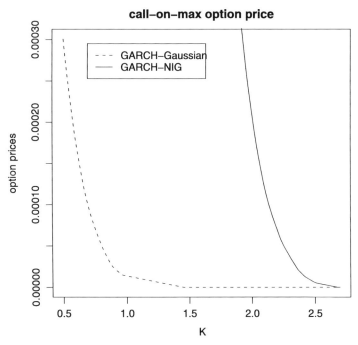

Figure 6. One-month maturity call-on-max option prices as a function of the strike from GARCH-NIG and GARCH-Gaussian models with dynamic copula.

(3) Repeat steps 1 and 2 until arriving at N simulated asset prices, $S_T^{(j)}$, $j = 1, \ldots, N$.

(4) Compute each of N option payoffs. Average N option payoffs, and discount the average, using the risk-free interest rate, back to the time of option valuation.

Our Monte Carlo study is based on $N = 100,000$ replications, resulting in simulation errors in the order of magnitude of 1 basis point for 1-month maturity claims.

5. Conclusion

In this paper, a systematic new approach for bivariate option pricing under GARCH-GH model with dynamic copula has been introduced. The introduction of GARCH-GH model on each asset permits to take into account most of the stylized facts observed on the data set; for recent development see Chorro, Guégan and Ielpo (2008a,2008b). The risk-neutral model permits to get an analytical expression for the fair value of the call-on-max option.

Concerning the adjustment of the dynamic copula, we use fixed moving windows, this approach could be extended to use other lengths of windows: the question which arises will be the good criterion to retain the copula. Indeed using AIC criterion, we need to know whether a change in the value of this criterion is relevant or not, which is not an easy task. In this work, we observe stability concerning the adjustment of the Student t copula, with changing parameters; thus, we keep static family and make varying the parameters.

Other extensions concern the choice of the type of GARCH process. For instance, the BL-GARCH (Storti and Vitale, 2003) could be interesting. Indeed this class of models permits to take into account explosion and clusters as stylized facts (Diongue, Guégan, and Wolff 2009).

Acknowledgements

The authors wish to thank the two referees for their precious remarks which permit to perform this paper.

References

Akaike, H. 1974. A new look to the statistical model identification. *IEEE Transactions on Automatic Control* AC-19: 716–23.

Barone-Adesi, G., R.F. Engle, and L. Mancini. 2004. Garch options in incomplete markets. Working Paper, NCCR-FinRisk.

Black, F. and M.S. Scholes. 1973. The pricing of options and corporate liabilities. *Journal of Political Economy* 81: 637–54.

Brennan, M. 1979. The pricing of contingent claims in discrete time models. *Journal of Finance* 34: 53–68.

Cherubini, U. and E. Luciano. 2002. Bivariate option pricing with copulas. *Applied Mathematical Finance* 9: 69–86.

Chorro, C., D. Guégan, and F. Ielpo. 2008a. Option pricing under GARCH models with generalised hyperbolic innovations (I): Methodology. Working Paper, CES-Université Paris 1, n 2008-37.

Chorro, C., D. Guégan, and F. Ielpo. 2008b. Option pricing under GARCH models with generalised hyperbolic innovations (I): data and Results. Working Paper, CES-Université Paris 1, n 2008-47.

Christoffersen, S., S. Heston, and K. Jacobs. 2006. Option valuation with conditional skewness. *Journal of Econometrics* 131: 253–84.

Cox, J. 1975. Notes on option pricing I: Constant elasticity of variance diffusions. Working Paper, Stanford University.

Dias, A. and P. Embrechts. 2003. Dynamic copula models for multivariate high-frequency data in finance. Working Paper, ETH Zurich.

Ding, Z., C.W.J. Granger, and R.F. Engle. 1993. A long memory property of stock market returns and a new model. *Journal of Empirical Finance* 1: 83–106.

Diongue, A.K., D. Guégan, and R. Wolff. 2009. BL-GARCH model with elliptical distributed innovations. To appear in SMA.

Duan, J.-C. 1995. The GARCH option pricing model. *Mathematical Finance* 5: 13–32.

Duan, J.-C. 1996. Cracking the smile. *RISK* 9: 55–9.

Duan, J.-C. 1999. Conditionally fat-tailed distributions and the volatility smile in options. Working Paper, University of Toronto.

Eberlein, E. and U. Keller. 1995. Hyperbolic distributions in finance. *Bernoulli* 1: 281–99.

Eberlein, E. and K. Prause. 2002. The generalized hyperbolic model: financial derivatives and risk measures. Paper presented in *Mathematical Finance-Bachelier Congress 2000*, ed. H. Geman, D. Madan, S. Pliska and T. Vorst, 245-267. Berlin: Springer Verlag.

Elliott R.J. and D.B. Madan. 1998. A discrete Time equivalent martingale Measure. *Mathematical finance* 8: 127–52.

Embrechts, P., A. McNeil, and D. Strausmann, 2002. Correlation and dependence in risk management: properties and pitfalls. In *Risk Management: Value at Risk and Beyond*, ed. M.A.H. Dempster, 176–223. Cambridge: Cambridge University Press.

Engle, R.F. 1982. Autoregressive conditional heteroscedasticity with estimates of the variance of United Kingdom inflation. *Econometrica* 50: 987–1007.

Forbes, K. and R. Rigobon, 2002. No contagion, only interdependence: Measuring stock market co-movements. *Journal of Finance* 57: 2223–61.

Gerber H.U. and S.W. Shiu. 1994. Option pricing by Esscher Transforms, *Transaction of Society of Actuaries* 20-2: 659–89.

Geske, R. 1979. The valuation of compound options. *Journal of Financial Economics* 7: 63–81.

Glosten, L.R., R. Jagannathan, and D.E. Runkle. 1993. On the relation between the expected value and the volatility of the Nominal excess return on stocks. *Journal of Finance* 48: 1779–C1801.

Gourieroux C. and A. Monfort. 2007. Econometric specifications of stochastic discount Factor Models, *Journal of Econometrics* 136: 509–30.

Granger, C.W.J., T. Teräsvirta, and A.J. Patton. 2006. Common factors in conditional distributions for bivariate time series. *Journal of Econometrics* 132: 43–57.

Guégan, D. and C. Caillault. 2009. Forecasting VaR and Expected Shortfall using Dynamical Systems: A Risk Management Strategy, *Frontiers and Finance*, April 2009.

Guégan, D. and C. Caillault. 2009. Change analysis of dynamic copula for measuring dependence in multivariate financial data. *Quantitative Finance*. In press.

Heston, S. and S. Nandi. 2000. A closed-form GARCH option pricing model. *The Review of Financial Studies* 13: 586–625.

Heynen, R., A. Kemna, and T. Vorst. 1994. Analysis of the term structure of implied volatilities. *Journal of Financial and Quantitative* 29: 31–56.

Hull, J. and A. White. 1987. The pricing of options on assets with stochastic volatilities. *Journal of Finance* 42: 281–300.

Jensen, M.B. and A. Lunde. 2001. The NIG-S&ARCH model: a fat-tailed, stochastic, and autoregressive conditional heteroskedastic volatility model. *Econometrics Journal* 4: 319–42.

Joe, H. 1997. *Multivariate Models and Dependence Concepts*. Chapman & Hall, London.

Johnson, H. 1987. Options on the maximum or the minimum of several assets. *Journal of Financial and Quantitative Analysis* 22: 277–83.

Jondeau, E. and M. Rockinger. 2004. Conditional dependency of financial series: the copula-GARCH model. *Journal of Money and Finance*, forthcoming.

Margrabe, W. 1978. The value of an option to exchange one asset for another. *Journal of Finance* 33: 177–86.

Merton, R. 1973. The theory of rational option pricing. *Bell Journal of Economics and Management Science* 4: 141–83.

Merton, R. 1976. Option pricing when underlying stock returns are discontinuous. *Journal of Financial Economics* 3: 125–44.

Nelsen, D.B. 1991. Conditional heteroskedasticity in asset returns: A new approach. *Econometrica* 59: 347–70.

Nelsen, R. 1999. *An introduction to copulas*. Lecture Notes in Statistics, vol. 139. Springer, New York.

Patton, A.J. 2006. Modelling Asymmetric Exchange Rate Dependence. *International Economic Review* 47: 527–56.

Reiner, E. 1992. Quanto mechanics. From Black-Scholes to Black Holes: New Frontiers in Options. *Risk Books* London: 147–54.

Rosenberg, J.V. 1999. Semiparametric pricing of multivariate contingent claims. Working Paper S-99-35, Stern School of Business, New York University, New York.

Rubinstein, M. 1976. The valuation of uncertain income streams and the pricing of options. *Bell Journal of Economics and Management Science* 7: 407–25.

Rubinstein, M. 1983. Displaced diffusion option pricing. *Journal of Finance* 38: 213–7.

Shimko, D.C. 1994. Options on futures spreads: Hedging, speculation, and valuation. *Journal of Futures Markets* 14: 183–13.

Sklar, A. 1959. Fonctions de répartition à n dimensions et leurs marges. *Publications de l'Institut de Statistique de L'Université de Paris* 8: 229–31.

Stentoft, L. 2006. Modelling the volatility of financial asset returns using the Normal Inverse Gaussian distribution: With an application to option pricing. Working Paper, Department of Economics, University of Aarhus, Denmark.

Storti, G. and C. Vitale. 2003. BL-GARCH models and asymmetries in volatility. *Statistical Methods and Applications* 12: 19–39.

Stulz, R.M. 1982. Options on the minimum or the maximum of two risky assets: analysis and applications. *Journal of Financial Economics* 10: 161–85.

Umberto, C., L. Elisa, and V. Walter. 2004. *Copula methods in finance.* New York: Wiley.

Van den Goorbergh, R.W.J., C. Genest, and B.J.M. Werker. 2005. Bivariate option pricing using dynamic copula models. *Insurance: Mathematics and Economics* 37: 101–C114.

Appendix 1. A short introduction for copulas (Joe 1997, Nelsen 1999)

Let $\mathbf{X} = (\mathbf{X}_n)_{n \in \mathbb{Z}} = \{(X_{i1}, X_{i2}, \ldots, X_{id}) : i = 1, 2, \ldots, n\}$ be a d-dimension random sample of n multivariate observations from the unknown multivariate distribution function $F(x_1, x_2, \ldots, x_d)$ with continuous marginal distributions $F_1, F_2, \ldots, F_d$. The characterization theorem of (Sklar, 1959) implies that there exists a unique copula C_θ such that

$$F(x_1, x_2, \ldots, x_d) = C_\theta(F_1(x_1), F_2(x_2), \ldots, F_d(x_d))$$

for all $x_1, x_2, \ldots, x_d \in \mathbb{R}$. Conversely, for any marginal distributions $F_1, F_2, \ldots, F_d$ and any copula function C_θ, the function $C_\theta(F_1(x_1), F_2(x_2), \ldots, F_d(x_d))$ is a multivariate distribution function with given marginal distributions $F_1, F_2, \ldots, F_d$. This theorem provides the theoretical foundation for the widespread use of the copula approach in generating multivariate distributions from univariate distributions.

In order to adjust a copula C_θ on a set of process, we will use maximum likelihood method and AIC criterion (Akaike, 1974). Details can be found in Umberto, Elisa, and Walter (2004).

A.1 *Gaussian copula*

The copula of the d-variate normal distribution with linear correlation matrix R is

$$C_R^{\text{Ga}}(\mathbf{u}) = \Phi_R^d(\Phi^{-1}(u_1), \Phi^{-1}(u_2), \ldots, \Phi^{-1}(u_d)),$$

where Φ_R^d denotes the joint distribution function of the d-variate standard normal distribution function with linear correlation matrix R, and Φ^{-1} denotes the inverse of the distribution function of the univariate standard Gaussian distribution. Copulas of the above form are called Gaussian copulas. In the bivariate case, we denote ρ as the linear correlation coefficient, then the copula's expression can be written as

$$C^{\text{Ga}}(u, v) = \int_{-\infty}^{\Phi^{-1}(u)} \int_{-\infty}^{\Phi^{-1}(v)} \frac{1}{2\pi(1 - \rho^2)^{1/2}} \exp\left\{-\frac{s^2 - 2\rho st + t^2}{2(1 - \rho^2)}\right\} \, ds \, dt.$$

The Gaussian copula C^{Ga} with $\rho < 1$ has neither upper tail dependence nor lower tail dependence.

A.2 *Student-t copula*

If $\mathbf{X}$ has the stochastic representation

$$\mathbf{X} \stackrel{\mathrm{d}}{=} \mu + \frac{\sqrt{\nu}}{\sqrt{S}} \mathbf{Z}, \tag{13}$$

where $\stackrel{\mathrm{d}}{=}$ represents the equality in distribution or stochastic equality, $\mu \in \mathbb{R}^d$, $S \sim \chi_\nu^2$ and $\mathbf{Z} \sim N_d(\mathbf{0}, \Sigma)$ are independent, then $\mathbf{X}$ has a d-variate t_ν distribution with mean μ (for $\nu > 1$) and covariance matrix $\nu/(\nu - 2)\Sigma$ (for $\nu > 2$). If $\nu \leq 2$ then $\mathrm{Cov}(\mathbf{X})$ is not defined. In this case we just interpret Σ as the shape parameter of the distribution of $\mathbf{X}$. The copula of

$\mathbf{X}$ given by Equation (13) can be written as

$$C_{\nu, R}^{t}(\mathbf{u}) = t_{\nu, R}^{d}(t_{\nu}^{-1}(u_1), t_{\nu}^{-1}(u_2), \ldots, t_{\nu}^{-1}(u_d)),$$

where $R_{ij} = \Sigma_{ij}/\sqrt{\Sigma_{ii}\Sigma_{jj}}$ for $i, j \in \{1, 2, \ldots, d\}$, $t_{\nu, R}^{d}$ denotes the distribution function of $\sqrt{\nu}\mathbf{Y}/\sqrt{S}$, $S \sim \chi_{\nu}^{2}$ and $\mathbf{Y} \sim \mathcal{N}_d(\mathbf{0}, R)$ are independent. Here t_{ν} denotes the margins of $t_{\nu, R}^{d}$, i.e. the distribution function of $\sqrt{\nu}Y_i/\sqrt{S}$ for $i = 1, 2, \ldots, d$. In the bivariate case with the linear correlation coefficient ρ, the copula's expression can be written as

$$C_{\nu, R}^{t}(u, v) = \int_{-\infty}^{t_{\nu}^{-1}(u)} \int_{-\infty}^{t_{\nu}^{-1}(v)} \frac{1}{2\pi(1-\rho^2)^{1/2}} \left\{ 1 + \frac{s^2 - 2\rho st + t^2}{\nu(1-\rho^2)} \right\}^{-(\nu+2)/2} ds\, dt.$$

Note that $\nu > 2$. And the upper tail dependence and the lower tail dependence for Student t copula have the equal value.

Index

Page numbers in **bold** type refer to **figures**
Page numbers in *italic* type refer to *tables*
Page number followed by 'n' refer to notes